THE
WINDSOR
SECRET

THE
WINDSOR

SECRET

New Revelations of
The Nazi Connection

Peter Allen

𝕤𝔻
STEIN AND DAY/*Publishers*/New York

First published in the United States of America in 1984
Copyright © 1983, 1984, by Peter Allen
All rights reserved, Stein and Day, Incorporated
Designed by Louis A. Ditizio
Printed in the United States of America
STEIN AND DAY/*Publishers*
Scarborough House
Briarcliff Manor, N.Y. 10510

Library of Congress Cataloging in Publication Data
Allen, Peter, 1937–
  The Windsor secret.

  Originally published in England under the title: The crown and
the swastika.
  Bibliography: p.
  Includes index.
  1. Windsor, Edward Duke of, 1894–1972—Political and
social views. 2. Germany—Politics and government—1933–1945.
3. Hitler, Adolf, 1889–1945. 4. Hess, Rudolf, 18 4–
5. Great Britain—Kings and rulers—Biography. I. Title.
DA580.A65 1984   941.084′092′4   84-40246
ISBN 0-8128-2975-1

Contents

Also by Peter Allen
One More River: The Rhine Crossings of 1945
The Yom Kippur War

List of Illustrations

1. The Duke and Duchess of Windsor in Paris, 1937
2. March 8, 1936; German troops crossing the Hohenzollern bridge into Cologne to reoccupy the Rhineland
3. Otto Abetz, German ambassador to Paris and later Nazi Gauleiter; a friend of Bedaux
4. Joachim von Ribbentrop, German Foreign Minister
5. Major E. D. ("Fruity") Metcalfe, the duke's companion
6. The Duke and Duchess of Windsor with Dr. Robert Ley, their official host in Germany
7. Windsor in deep conversation with Dr. Joseph Goebbels, Nazi propaganda minister, at dinner, October 12, 1937
8. Rudolf Hess, Hitler's deputy, with General Professor Karl Haushofer, who greatly influenced his thinking
9. Sir Samuel Hoare, Britain's wartime ambassador to Madrid, arrives at 10 Downing Street, September 12, 1938
10. The sinister Reinhard Heydrich, known as "C," who masterminded the SS/SD
11. The Windsors are greeted by Hitler at Berchtesgaden
12. Albrecht Haushofer's earlier letter to the Duke of Hamilton, dated July 16, 1939
13. Hess sits with Hitler, who has just made his peace offer to Britain in the Reichstag, July 19, 1940
14. SS-Brigadeführer Walter Schellenberg who was sent to Spain to "kidnap" the Duke of Windsor
15. The *Daily Record* reports Hess's arrival in Britain

Picture Credits
Popperfoto: 1, 2, 4, 6, 7, 9, 10, 11, 14; BBC Hulton Picture Library: 5; W. G. Fitzgerald: 8; Professor Dr. Heinz Haushofer: 12; United Press International: 13.

Acknowledgments

I wish to acknowledge and thank the following, who have given permission for me to quote from their publications or correspondence, and also those individuals who have been kind enough to correspond with me, or who discussed various aspects of the research and have allowed me to draw on their experiences:

The Bodley Head for permission to quote short extracts from *The Nazi Secret Service* by André Brissaud; Monsieur André Brissaud for his correspondence; Bundesarchiv, Koblenz, for copies of various German documents relating to political and military activities during the war; the director of the Central Museum of the Soviet Army, Moscow, for their correspondence; Dokumentationarchiv des Osterreichischen Widerstandes, Vienna; A. J. Davies; Lord James Douglas-Hamilton, MA, LLB, MP, for permission to quote passages from *Motive for a Mission*, published by Mainstream Ltd; Herr J. Ebert im Heusse, MBB Flugzeuge, Munich; The chief librarian and his staff, the Grand Rapids Public Library, Grand Rapids, Michigan, for their help in researching Charles Eugene Bedaux; Otto K. Hahn; Hoover Institution on War, Revolution and Peace, Stanford, California; The Imperial War Museum, Departments of Documents and Printed Books; Michael Joseph Ltd for permission to quote short extracts from *The Heart Has its Reasons* by the Duchess of Windsor; Kimber Press Ltd

9

for permission to quote two short extracts from *Secret & Personal* by F. W. Winterbotham; Ralph G. Martin for permission to quote five short extracts from his book *The Woman He Loved—The Story of the Duke and Duchess of Windsor*, published by W. H. Allen & Co. Ltd; Martin Secker & Warburg Ltd for permission to quote several short extracts from *The Rise and Fall of the Third Reich* by William F. Shirer; Major R. B. McNicol; Ministère de L'Interieur et de la Décentralisation, Paris; The National Archives and Record Service, General Services Administration, Washington, for records of German individuals and for American military intelligence records; Orbis Publications Ltd for permission to quote short extracts from their part-weekly publication *World War II*; Paul Paget, CVO, FSA, FRIBA, for giving his permission for the inclusion of extracts from the Templewood Papers; René Picot; Lyndon Prossor, *The Abergavenney Chronicle*; Public Records Office for authority to quote from the texts of Crown Copyright documents in their custody; Gerda Sorge; Kurt Stahl; Franz Svoboda; Hugh Thomas, author of *The Murder of Rudolf Hess*, for his time; George Weidenfeld & Nicolson Ltd for permission to quote several passages from *Edward VIII* by Frances Donaldson, for three extracts from *Inside the Third Reich* by Albert Speer, and three short extracts from *The Nazi Connection* by F. W. Winterbotham; Group Captain F. W. Winterbotham for his time in correspondence and personal discussion and his advice.

If I have inadvertently omitted to mention any other copyright-holder of material I have quoted, I apologize in advance.

Foreword

Four years ago I was doing research for a book on the Allies' Rhine crossings in 1945. My work included the examination of a great many records and documents from British, Canadian, American, and German sources. Among those that I obtained from the German Bundesarchiv was a report that had nothing to do with my current research but was by a man named Schellenberg; at that time I set the report aside. Only later, when that particular book had been published, did I again pay attention to the Schellenberg report, and on close examination I realized it was connected with a quite short passage that I had read in William F. Shirer's monumental *Rise and Fall of the Third Reich.* That passage dealt with the German attempt to "kidnap" the Duke of Windsor from Portugal in the summer of 1940. The report that I had did not seem to substantiate Shirer's account and set me thinking.

From that incidental beginning I have carried out several years of research in archives, libraries, military museums, and personal sources in Britain, Holland, Germany, Austria, France, Spain, Portugal, and the United States. My investigation was originally concentrated on July and August 1940, the period of the German plot as it has been described, but as the research progressed, it became obvious that whatever happened in Spain and Portugal was only part of a much wider conspiracy and intrigue that was itself central to Adolf Hitler's overall strategy for expansion and aggression.

11

It became evident that the Duke of Windsor was pushed by force of his personal circumstances into the dubious company of sympathizers who had ulterior motives; they believed that the duke was potentially an alternative British leader who would be pliant and acquiescent to the German cause. There can be no doubt from the evidence that he lent himself to their intrigues, although whether he did so by inclination or foolishness, readers will have to judge for themselves.

On the publication of the Documents on German Foreign Policy, Series D, Volume X, a notice was inserted, headed: "Statement to be Made by Her Majesty's Government on Publication of Volume X of the German Documents."

This includes the following passage: "The Duke was subjected to heavy pressure from many quarters to stay in Europe, where the Germans hoped that he would exert his influence against the policy of His Majesty's Government. His Royal Highness never wavered in his loyalty to the British cause or in his determination to take up his official post as Governor of the Bahamas on the date agreed. The German records are necessarily a much tainted source. The only firm evidence which they provide is of what the Germans were trying to do in this matter, and of how completely they failed to do it."

On the evidence I have acquired, I do not believe that the German records are necessarily a tainted source because, as I have pointed out in the text, they were never intended for publication but were the secret records of the German Foreign Ministry and its embassies. They were not discovered until after the collapse of Germany in May 1945, when many of the more notorious leaders were already dead and when their revelation would do the remaining Germans no good at all. But, in addition to the German records, there are other sources that have confirmed the veracity of many of those German records.

This story is about extensive German intrigue over many years, involving people in the highest positions in the land. It is, by its nature, complex and entwines the threads of many spools to weave a tale involving several of the major unanswered puzzles of the Second World War.

Peter Allen, 1983

THE
WINDSOR
SECRET

1

Intrigue in Spain

IT WAS appallingly hot in Madrid. Heat shimmered in waves from the roofs, distorting the already curled earthen tiles. Sunlight bounced off whitened walls in a blinding, eye-watering glare. Sunshades hung listless above dark, sightless windows, while paint-peeled shutters hid the sleeping, drowsy world within. The midday heat lay heavy on the city. Only a few days past midsummer, the brazen sun had driven the Madrileños to the refuge of their cool homes.

Madrid is the highest capital city in Europe, and from its heights one has views across parched valleys to the chilly snow-capped peaks of the distant Sierra de Guadarrama. Despite the parched summer's habitual shortage of water, the city's myriad fountains still splashed coolly in the parks, which provided the city with shady woodlands right to its heart; dark cypresses, bright green cork oaks, and delicate fronds of beech contrasted with great daubs of tropical scarlet, yellow, and flame of bougainvillea, hibiscus, and oleanders.

Since 1933 Spain had been plunged into the incalculable turmoil of civil war between the Soviet-backed Communist Republicans and the right-wing Nationalists, who had finally triumphed under the dynamic General Franco. That triumph, however, had been largely provided by the arms of Fascist Italy and National Socialist Germany. Hitler's Germany, especially, had learned in Spain the techniques of modern warfare

15

and conceived the blitzkrieg in the Spanish proving grounds. Although the civil war had ended eighteen months before, Madrid still showed many signs of the carnage, as little of the bomb and shell damage had been repaired. Evidently the population was far from recovered from the effects of the prolonged and bitter strife. An atmosphere of poverty and despair pervaded everything. There were lines of dejected people outside the depleted food shops, and most of the poorer people were clothed in little better than rags.

In the summer of 1940 war was spreading across Europe like a plague. Already Hitler's Wehrmacht, which occupied a cowed Austria and prostrate Czechoslovakia, had demonstrated how well it had learned its Spanish lessons and that it was truly the greatest war machine ever assembled. It had smashed its way across Poland in less than the month of September 1939 and then, after lying dormant during the bitter winter's phony war, had been unleashed in the following spring. Norway, Denmark, the Netherlands, Belgium, Luxembourg, and even France had fallen before the ruthless blitzkrieg machine. Only Britain remained, breathless and half-beaten on the far side of the narrow English Channel. After the débâcle of Dunkirk the British were awaiting the final onslaught. Few in Europe and the world believed that they would have long before the victorious and seemingly invincible German Army, Luftwaffe, and Navy hurled themselves on the barely defensible island. Few people would give Britain much hope then.

Fringed awnings veiled the sun's glare from the room of the German Ambassador to Spain, Eberhard von Stohrer. It was a large room where a thick carpet hushed the footsteps of those who deferentially visited this powerful representative of the all-conquering Führer. Around the carpet the parquet floor gleamed, and the room was pervaded with the Prussian smell of polish. The furniture was heavy with quality and the desk imposing; on its leather-topped surface stood a heavy paperweight adorned with the Nazi eagle. On the wall above Stohrer's desk hung a large portrait of the uniformed Führer gazing autocratically down, his slightly protruding pale eyes fixedly following whoever was in the room. It was not a room in which one relaxed, this outpost of the Third Reich.

Eberhard von Stohrer was a career diplomat who early on had firmly and resolutely embraced the Nazi doctrine. Orthodox in his views, he always ensured that his opinions were those of the party and never likely to be embarrassingly right or fatally wrong. He was, at that time, no doubt, contemplating a cable that he had instructed his cipher clerk to dispatch urgently to the German foreign minister, Joachim von Ribbentrop, in Berlin.

Earlier that day Stohrer had been approached by the Spanish foreign minister, Colonel Juan Beigbeder y Atienza, one of the military men who ruled pro-Nazi Spain. Beigbeder had confirmed to Stohrer that Britain's Duke and Duchess of Windsor were arriving in Madrid that day. Stohrer had already known that the duke and his wife were in Spain, for his agents at the Spanish border town of Port Bou had confirmed their arrival from war-torn France two days before. What intrigued the ambassador, though, was Beigbeder's request for advice regarding their treatment while in Spain. His information was that the couple were on their way to the Portuguese capital of Lisbon, whence, presumably, they would return to Britain. But that was not the entire story.

Beigbeder had pointed out to Stohrer that, when their own General Vigon, head of the Supreme Army Defense Council, had visited Hitler on June 16, exactly a week previously, the Führer had actually spoken of the Duke of Windsor and implied that Germany was very interested in detaining him and his wife in Spain in order to establish contact with him once more.[1] Hitler had, of course, known that the Windsors had been living in the south of France until the Italian invasion had begun, and he had, so it would seem, also known that the duke and his wife were going to make for Spain.

Ambassador Stohrer could well perceive the importance of the duke's arrival in Spain. His cable to Berlin, therefore, had repeated Beigbeder's information, and he had concluded this "strictly confidential" cable: "Please telegraph instructions. Stohrer."[2]

Nearly thirteen hundred miles away to the northeast, Stohrer's cable arrived on the desk of Joachim von Ribbentrop. Ribbentrop had capped a successful career as a salesman of sparkling German wine by marrying Anneliese Henkel, the heiress daughter of the owner of the great German house. He had shortly afterward been introduced to Adolf Hitler by the future German chancellor von Papen, with whom Ribbentrop had served in the army in Turkey. He had quickly attracted Hitler's admiration by his linguistic abilities, for while the struggling, impecunious leader of the embryonic Nazi Party spoke only German with an Austrian patois, Ribbentrop could speak both English and French. Soon Ribbentrop was regularly inviting Hitler to his smart home in the exclusive Berlin-Dahlem suburb. The story may be apocryphal, but it is said that Hitler, who was then very down-at-the-heels, was obliged to scale the back wall on arriving and leaving Ribbentrop's home to avoid being seen by the snobbish neighbors. Ribbentrop had been the Reich foreign minister since 1937, although his had not been a popular appointment. Ribbentrop's obtuse manner, his haughtiness and arrogance had won him few friends and alienated a great many people at home and abroad. In spite of his arrogance, though, it was well known that he stammered nervously whenever he spoke to his Führer.

Stohrer's cable was undoubtedly welcomed by Ribbentrop, who was only too aware that his star had ceased to ascend in Hitler's sky. After all, many Germans said that it was his assurances to the Führer that Britain was effete and would not fight Germany that had led Hitler along the warpath. But, as we shall see, many of Ribbentrop's now-scorned opinions were based on sound advice and determined assurances given by his well-placed and powerful British friends in the 1930s, including the Prince of Wales, as the Duke of Windsor then was. So Ribbentrop was very keen to renew contacts with the duke, who had shown himself very sympathetic to Germany's problems. Much advice to the Führer had emanated from a variety of sources in Edward's confidence when he was first prince and then uncrowned king. The foreign minister therefore replied to Stohrer's cable with alacrity: "Is it possible in the first place," he cabled, "to detain the Duke and Duchess of Windsor for a couple of weeks in Spain before they are granted an exit visa? It would be necessary at all events," he cautioned, "to be sure it did not appear in any way the suggestion came from Germany."[3] The cable was not decisive, though, but merely a holding action to delay the duke's departure long enough for some scheme to be worked out. Ribbentrop was not the man to instigate subtle plans quickly. However, it would give him time to contact the Führer.

Stohrer, back in Madrid, received the cable the following day, Monday, June 24. He wasted no time but promptly called the Spanish foreign minister, Beigbeder, told him what was wanted, and asked for help. Within hours he was able to send a reply to Ribbentrop assuring him that Beigbeder had "promised me to do everything possible to detain Windsor here for a time."[4]

In fact, once the German ambassador had finished, the tall, dark-haired Spanish foreign minister called for his limousine and was driven through the hot afternoon to the imposing Ritz Hotel, in the Plaza de la Lealtad, where the Duke and Duchess of Windsor had newly taken up residence. With a flourish Beigbeder swept into the hotel and with the very minimum of delay had himself announced to the duke.

The Duke of Windsor was then forty-four years old. He and his wife, together with their retinue, had arrived at the hotel the day before by train from Barcelona, where they had rested for forty-eight hours following a tiring, frustrating, and quite dangerous drive across a disintegrating France from their home at Cap d'Antibes. Once in Madrid they had gone first to the British Embassy in the nearby Calle Fernando el Santo where they were received with all the respect and slight awe due to the former king. Sir Samuel Hoare, the British ambassador, had already been forewarned by the Foreign Office in London when the duke had set out for Spain, and indeed he had intervened with the Spanish authorities on the previous Sunday when the duke's party had been held up at the Port Bou customs post because they had no entry visas. But, as Hoare tactfully explained on their arrival, the embassy was not considered suitable accommodation for the duke and duchess, and arrangements had accordingly been made for them to stay at the Ritz Hotel.

Behind the official welcome and outward honor at His Royal Highness's safe arrival in Madrid, there was also acute embarrassment. Ever since his abdication and subsequent marriage to American, twice-divorced Mrs. Wallis Simpson, protocol determined that wherever possible the duke and his wife should receive no official reception; the duchess, of course, had even been denied the right to the title of Royal Highness on the day before their marriage.

Receiving Colonel Beigbeder in his suite, the duke was, as usual, lounging relaxed in the wide-bottomed checked trousers of his habitual double-breasted suit, with an open-necked shirt. (Although he had the reputation in the thirties of being one of the world's best-dressed men, in private he loved to dress casually and took the opportunity to do so whenever he could.) The only information on Beigbeder's visit relates how the duke chatted pleasantly and, with his usual ingenuousness, expressed his views frankly on a number of subjects to which the Spanish foreign minister listened attentively, while the duke chain-smoked nervously. The interview was pleasant and relaxed in the cool of the suite but did not last long, and soon Beigbeder was being driven back to the Foreign Ministry.

Once back in his own imposing office, Beigbeder lost no time in telephoning Stohrer to report on his interview with the duke. The portly German ambassador nodded his head in satisfaction. The gist of the conversation was that the duke had been firm: He would not return to Britain unless his wife was given official recognition as a member of the royal family and unless he himself could be given a position of importance. Yes, the duke had made his attitude quite clear.[5]

The duke, however, could have had no illusions that he was talking to the foreign minister of a country that, while declaring itself neutral in the war between the Axis powers and Britain, was, nevertheless, on the closest possible terms with Germany and Italy and could well be expected to join the war on the Axis side at any time. So when Stohrer cabled Berlin again that evening, it was to provide information of the highest importance to the Führer and Ribbentrop.

The Reich's armies had defeated all the Continental forces that had opposed them; only Britain remained. As will soon become apparent, Hitler had long believed that he could find an accommodation with Britain that would leave him undisputed master of Europe and free to pursue his declared dream of turning east to seize the Lebensraum (living space) to which he profoundly believed the German people were historically entitled.

Thus began a German-Spanish intrigue that has never before been fully investigated or explained. The real, underlying explanation, however, to what has been loosely called an attempt to kidnap the Duke of Windsor is that strong and powerful people in high places in Britain had long planned that Britain would not be drawn into conflict with Nazi Germany but would permit that country to destroy the Bolshevik evil that had spread from the east since 1917 and which they clearly and realistically perceived as the major threat to the roots of Western democracy.

The Windsors were to stay in the Spanish capital for just over a week before escaping the arid heat of Madrid in June for the cooler sea breezes of Portugal. The duke and duchess attended several receptions, for they were international figures whose society had long been sought after wherever they went. The most important reception was given by the ambassador Sir Samuel Hoare at the embassy on the evening of Friday, June 28. The *Times* reported in its "News in Brief" column on Monday, July 1: "More than 300 guests attended a reception given by Sir Samuel Hoare at the British Embassy in Madrid on Friday night. Among them were the Duke and Duchess of Windsor, the Spanish Foreign Minister, Don Miguel Primo de Rivera, the Papal Nuncio and the American Ambassador...."

Although people who knew the duke believed that he was thoroughly patriotic, there were many others who worried because he had his own very definite ideas as to where his responsibility lay. As the events both before and after that week in Madrid have shown, the duke's notions of Britain's relationship with Germany hardly accorded with those of a country fighting for its very life.

Nothing pleased the duke more than for his wife to be accorded the respect he believed her due; she had after all married the former head of a mighty empire. It was inevitable then that when they entertained Spanish friends at their hotel suite, the duke would derive enormous satisfaction and pleasure at the respect they gave to his wife, who had suffered snubs that would have been considered churlish had they emanated from any family other than the royal family. He was delighted when, for example, Doña Sol, sister of the Duke of

Alba—Spain's ambassador to London—and a leading Falangist, gave them a smart Fascist salute on entering their luxurious hotel suite. The Infante Alfonso, the second son of King
Alfonso XIII and then a Spanish Air Force general, also
showed his respect when he bowed low, kissed the duchess's
hand and addressed her as "Highness," the title to which she
aspired but which she had been denied by the royal family.
These acts, of course, gave great delectation to both the Windsors, for the duchess slipped easily into the role of royalty
despite the royal family's resolve to keep her out.

In 1936 "Chips" Channon had described Mrs. Ernest Simpson, as the duchess was then, as "a jolly, plain, intelligent, quiet,
unpretentious and unprepossessing little woman," but he had
soon ruefully to revise his condescension and add: "She has
already the aim of a personage who walks into a room as
though she almost expected to be curtsied to."[6] She had since
found in her visits to Germany in 1937 and now in Spain that if
the British would not curtsy, the Fascists would.

Britain's new prime minister, Winston Churchill, who had
taken over from the ailing and discredited Chamberlain only
some six weeks before, did not need to be told of the danger that
lay in the duke's presence in Spain. He was only too well aware
of the duke's mercurial temperament and his unshakable, if
misguided, faith in his own judgment and omniscience, which,
as the events of the abdication crisis had shown, could be
completely remote from reality. But Churchill was also ominously aware of the danger of the duchess's distorted view of
the duke's potential as a rallying point for the British people. It
has long been claimed that she was also too friendly with the
Germans, a fact that had been noted by many of their contem-
porary friends and acquaintances. On the day of the abdication, Blanche Dugdale, a society confidante of the then king,
wrote in her diary: "Lunched at Ritz with Jack Wheeler
Bennet. He talked about Germany. He is convinced that Ribbentrop used Mrs. Simpson but proofs are hard to come by. But
I think government and *Times* have them."[7] They were wrong,
however, and it seems much more likely that this charge was a
convenient cover-up for something far more sinister and that
the duchess had been used as a scapegoat to remove the pro-
German king. When Ribbentrop was Nazi ambassador to Lon-

don, he had, indeed, been a companion of the then prince and Mrs. Simpson, but the prince's connection with the Germans, including the Nazis, predated Mrs. Simpson by many years and was a part of a much wider network of such contacts at the highest level. Nevertheless, in the circumstances of June 1940, Churchill did immediately recognize the necessity of getting the ducal couple back to Britain before the Germans began to show their hand, for he must have feared the sympathy they would get.

The neutral capitals of Spain and Portugal, to which the duke would soon go, were already hotbeds of espionage and intrigue and were to become during the war years labyrinths where entwined the plots of Nazis, Fascists, and Falangists as well as the British SIS and eventually the American OSS, precursor of the CIA. It was an atmosphere, even in the summer of 1940, where all the belligerents spied and bribed and where the neutrals, too, picked up what they could. In that volatile atmosphere of conspiracy, where every official utterance was analyzed for some clue as to diplomatic feelings and intentions, the duke went about speaking his mind with careless abandon. While in besieged Britain posters were going up to warn about careless talk, in Spain, where every wall had Nazi ears as a fixture, he does not appear to have thought twice about what he was saying.

At that embassy reception on the Friday night he was, naturally, the center of attention; he would have expected no less after all. Outside, the altitude of the Spanish capital quickly cooled the summer air, but inside the ballroom the only frigidity occurred when diplomats of competing powers inadvertently encountered one another.

Among the guests was A. W. Weddall, the ambassador of the United States of America. He was conscientiously seeking evidence of Britain's intentions and prospects so that he could report back to Washington where President Roosevelt and his advisers were struggling to assess whether or not it was worth supplying arms and credit to a country on the verge of invasion and defeat. The President was already getting extremely defeatist reports from the venerable anti-British U.S. ambassador to London, Joseph Kennedy. Would the arms fall into German hands when they overran Britain? Would the Royal

Navy be interned, only to be used against the United States at a later date? These were the perplexing questions occupying the American government and Weddall. To this influential man, upon whose country's goodwill Britain's very survival depended, the duke nevertheless opened his mind in disturbing frank conversation. The duke, of course, loved to talk and was a noted raconteur; the trouble was that he regarded his own views as self-evident truths and rarely reflected that others might think otherwise. Weddall listened carefully and clearly retained a great deal of what the duke told him. Like most ambassadors, he probably made a written report of everything said, for the next day he sent a long and revealing cable to the U.S. secretary of state:

> In a conversation last night, the Duke of Windsor declared that the most important thing now was to end the war before thousands more were killed or maimed to save the faces of a few politicians.
>
> With regard to the defeat of France, he stated that stories that the French troops would not fight were not true. They had fought magnificently, but the organization behind them was totally inadequate. In the past ten years Germany has totally reorganized the order of its society in preparation for this war. Countries which were unwilling to accept such a reorganization of society and concommitant sacrifices should direct their policies accordingly and thereby avoid dangerous adventures. He stated this applied not merely to Europe, but to the United States also. The Duchess put the same thing more directly by declaring that France had lost because it was internally diseased and that a country which was not in a condition to fight a war should never have declared war.
>
> These observations [the ambassador declared] have their value, if any, as doubtless reflecting the views of an element in England, possibly a growing one, who would find in Windsor and his circle of friends a group who are realists in world politics and who hope to come into their own in the event of peace. Weddall.[8]

Everyone in his right mind wanted peace by June 1940, but the "peace" notion that had formed in Weddall's mind after talking with the Windsors was clearly to be the peace of surrender, rather than of victory, while the circle of friends who would come into their own, in that event, evidently presaged a change of rule. Weddall must have known, though, much of the duke's views on war and on Nazi Germany before he met the Windsors that evening. His counterpart in Paris, U.S. ambassador William C. Bullitt, was a frequent companion of the Windsors, which was natural in view of the duchess's American birth. While living in France, too, during the previous three years, they had moved in the company of leading French families who between them exerted considerable influence and control over their country's policies, and as will become apparent later, France's quick defeat was not entirely a military matter but rather an international conspiracy to erect a powerful, industrial-based power bloc against Bolshevism, the bogey of all conservative thinking in the twenties and thirties.

Weddall was correct to surmise that the Windsors had indeed a circle of appeasers; certainly his host, Sir Samuel Hoare, was one. He had been British foreign secretary in 1935, until he lost favor even with his own party after the notorious Hoare-Laval Pact, and Laval, who had done much to hinder unity in France, was about to become the Vichy servant of the Nazis. Hoare had been appointed British Ambassador to Madrid, where it was assumed, rightly, that his reputation as an arch appeaser would make him highly acceptable to the French. Sir Alexander Cadogan deduced from a remark made by Lady Hoare on May 20, 1940 that she was already anticipating Britain's defeat, and he later confided to his diary: "The quicker we get them out of the country the better. But I'd sooner send them to a penal settlement. He'll be the Quisling of England when Germany conquers us and I'm dead."[9]

But it was not only to Weddall that the duke and duchess expressed their urbane views that evening. There were many eavesdroppers present, and there were also high officials of the Spanish government and the ruling Falangist party. One who pricked up his ears on hearing the duke's forthright views was Don Miguel Primo de Rivera, the leader of the Madrid Falange, the son of a former Spanish dictator, and an influential Fascist friend of Germany. De Rivera, who was to play a leading role in the forthcoming German intrigues to encourage the duke into cooperation with them, listened carefully to the duke discussing the war's progress and the international situation. Once the reception ended that evening, de Rivera, too, wasted no time in quickly reporting the duke's views to Stohrer. The report was on Ribbentrop's desk in the early hours of July 2. "Windsor has expressed himself to the Foreign Minister and other acquaintances against Churchill and against this war. . . ."[10]

The Germans did not, though, have to rely solely on Spanish friends to get such information. In became known only after the war that the Abwehr—the German military secret service—had from the very earliest days of the war, and maybe before, penetrated American diplomatic security in Spain. According to captured Abwehr documents, Weddall himself was under a continual and dual surveillance. First the Abwehr's agents and then the infinitely more sinister SS Internal Security Service (SD) agents of Walter Schellenberg—the young and boundlessly ambitious protégé of "hangman" SS General Reinhard Heydrich, both of whom were to play leading roles in the coming conspiracy—were reading the American ambassador's confidential correspondence. Through the Abwehr's Amt (Dept.) VI, they had an agent in the section of the postal administration that handled the diplomatic mail. According to the late Ladislas Farrago, "A high official in the Spanish Foreign Ministry (who shows up in both the Abwehr's and SD's papers with the code name 'Guillermo') reported practically everything that came to his attention about Weddall and his successor Professor Carlton Hayes."[11]

With these notable agents and contacts insinuated into virtually every important aspect of diplomacy in Spain and Portugal, the Germans were well placed to take advantage of opportunities to harm the Allied cause as they arose.

Those careless utterances by the duke and his wife in Madrid were by themselves, however, hardly enough to set in motion the intrigue that followed. They were not isolated instances, though, but rather the culmination of what the duke had said and done in the previous years, especially since his abdication and marriage, when he had become a well-known sympathizer with Nazi Germany. His ingenuous behavior, his overwhelming sense of self-importance engendered by a lifetime of flattery when his every rehearsed speech and prompted remark was received with acclaim, encouraged in him a belief in his own correctness and infallibility. His controversial visit to Germany, when he had reveled in the fawning attention of Nazis, his polite indifference to the fate of the Jews, Austrians, and Czechs, his Nelsonian blind eye turned to the venomous Nazi propaganda aimed at Britain, his courting of known Nazis and his willingness to entertain them on the very brink of war and afterward, and above all his constant criticism of his country's war effort and leaders left no doubt in the minds of Nazi leaders—here, they declared, was a rejected but popular leader of his people, waiting for the opportunity to regain his eminence. Then, they were sure, he would be willing to bring about a solution to Britain's struggle against Nazi Germany.

The plot, nevertheless, goes deeper than laying the mantle of collusion upon the duke, for throughout the interwar period there had been a powerful lobby at work in Britain, in industry, in the great houses, and, most worrying of all, among those most secretive of services upon whose loyalty and discretion any country relies ultimately for its security. All these institutions had played their part in preparing the Nazis for a war in which they really did not believe that Britain would be their enemy. At the apex of this pyramid of conspiracy was the Duke of Windsor, and as this book will show, the German belief that he was their friend was not far wrong.

2

Roots of the Conspiracy

B Y AUGUST 1933 the Nazi party had been governing Germany for six months. In that time they had dissolved the Reichstag, which Hitler had taken over on his appointment as chancellor on January 30, 1933, and had called for new elections for March 5. In the intervening weeks, however, the Nazis harnessed all the vast resources of government to win votes. Joseph Goebbels, Hitler's gnomelike propaganda minister, wrote in his diary on February 3: "Now it will be easy to carry on the fight, for we can call on all the resources of the State. Radio and Press are at our disposal. We shall stage a masterpiece of propaganda."[1]

The big businessmen who had been frightened by the Communist revolt at the end of the First World War were pleased that the new government was going to put labor in its place and coughed up the millions needed for the election. The Communist party and its press were eliminated either by government order or by the Stormtroopers, and even the Catholic Center party was cowed into submission. Hermann Goering, the fat, rambunctious ex-air force ace—who was in the key position of minister of the interior of Prussia—simply removed from office hundreds of republican officials and replaced them with loyal Nazis. Then, when even all this deliberate provocation failed to produce the expected "Bolshevik revolution," which was to be the raison d'être for Hitler's dictatorship, more direct

29

action was taken. Goering's police raided the Communist party headquarters in Berlin on February 24, and from the piles of propaganda leaflets that they found, Goering was able to announce "proof" that the Communists were about to launch a revolution. But even that threat failed to arouse the masses before the election. Then, on the night of February 27, the Reichstag was burned down. Whether or not the fire was begun on Goering's orders, as was alleged by Socialists and Communists, it did arouse great indignation in Germany. The Communist party was banned amid a storm of Nazi propaganda. Nevertheless, on March 5, in the last democratic election in Hitler's lifetime, the German people still did not give him the overwhelming mandate he sought and which he needed to establish his dictatorship legally.

On March 23, just over a fortnight after the election, in the Kroll Opera House in Berlin, which served as a temporary parliament building, the last rites of German democracy were enacted. By a mixture of bullying and bribing, Hitler passed his Enabling Act, which gave him extraordinary powers and alone formed the legal basis for his dictatorship. When the vote had been counted and revealed their success, the Nazi deputies shouted and stamped, and the venerable opera house echoed to Nazi marching songs. As Alan Bullock put it, ". . . the gutter had come to power,"[2] but they had done it legally, nevertheless.

Once firmly in power, the Nazis lost no time in turning their attention to the new Reich's foreign policy.

At the heart of the Nazis' philosophy and, therefore, the guiding principle of their foreign policy, was Hitler's own monumental book, *Mein Kampf.* The book had been dictated by Adolf Hitler while he was imprisoned for a comfortable nine months in the old fortress of Landsberg, his sentence for leading the abortive 1923 Munich Beer Hall *Putsch.* The man who took Hitler's far from erudite dictation and put it into more literate form was Rudolf Hess, who was to become his deputy Führer and play one of the strangest and most intriguing roles in the Second World War and in this story, too.

Hitler wanted to call his book *Four and a Half Years of Struggle against Lies, Stupidity and Cowardice* but was firmly persuaded by Nazi publisher Max Amann to shorten it to *My Struggle (Mein Kampf).* The book was generally regarded as pretty turgid reading, but whatever criticisms are leveled at its literary merit, no one could accuse Hitler of not expressing his intentions for Germany and Europe. His basic ideas had been formulated in his early twenties in Vienna, and throughout the remainder of his life he altered nothing in his thinking. He had arrived in Germany from his native Austria in 1913, aged twenty-four, with a burning passion for German patriotism and a bitter hatred for democracy, Marxism, and Jews.

In *Mein Kampf*, Hitler plainly declared his intention of restoring a defeated Germany to a stronger and even more illustrious position than ever before. It would be, he insisted, a state based upon racial principles and would include all Germans then living outside the frontiers of the Reich. In order to achieve these momentous objectives, Hitler made it absolutely clear that he would have to deal with France, which he called "the inexorable mortal enemy of the German people." The destruction of France, all the same, was to be only a means to an end, to remove France's military threat in the west while his German legions struck out eastward. "Germans," Hitler exclaimed bluntly, "must expand in the East—largely at the expense of Russia."

So there it was for all to see who would read it. Hitler's fundamental objective from the very beginning was to drive eastward to carve out an empire in Poland, White Russia, and the Ukraine. In so doing he would gain the living space that the industrious, expanding German people demanded. He would not seek an empire in Africa, as had the Hohenzollern kaisers, but instead, ". . . the new Reich must again set itself on the march along the road of the Teutonic Knights of old, to obtain by the German sword sod for the German plough and daily bread for the nation."[3] "If we speak of soil in Europe today," he continued, "we can primarily have in mind only Russia and the vassal states." This new Teutonic crusade would, in Hitler's eyes, not only give living space to Germans; it would also destroy what he saw as the twin roots of all evil, Bolshevism and the Jews, which in his mind were inseparable. "The giant empire in the East is ripe for collapse," he exulted in *Mein Kampf*, "and the end of Jewish rule in Russia will also be the end of Russia as a state."[2]

Hitler's declared objectives, then, necessitated taking a se-

ries of steps in which intermediate obstacles would first have to
be dealt with. To invade Russia, Germany would need to have a
common frontier with that great state; otherwise Russia would
have time to prepare its notoriously slow mobilization. Germany, therefore, would have to absorb, or otherwise take over,
the intervening buffer states between Germany and Russia,
i.e., Poland, Czechoslovakia, and Austria. As an Austrian,
Hitler, in any case, hated the creation of these succession states
out of the ruins of the great Austro-Hungarian Empire that
had been dismembered by the victorious Western Allies in the
postwar peace treaties.

Hitler knew well enough, however, that France would not sit
by and allow a resurgent Germany to gobble up these buffer
states, and indeed, during the 1930s France signed mutual-aid
treaties with Czechoslovakia, Yugoslavia, and Romania as well
as Russia, in an endeavor to hem in the German military
machine. It was in France's interest, too, to have these mutu-
ally helpful pacts so that, if Germany should ever attack
France again, counterattacks on her eastern frontier would
force Germany to divide her forces.

Germany's military strategy in the First World War, in
which France and Russia were allied, had been to hold the
Russians on her eastern frontier while five-sixths of the German Army dealt a massive knockout blow against France.
Germany's timetable had been to defeat France in just forty
days, by which time the Russians would be nearing completion
of their mobilization; Germany would then switch her victorious divisions eastward, using a well-planned railway system,
from France to Russia, in time to meet the Russians with her
full force again. This was called the Schlieffen Plan. It just
failed to work because the Germans had not foreseen the presence of a small but experienced and very determined British
Army which bolstered up the French, who made a last-ditch
stand on the Marne, where they defeated the Germans and
drove them back to the Aisne, creating the stalemate that was
to last for four years. In the early 1930s the Germans were
already planning that in any future war they would not again
allow themselves to be committed to fighting on two fronts
simultaneously, a promise Hitler explicitly made in *Mein
Kampf.*

It was obvious, therefore, that for Germany's Eastern Plan to succeed, France had to be neutralized. France had suffered appalling casualties in the First World War, and few French people could envisage themselves fighting another protracted war; they were both exhausted and disillusioned. France's one hope in a future conflict was that Britain would again fight with her. But Britain had also suffered terribly; every town and village had its granite cross bearing a long list of names to remind those who remained that they could not let it happen again. In any case, Britain was essentially a great seapower with only a small regular army, mostly in India—although in the latter part of the First World War the British had formed the main opposition to Germany. It was, therefore, important to the Nazis that in making their long-term plans, they keep two aims in mind: to discover as soon as possible what Britain's attitude might be and to keep Britain out of a future war at all costs.

On August 16, 1933, the German ambassador to London, Leopold von Hoesch, sent a long and detailed dispatch to the German foreign minister, Baron Konstantin von Neurath. It was No. A2705 and headed: "Subject: German-English Relations."

Hoesch was a correct, old-world German diplomat of impeccable dress who moved in the best circles in London and was on friendly terms with most people who mattered. He began his dispatch with a general summation of the atmosphere in Britain that summer, commenting that, "England . . . vacationed on an especially large scale this year." There was an air of political calm, he wrote, and after the World Economic Conference the British ministers and parliament "adjourned in harmony." Then he continued in a more specific vein: "This pause in political activity suggests the idea of drawing up a balance sheet showing the present status of our relations with England." He explained that the Nazi revolution in Germany had inevitably lost the sympathies of the "Socialist, labor unions, pacifist and liberal circles" that hitherto had been "the most pro-German element in England. In fact," he added, "we must for the present write off from our account this numerically significant portion of the English people."

He continued: "On the other hand, on the extreme right, a

certain sympathy has developed for the way things have shaped up in Germany. This sympathy is based primarily on the interest that is growing in these circles, in the idea of authority which had been carried out in Germany. As typical of persons with this attitude I would think of politicians such as Lord Lloyd and in the sphere of the press, organizations such as the *Morning Post* and the press of Lord Rothermere." Nevertheless, so shrewd an observer as Hoesch, who was no Nazi either, had no illusions about that Government's low popularity in Britain.

> It must be stated that a glance at the general lineup of the English political parties and groupings at present no longer reveals any real rallying point for a pro-German attitude.
>
> The picture is somewhat brighter if one disregards political groupings and examines the development of public sentiment in accord with the class structure of the country.
>
> Here we must mention the English Court, where true sympathy for Germany is still to be found. To be sure, King George [V] has become more and more critical in his attitude toward the German revolution, and various statements which I know him to have made recently are in fact anything but friendly. On the other hand, the Queen [Mary] and various princes and princesses who are connected by family ties with Germany still entertain a warm feeling for our people and country, and also a certain sympathy, or at any rate a lively interest, in the most recent German developments. Most pronounced are the sympathies and the interest in the case of the successor to the throne [the Prince of Wales], with whom I have often had opportunities for a frank and detailed discussion.[4]

It was natural that the king and his family should feel sympathy toward Germany. They were, after all, basically a German family. Queen Mary was German by birth, and according to one of the duke's biographers, when they were together he and his mother conversed quite often and naturally in German. Kaiser Wilhelm II had also been the king's cousin, and it was with "Uncle Willi," the young Prince of Wales's favorite uncle, that Edward spent many long and pleasant summers before the First World War.

It is also important to remember that, in the past, war had been strictly a matter of military operations that did not fundamentally affect the personal relationships of individuals, certainly not royal families, who regarded their international relations as something apart. Napoleon Bonaparte had introduced a new and unpleasant professionalism into war by interning foreign nationals, but royalty still regarded itself as above the day-to-day unpleasantness of aggression. In most respects this situation was swept away in the First World War, and the war that began to loom once the Nazis came to power was going to be a very different one from the comparatively simple concept of fighting for territorial gain. It would be a civil war setting countrymen against one another. Both Nazism and Communism were about men's minds, and the racialism of the one and the nihilism of the other were to bring a new dimension to a war that devastated innocent people in a way hitherto undreamed of.

The Bolshevik revolution, too, had left in its wake a deep-rooted fear among Europe's ruling classes. King George V had a constant terror of revolution breaking out in Britain and imbued his heir, Edward, the Prince of Wales, with a similar underlying suspicion of Communism. It was the opinion of many influential people, the hereditary wealthy and the industrialists especially, that the real enemy in the 1920s and 1930s and for the foreseeable future was Soviet Communism.

Long before Hitler's Nazis assumed power in Germany in 1933, they were attracting the attention of people in Britain and France, who perceived that the only answer to the constant threat of Communist expansion westward was a strong, rearmed, and anti-Communist Germany. Germany had experienced "workers'" revolutions in Munich, Berlin, and elsewhere in the years after the First World War and had produced the dynamic firebrand Adolf Hitler and his Nazi Party, which, as newspapers and travelers reported, stood no nonsense from the Communists. So, although Hitler was personally not well known in Britain in 1930, interest was growing in the Nazis, and an increasing number of people were visiting Germany and the Berlin offices of the Nazi party's own newspaper, the *Volkischer Beobachter*.

The editor of the *Volkischer Beobachter*, which had been a

pretty insignificant provincial paper until the party bought it, was Alfred Rosenberg, a man who rose to power in the party and was eventually executed as a war criminal. Rosenberg grew up in the Baltic province of Latvia when it was a part of Czarist Russia. He went to the USSR as a student during the revolution in 1917 and there first became aware of the close association between the Jews in Russia and Communism. Leon Trotsky was a Jew, and somehow the impression that all Jews were Communists was imprinted on Rosenberg's mind. In spite of his own Jewish-sounding name, Rosenberg was not Jewish; the name was apparently common among Germans who had settled in Latvia generations before.

From Russia the young and politically ambitious Rosenberg traveled to Munich, where he joined Hitler's movement in 1920. There is a story that he had brought with him to Munich some spurious document showing that at a Jewish convention in Geneva plans had been drawn up to take over the finances of Germany and the rest of Europe. This proved to be his passport into the Nazi party, for no one bothered to authenticate the document. But, whether or not this is true, Rosenberg was well read, had a good education, and certainly impressed Hitler with the soundness of his views on racism and Communism. Before long he was the accepted philosopher of the Nazi party and became editor of the *Volkischer Beobachter.*

It was to Rosenberg that a number of eminent British people went as the Nazi party struggled for power in Germany. The parliamentary private secretary of Sir Neville Henderson, the foreign secretary, and Thomas Jones, the former assistant to Lloyd George when he was prime minister, were among the visitors, and both were given a copy of Alfred Rosenberg's book, *The Future Course of German Foreign Policy.* Anyone who read this book could have had few illusions about Germany's intentions. It was also from Rosenberg that a thread unwound that would reach out in time to the Duke of Windsor and to Rudolf Hess.

On the staff of the *Volkischer Beobachter* at that time was another Balt, named Arno Schickendanz, a friend of Rosenberg. Schickendanz was by all accounts a rather reserved man, but he had a flair for research and was useful in developing contacts. One of these contacts was a third Balt, Baron William de Ropp.

De Ropp had been born into a wealthy, aristocratic Baltic family, but for some unexplained reason he had chosen to live in Britain since 1910. During the First World War he had become a British subject and joined the Wiltshire Regiment in which he served until transferring to the Royal Flying Corps. After the war de Ropp found that his estates in Lithuania had been seized by the Bolsheviks, and he turned to freelance journalism for a living, contributing political articles to *The London Times*. By the late 1920s he had moved to Berlin, where he wrote on the political developments in Germany.

During his war service in the RFC de Ropp had served with squadron leader F. W. Winterbotham, who would later become eminent in the Second World War for his role in developing the Ultra system, which British Intelligence used to decipher the German secret codes. This particular ability also has its place in the story here being unfolded. According to Winterbotham, after the First World War ended, he had retired to his Devonshire farm only to be recalled in 1930 and given the task of establishing the Air Intelligence section of the Secret Intelligence Service (SIS). The SIS organization came under the Foreign Office, to whom it was responsible for gathering foreign intelligence, which was then supposed to be disseminated for the needs of foreign affairs decisions. However, the SIS spread its inquiring tentacles very widely and turned up doing some curious things, not always with Foreign Office knowledge.

De Ropp was by then married to an Englishwoman, with whom he lived in a very comfortable apartment on the fashionable Kurfurstendamm, one of Berlin's gayest and liveliest streets. He was a big man, almost six feet tall and of robust build, with blue eyes and sandy hair and mustache. In dress and appearance de Ropp epitomized an Englishman, but his linguistic abilities enabled him, if he wished, to pass for a German or a Russian. He was also to play a curiously nebulous though persistent role in the German intrigue leading to the Duke of Windsor.

Having their Baltic origin in common, de Ropp and Schickendanz soon established a friendly relationship from which de Ropp could satisfy his curiosity about the rising Nazi Party, whose significance he had quickly realized. Its crusading philosophy regarding Bolshevism could not be missed. Then, during 1930 to 1931, Schickendanz introduced de Ropp to Rosenberg and so set in motion a curious sequence of events, for de Ropp sought to make use of this quite important contact by introducing Rosenberg in turn to the British Secret Intelligence Service.

It did not take de Ropp long to establish himself in Nazi society; he was, after all, a journalist who regularly contributed to the highly respectable *Times*. Rosenberg, it seems, took the first opportunity to introduce de Ropp to Hitler, who took an instant liking to the engaging Balt who was so well informed about events and opinions in London. Soon a close personal relationship had developed between de Ropp and Hitler, who took to using him as his confidential consultant about British affairs and in return, Winterbotham says, outlined to him very frankly his grandiose plans, even confiding to him some of his intentions. This was a trust no other foreigner enjoyed to this extent, although in Hitler's eyes de Ropp was a German Balt, as were many leading Nazis.

De Ropp reciprocated Hitler's confidence by becoming his chief agent of Anglo-German rapprochement. He acted as Hitler's mouthpiece with influential Britishers whom the Führer was anxious to reach and influence. Whether or not he was already a British agent is hard to say; he was not supposed to be, and yet many journalists were involved in intelligence gathering. In all events de Ropp soon became a British agent, but, he was really a double agent, for he was acting for the Germans, too. In the shadowy world of espionage and intelligence, loyalties often became blurred, and even so-called double agents could well be getting from one side much more than they were giving to the other.

Before long, Bill de Ropp was firmly entrenched as Rosenberg's English agent, with a direct pipeline to Whitehall and Buckingham Palace at one end and Hitler at the other. He brought to Germany many of his highly placed British friends —"several peers," as he himself boasted, two generals, an admiral, a number of journalists, and a sporting parson. Indeed, as we shall discover, in the weeks following the outbreak of war in 1939, de Ropp was offering advice to the Germans on how they should deal with Britain.

Winterbotham, a tall distinguished man with a millimetrically clipped moustache and rather devilish eyebrows, reverted to his RAF rank and to all intents and purposes was a serving RAF officer, a point with not a little bearing on this story's conclusion. He had, he says, kept up his friendship with de Ropp, who told him about his contact with Rosenberg. At that time Rosenberg was not just the *Volkischer Beobachter*'s editor but also one of the top men in the Nazi hierarchy, although in later years he was to be shunted aside by such men as Ribbentrop, Himmler, and Martin Bormann. Now, since Winterbotham was supposed to be only a serving RAF officer, it is puzzling why de Ropp went to him with his political contacts. It seems that either Winterbotham had told him of his SIS role, which is unlikely given the secrecy he maintained until after the war, or which appears more likely, de Ropp too was in the service of the SIS. When I asked Winterbotham about this point, he was very vague and said that it was all a long time ago.

Winterbotham and de Ropp met in London in 1931. They discussed the aims and methods of the Nazi movements, and then, apparently on their own initiative, Winterbotham said, they decided to learn all they could about the dynamic new movement that was sweeping Germany. According to Winterbotham, it was de Ropp who proposed inviting Rosenberg to London so that they could establish closer contacts with the Nazi leadership. This they both agreed to do.

Alfred Rosenberg was accompanied by de Ropp when he arrived in Britain in late 1931 on a still, bleak autumn day of leaden sky and pewter seas. They caught the Harwich boat train and arrived at a dreary Liverpool street station, where they were met by a smiling Winterbotham. He greeted his old friend warmly and was in turn introduced to Rosenberg. Winterbotham remembers that his first impression of Rosenberg was of a "keen, intelligent, cheerful type, rather heavily built, in his later thirties like himself, height about five feet-ten, coarse features, anxious to make a good impression; and, above all, to talk of his beloved movement.."[5]

Once the greetings were over, Rosenberg was whisked off to a luxury London hotel where they had reserved him a room. For the next few days de Ropp and Winterbotham gave the Nazi leader a whirlwind tour around London to see the sights, and in particular they included a visit to the exclusive Carlton Club, whose members were noted for their right-wing political opinions. They also took Rosenberg on a mysterious car trip into the Surrey countryside, although it has not been explained why. Later, when they compared impressions, they agreed that their important Nazi guest had liked all he saw; he had been especially impressed with the charming and friendly manners of English people. But, besides these pleasant interludes and excursions, Winterbotham and de Ropp were significantly introducing Rosenberg to some very influential people, one of whom was Geoffrey Dawson, the editor of *The Times*. De Ropp had been able to arrange this meeting easily by reason of his connection with the paper. Wearing a gray pinstripe suit, with round tortoiseshell-rimmed glasses perched on the end of his beaky nose, Dawson was the essence of conservative respectability. As editor and controlling influence of the *Times*, he was also a very important channel for communicating views in both directions.

Rosenberg did not speak English, and so when he and Dawson settled down to talk, de Ropp acted as their interpreter. From the onset they found a coincidence of views on many topics. Both men favored, for example, good relations between Britain and Germany, and Dawson wholeheartedly agreed that the Versailles Treaty was pernicious and threatened Europe's economic recovery, fully accepting the Nazis' grievances on this issue. They had similar views on other matters too. Dawson's political philosophy pivoted on the preservation of the British Empire, and he was accordingly sympathetic to Germany's loss of her colonial empire. Nevertheless, the *Times* view did not extend to restoring Germany's colonies, most of which had gone to Britain anyway, but Dawson did agree that a rectification of the Versailles Treaty should undoubtedly reconsider the expropriation of the colonies. Again the two men were in agreement, and Rosenberg must have been heartened and hopeful of a Britain sympathetic to Nazi policies.

It is not possible to say to what extent Rosenberg's opinions influenced Dawson's own views of the Nazis, although in the next few years the *Times* was far from hostile to them, at least until the outbreak of war. For instance, on February 3, 1933, while Goering and his Stormtroopers were cowing the electorate and Goebbels was honing his propaganda to a fine art, the *Times* carefully wrote of Hitler: "No one doubts Herr Hitler's sincerity. That nearly 12 million Germans follow him blindly says much for his personal magnetism."[6] Needless to say, the Nazis derived priceless esteem from such favorable comments by a newspaper which many foreigners equated with official British government views. Dawson was indeed often accused of being soft on the Nazis after Hitler came to power, and the *Daily Herald*'s editor, Francis Williams, accused Dawson of watering down news dispatched from correspondents in Berlin so as to keep stories of Nazi atrocities out of the paper.

Rosenberg's visit to Britain has always been cloaked in an aura of mystery, and it is difficult to reconstruct exactly what he did. Notwithstanding this, from snippets of information it is possible to extricate a few more details. He is said to have visited Lord Hailsham, who was then secretary for war, and Lord Lloyd, of whose Nazi sympathies Leopold von Hoesch was to write in 1933. Surely, however, the acme of Rosenberg's visit was the private meeting that he had with Montague Norman, the governor of the Bank of England.

Montague Norman's biographer Andrew Boyle says Rosenberg met with him because the governor was instinctively pro-German—which did not make him a collaborator with the Nazis. But he also had a reputation for hating the Jews, which arouses more suspicions. It is a fact that Norman did make substantial loans to Hitler's regime not long after it took office, but did the governor finance the Nazis before they were in power? Another of Norman's biographers, John Hargrave, thought he did: "It is quite certain that Norman did all he could to assist Hitlerism to gain and maintain political power, operating on the financial plane from Threadneedle Street."[7]

One of Rosenberg's final appointments in Britain in 1931 was to meet with Lord Beaverbrook, the ebullient Canadian press baron. Contacts with the British press were invaluable, for it was to play a very important role in helping the Nazis to obtain money. German industrialists, aristocrats, and bankers were all very sensitive to how foreign opinion regarded the Nazis, so whenever moderate Germans were debating the merits of joining Hitler's bandwagon, favorable comments in the respectable, neutral British press were very encouraging.

For the Nazis to fight several successive elections, they needed a great deal of financing. There has been much speculation as to where that financing came from. Of course, German industrialists such as Krupp, Thyssen, and Farben provided millions of marks, and countless thousands of small businesses provided accumulated millions, but this did not account for all the money. There is strong evidence that the Nazis had also attracted a very substantial amount of international finance, especially from Britain and France.

In mid-1933 Rosenberg made a second and last visit to Britain. It was on this occasion not an outstanding success, however, because by then the Nazis were firmly in power and Rosenberg's innate pomposity and blundering got the better of him. He could not resist spouting tactless remarks about the Jews, which were then reported in the press. Despite this setback, his visit included one particularly noteworthy event: He spent an entire weekend at the palatial home at Ascot of Sir Henry Deterding. Several newspapers gave reliable accounts of the visit. *Reynolds Illustrated News* wrote: "In the light of the present European situation, this purely private talk between Hitler's foreign adviser (Rosenberg) and the dominant figure in European oil politics is of profound interest. It supports the suggestions current in well-informed political circles that the big oil interests have been closely in touch with the Nazi Party in Germany."[8] Another source claimed they had met in 1931 as well—perhaps the reason for the drive into the countryside that had so pleased Rosenberg?

The meeting between Rosenberg and Deterding was significant because Deterding was one of the wealthiest men in the world, and it is a fact that in the 1930s he loaned Hitler between 30 and 55 million pounds. His clandestine meetings with Rosenberg, though, gave little indication of the plots, intrigues, and secret transfers of money that were occurring between Hitler and Deterding. Deterding's oil business had suffered severe financial losses as a result of the Soviet takeover of his interests in Russia, and he was, per se, another dedicated anti-Communist.

Why should such substantial men as Deterding, Dawson, and Beaverbrook, and many others, go out of their way to aid Hitler? A rowdy political pariah until quite recently, Hitler had been a figure of fun in his ill-fitting raincoat, porkpie hat, and silly mustache. F. W. Winterbotham, who, as we shall see, was to spend a great deal of time in the Reich in the 1930s and met frequently with both Hitler and Hess, explained it:

> The reader must realise that the Nazis, who were themselves daily gaining experience in the battle for men's minds, saw at much closer quarters than ourselves the tyranny of Communism, the massacre of farmers, and intellectuals, the police state in which families were made to spy on each other and where murder was the reward for one word out of place. In those early days the Nazis felt that they had saved their country from Communism, they could not understand why we too were not violently opposed to Stalin's regime. They felt that we should welcome the destruction of the Bolsheviks. Some of them even felt that we should help in this anti-Russian drive; or, if we would not offer positive help, then the least we could do was to stay neutral and well out of the way while the Nazis got on with the job.[9]

By the end of 1933, then, the Nazis were firmly in control of Germany. The Communists had been smashed, and an enthusiastic new Nazi dawn was well risen. It would be a few years before Hitler would be able to rebuild his Wehrmacht to the point where he would begin to flex the Nazi muscle and start his territorial expansion along the path eastward. Nevertheless, he must have been well satisfied with his progress. When Rosenberg returned to Berlin after his May visit to Britain, he took back a great deal of hope for friendship from the people who counted in Britain, and soon that connection would be extended firmly and decisively toward the throne itself, with considerable success. Hitler's plan to keep Britain out of the next war seemed well on the way to success, and the events of 1935 and 1936 were to confirm these hopes and lay the foundation of his intuition.

3

The Rhineland
Retaken

A GRAY, misty, and chill dawn crept over Germany on March 7, 1936, burnishing the leaden surface of the Rhine. The great river sometimes ran swift between towering Lorelei crags capped with turreted castles, and sometimes it ran broad and strong, sweeping away the debris of sprawling industrial towns. It swirled past historic German cities—Karlsruhe, Mannheim, Mainz, Koblenz, Bonn, Cologne, Düsseldorf, and on into the Netherlands toward the still dark and cold North Sea. On the right bank the cities and farms were a part of the full trappings of Hitler's three-year-old Third Reich. The left bank, however, had been demilitarized and estranged from the fatherland since 1920 by order of the Western Allies, as a guarantee that Germany would never again march into Belgium and France. That assurance was about to expire.

As night dissolved into the damp early spring morning, there was a hubbub of activity among the troops assembled along the wide, well-made roads leading to the Rhine bridges. At the appointed hour the commands were given and the gray-uniformed, steel-helmeted German Army surged forward across the bridges and set off to recover the frontier cities of Aachen, Trier, and Saarbrücken. The Nazi reoccupation of the Rhineland had begun.

On May 21, 1935, Hitler had made a "peace speech" in the

Reichstag that greatly affected the world with its conciliatory tone; Britain, especially, had been impressed. But into this oration Hitler had, nevertheless, slipped a definite warning that "an element of legal insecurity" had been brought into the Locarno Pact by the Franco-Soviet Mutual-Assistance Pact that had been signed on that March 2, 1935 in Paris and on March 14 in Moscow. Although it had still to be ratified by the French parliament by the end of the year, the German Foreign Office, nevertheless, sent a formal note about this "element" to the French government. Then, on November 21, Francois-Poncet, France's very shrewd ambassador to Berlin, was subjected to a long tirade by Hitler against the Franco-Soviet Pact. Francois-Poncet forthwith reported to Paris that he was certain Hitler would use the pact as an excuse to reoccupy the Rhineland. "Hitler's sole hesitancy," he warned, "is now concerned with the appropriate moment to act."[1]

Francois-Poncet knew what he was talking about and had inside information that as early as May 2 General von Blomberg, the minister of defense and commander-in-chief of the Wehrmacht, had issued the first directive to the forces to plan for the reoccupation of the Rhineland. This operation, given the code name *Schulung*, was to be executed by a "surprise blow at lightning speed." Its planning was so secret that Blomberg himself wrote out the order, and only the very smallest number of officers were informed.

More detailed discussion of operation *Schulung* took place on June 16, when the Working Committee of the Reich Defense Council met. Colonel Alfred Jodl, head of the Home Defense Department—later to become Hitler's chief of operations and to hang at Nuremberg, reported on the plans and again stressed the need for the strictest secrecy. Nothing was to be committed to writing, he warned, unless absolutely necessary, and "without exception such material must be kept in safes."[2]

And so it was that at 10 A.M. on that chilly morning of March 7 Baron Konstantin von Neurath, Hitler's compliant foreign minister, called to his office in the Wilhelmstrasse the ambassadors of Britain, France, and Italy. He coldly informed them that German troops had entered the Rhineland and formally denounced the Locarno Pact, the basis of the European peace settlement and Germany's entry into the League of Nations. Then, with Hitler's first treaty broken only a few hours before, Neurath used the occasion to propose Hitler's latest plans. By 10:17 A.M., Sir Eric Phipps, the British ambassador to Berlin, had got back to his office and sent a telegram to London: "Most immediate," it began. "Minister for Foreign Affairs has just handed me the German memorandum (No. 42). In doing so he told me that the Chancellor would announce today in the Reichstag that German armed military detachments had this morning entered the demilitarised zone. . . ."[3]

At noon the Führer himself rose to face the Reichstag, and with exceptional guile, even by his standards, he too expanded his ideas on peace. The Kroll Opera House reverberated to his harangue and the restlessness of his deliriously excited audience. Then, fixing the members with his mesmeric gaze, he calmly announced what they had expectantly awaited. American correspondent William L. Shirer was there: "Germany no longer feels bound by the Locarno Treaty," Hitler rasped. "In the interests of the primitive rights of its people to the security of their frontier and the safeguarding of their defense, the German Government has reestablished, as from today, the absolute and unrestricted sovereignty of the Reich in the demilitarized zone!"

Six hundred deputies, all personal appointees of the Führer, leapt to their feet, their jackboots thudding. "They all seemed to be small men," Shirer recalled, "with big bodies, bulging necks, and cropped hair, with brown uniforms stretched over fat bellies." Together they upstretched their right arms: *"Heil! Sieg Heil!"*

Hitler raised his hand for silence . . . and said in a deep, resonant voice, "Men of the German Reichstag!" The silence was absolute. "In this historical hour, when in the Reich's western provinces, German troops are at this minute marching to their peacetime garrisons, we all unite in two sacred vows. . . ." The Führer could get no further. Even his stentorian voice was overwhelmed by the storm of delirium that burst from the Reichstag mob. "All the militarism in their German blood surges to their heads. They spring yelling and crying to their feet. . . . Their hands are raised in slavish salute, their faces contorted with hysteria, their mouths wide open, shouting, shouting, their eyes burning with fanaticism, glued to the new God, the Messiah. . . ."[4]

Again Phipps wasted no time, and by 12:15 P.M. another cable was on its way to London. It gave the gist of Hitler's speech but added, ". . . I know, however, from a private source that final military discussion only took place yesterday. . . . Even yesterday the army chiefs deprecated military occupation. They were eventually overruled. . . . General Goering, who has always urged drastic action at all great crises in the Chancellor's career and has so far always proved right, helped to carry the day." Evidently Phipps and the embassy were in a flurry of activity.[5]

Away from the fanatical hysteria of the Reichstag, however, there was a singular lack of enthusiasm among Hitler's generals, who had good reason for their apprehension. They knew that behind Hitler's façade of force and the bravura of reoccupying the German Rhineland was a mere shadow of an army. Only three battalions had crossed the Rhine, and they were heavily dependent on horse-drawn transport. While they trundled bravely across the rich farming land of the Rhineland to the far frontiers, welcomed and feted by their own ecstatic people, their sole remaining division was setting about occupying the entire west bank of the Rhine. Meanwhile, facing them across the frontier was the mighty French Army. This, the German generals were convinced, was about to make mincemeat of them.

It was only after a protracted and futile argument with Hitler against this dangerous maneuver that Blomberg had admitted he thought that it could be a peaceful operation. Nevertheless, if the French decided to fight, he still reserved the right to decide on any military countermeasures. At Nuremberg in 1946 the generals' testimonies confirmed that these countermeasures were to have been a hasty retreat back across the Rhine. If the French Army had moved, the Germans would have retreated. Hitler's intuitive invincibility—which was to prove so troublesome in the coming years—would have been stillborn, and he would have been deposed by the army. But the French did not act, largely because Britain would not commit her forces alongside them, and the answers to the questions this attitude raised are revealing. But to seek the causes of Franco-British reticence in the face of German aggression, one has to go back some years.

In 1932, it will be recalled, William de Ropp had made his successful trip to Britain when he had brought Rosenberg and introduced him to many influential people who were to be useful to the Nazis in the years ahead. He had suggested then to his colleague Frederick W. Winterbotham that they should make use of this valuable Nazi connection to try to discover their aims. In particular, he proposed, they should investigate how the Nazis intended to develop their air force, which was, of course, of special interest to Winterbotham. The SIS and the Foreign Office, however, were far from keen on having a senior air force officer getting too involved with the Nazis, and so, Winterbotham says, he decided to string the Nazis along, pretending to be an individual with sympathetic views. During the coming years he was to make a number of trips to Germany and at one time or another met most of the leading Nazis, including Hitler, with whom he had a very interesting discussion in 1934. He also met the man who would become Hitler's deputy Führer, Rudolf Hess, who, with Rosenberg, was among Hitler's closest associates. Hess impressed Winterbotham with his honesty. In view of the events that developed later, this early association between Rosenberg, Hess, and the SIS is notable.

At his 1934 meeting, when Winterbotham had got over the introductions to the Führer, who warmly shook his hand—as he did habitually with everybody he met—they sat in easy chairs around a small table to one side of Hitler's vast and splendid office. Hitler was expansive on that occasion and evidently took the RAF officer's similarity of views to heart. He discussed foreign policy frankly and told Winterbotham: "There should be only three major powers in the world, the British Empire, the Americas and the German Empire of the future," which, he explained, "would include the rest of Europe and the lands to the east. England," he said enthusiastically, "with one or two exceptions, would continue her role in Africa and India, while Germany would take Russia and together we could decide the policy for China and the Far East."[6]

He continued to digress in his usual overbearing manner, and Winterbotham seized upon the following as being especially important: It was, he says, the basis of the theme he was to hear persistently in his visits to Germany in next few years. "All we ask," Hitler declared, "is that Britain should be content to look after her Empire and not to interfere with Germany's plans of expansion." He wanted Britain to keep her nose out of European affairs as they were going to evolve in the years ahead. It would do Britain no good, he declared like a benevolent schoolmaster, to get involved in another war. He went on patronizingly to assure Winterbotham that the Germans themselves would look after the "crushing of Communism" in Russia. They really did not need any help at all.

Hitler's surprising candor and frankness with Winterbotham and de Ropp has to be attributed to this single, important point: *"The main reason must be that the Nazi plans necessitated a neutral Britain."* Evidently Rosenberg believed that he could build up an important collaborationist connection in Britain that would oil the wheels when the time came for Hitler to begin his drive to realize his foreign policy ambitions. Perhaps the most terrifying aspect of all this Nazi scheming, the territorial ambitions, and the treaties that would be made and broken at the Führer's whim before war finally laid Europe prostrate and opened the door to Communism, was that it was frighteningly deliberate. Many people saw his plans; many were certainly sympathetic to these plans; and yet few even tried to head off this juggernaut as it rumbled unswervingly forward on its path of destruction.

Meanwhile, Rosenberg was gradually becoming wrapped up in many other areas of the Nazi party's seemingly endless projects and hairy schemes, so that, as 1934 passed, he faded out of the direct connection with Winterbotham. He went back to his own favorite pastime of secret diplomacy and concentrated his political intrigues behind the scenes in Britain, where he was developing his own high-level collaborationist connections. Then, in January 1935, Rosenberg's scheming paid off, for he received a report from de Ropp, who was at work in London, advising in the strictest confidence that he had succeeded in enlisting a man he called the "political adviser" of King George V as a confidential broker of Hitler's cause. This, Rosenberg claimed, established a "direct pipeline to Buckingham Palace." So delicate and secret was this contact, though, that the details could not be entrusted to the mails, so on February 2 de Ropp made the journey to Berlin to report to the enraptured Rosenberg that the new contact was none other than the Duke of Kent, the king's youngest son. Rosenberg was so elated that, as soon as he could get away, he rushed to the Chancellery to tell Hitler about his latest coup.

It was late in the evening of January 23, 1935, when de Ropp paid his prearranged clandestine visit to the Duke of Kent at one of the royal residences. It goes without saying that very little has ever been revealed about what went on at that late-night meeting, although, according to Ladislas Farrago, the duke definitely knew that de Ropp was a German agent. De Ropp always insisted that it was the Duke of Kent who pumped him for information and not the other way around and claimed that the initiative for the meeting also came from Kent. As de Ropp was evidently working for the Germans then, and since, as evidence will show, he continued to do so through the early years of the war at least, this was an occasion when de Ropp's role was to influence the duke and, through him, someone else. Was that other person the king or the Prince of Wales, and was this laying the foundations of what Francois-Poncet had called Hitler's appropriate moment to act in relation to the Rhineland? In the years ahead the Duke of Kent was to crop up several times as an emissary between the Nazis and his eldest brother—the future Duke of Windsor. But the Duke of Kent— Prince George—was certainly privy to his father's political thinking, and indeed de Ropp terms him the king's political adviser. He had been with his parents, King George V and Queen Mary, when they had entertained Hoesch at dinner at Windsor Castle the previous April 25. Following that, Hoesch had sent off a cable at 11:15 P.M. hastening to inform the German foreign minister about his conversation at Windsor.

That meeting at Windsor had been interesting for the German ambassador. The king, he cabled, "engaged me in a long political conversation" after dinner. He said the king had been well informed on current issues and began with a brief review of German-British relations in the postwar period; these, he thought, had deteriorated after the Nazis came to power following their rapid improvement after the war. The king was sure this was due to the treatment of the Jews, and to the concentration camps, of which he had evidently heard already! One point that especially interested Hoesch was that "King George did not hesitate to express some adverse criticism of the dictated peace of Versailles; in this connection he made the war itself, as a human madness, responsible for such deplorable consequences." A human enough judgment on a harsh treaty that many statesmen regretted by the 1930s, but, nevertheless, honey to the lips of the Nazis. The crux of the talk had come later, though, when the king said that, "as long as he was living England would not again become involved in war. Accordingly, out of his firm conviction that a new war would mean the ruin of everybody, he would do everything in his power to forestall every possibility of war."[7]

Many of the sentiments being expressed by the king on that occasion were to form his son Edward's theme during the grind toward the Second World War. But his words "the ruin of everybody" perhaps reflected his own deep-rooted fear of Bolshevism, which he was convinced would be the only winner in the next conflict. Indeed, as we shall see, on the outbreak of war, this was to be the Duke of Windsor's first and instinctive response. Their cousins in Saint Petersburg had, after all, been swept away in the Russian Revolution and their German relatives bereft of their royal status after the war.

So, when de Ropp met the Duke of Kent that night in January 1935, it was no new experience for the duke to talk with the Germans. De Ropp records that at that time the duke declared that Britain was reconciled to Hitler's determination to rearm Germany, but what after that, he wanted to know. And what was the real "mentality" of Germany's new masters? Were they aggressive, congenital troublemakers, or could they be tamed to work in traditional diplomatic ways? He was deeply interested, too, to know what made Hitler tick, and Hess, Goering, and Goebbels as well.

There has been a great deal of derision expressed about the references to the royal family that appear in German documents. Later in this story we will find much supportive evidence among these documents about Windsor's activities in Portugal. But all too frequently, whenever the documentary evidence looks like it is becoming compromising, it ceases abruptly. The usual footnote in the records is, "This document had never been found." It is suggested by those who seek to protect eminent people that the whole affair of the duke and the Nazis was concocted by them to discredit the duke and his family. This view is irrational, however, since the papers are records made at the time of the events when the Nazis' star was ascending rapidly and were not discovered until after Germany's total defeat. By that time most of Germany's leaders were dead. The documents were never intended for publication and were hidden among literally hundreds of tons of German records, correspondence, and reports amassed in the everyday business of the Reich and took years to sort and catalogue. When the German Foreign Policy Documents were in preparation for publication, the British government wanted certain documents stopped, and Churchill appealed to the Americans not to publish them. Eventually, however, the papers were published in America and France, and so, reluctantly, they were published in Britain too. Nevertheless, Volume X, which is especially concerned with the Duke of Windsor, carries an official note, cautioning readers not to believe all they read, a clear attempt at censorship. As this story progresses, there will be several instances where the evidence stops short, because papers "have not been found," or "official records are closed"; some, it is said officially, will never be made available. What is being hidden more than forty years after the events?

While Hitler was consolidating his position as Germany's dictator and cautiously preparing to reoccupy the Rhineland as an opening gambit for the Reich's path of conquest, in Britain, Edward, Prince of Wales, had been growing increasingly fond of Mrs. Wallis Simpson, who exerted a great influence over him. Her story has been told many times, and here it is necessary only to recount the broad outlines. Her involvement with the prince rocked the throne and confused vital foreign issues at one of the most dangerous periods in the country's history. That the result was not more cataclysmic can only be attributed to the manner in which Edward's brother Albert accepted a daunting responsibility as King George VI and especially in the way that he was backed by the redoubtable common sense of his queen, Elizabeth.

Mrs. Simpson had been introduced to the eminently attractive bachelor prince at a reception given by Lady Furness, an American with whom she had cultivated a friendship soon after setting up home in London with her businessman husband, Ernest Simpson. That was in the autumn of 1930. Mrs. Simpson later claimed that she saw the prince only once during the next twelve months, although Lady Furness's recollection was that Mrs. Simpson and the Prince met at least once a week for three and a half years. There was certainly ample opportunity for them to do so in the gay whirl of the London season of the time—luncheons at one or another sumptuous house, dinner parties where the latest music of the twenties and thirties set the taffeta swirling; a world of men's capaciously wide trousers and long cigarette holders. Eventually, in the fullness of time, the prince and Mrs. Simpson's relationship developed, until in January 1932 he unexpectedly sent her an invitation to Fort Belvedere, then the very acme of social acceptance.

Fort Belvedere was situated in the grounds of Windsor Great Park. It was a romantic enough setting for the prince and his friend, who could look across the delightful view to Virginia Water from the semicircular stone battlement where some thirty eighteenth-century Belgian cannons were emplaced. Edward had made the fort his home some years before, had it modernized, and installed a tennis court and a swimming pool.

The relationship between them developed convivially enough and to the virtual exclusion of all the former close friends of the duke. This was not conducive to concord among Edward's well-established society circle, and most biographies of the Prince of Wales are peppered with patronizingly catty remarks about Mrs. Simpson's appearance, her sharp wit, her obsession with perfection in decor, dress, and dinner; terms like "educable" appear to sum up society's attitude to her in the thirties. Nevertheless, people agreed that she was having a favorable impact on the prince. As Chips Channon put it, "Mrs. Simpson has enormously improved the Prince.... I was interested to see what an extraordinary hold Mrs. Simpson has over the Prince. In the interval [at the theater] she told him to hurry away as he would be late in joining the Queen at the L.C.C. ball—and she made him take a cigar from out of his breast pocket. 'It doesn't look very pretty,' she said."[8]

This concern over his appearance and his punctuality was, perhaps, the magic of her attraction for him; it made up for the lack of affection from his parents. His biographer Donaldson says: "There is no doubt that King George and Queen Mary failed in their relationships with their children and were for different reasons temperamentally unsuited to parenthood."[9] Mrs. Simpson's manner was a refreshing change from the obsequiousness of his usual hangers-on. She was both direct and outspoken, and her very ignorance of protocol and court ritual was a welcome change to a man who had grown up in a veritable hothouse of both. Throughout his adult life he had defied tradition and the sentiments of the royal household; in his own favorite expression, he "had got away with it." He clearly perceived himself upholding the principles of the young of the postwar years against the old and failed, who had all but decimated his generation. It is significant that he was only six years younger than Adolf Hitler, whose ideas he evidently found new and exciting. Of course, he was not alone in his 1930s outlook. Edward has often been compared with the American aviator Charles Lindbergh: both were youthful heroes to a generation of a troubled and unheroic time, and they both had exceptional opportunities to form erroneous judgments. Although both believed in the phoenix-like power and might of the new Germany, neither recognized that eventually this would have to be fought, if necessary to the death.

Mrs. Simpson's attention and outspoken advice, which was often given in ignorance of the wider implications of a king's role, undoubtedly gave Edward confidence and hardened his own attitudes, putting steel into the shyness that hid behind the public smile. Perhaps in those long conversations they had together in the middle 1930s, holidaying at Biarritz or cruising the Mediterranean in the *Rosauros* and the *Nahlin*, she was able to give him the chance to round out his views. No doubt he also learned a great deal from her about the way in which Americans looked at things, for Edward regarded himself as very much a twentieth-century man and was delighted by the go-ahead drive of America. He was, similarly, very enthusiastic about the way in which Nazi Germany was solving its economic and social problems, too, which, he could not fail to observe, Britain and France were manifestly unable to do despite all their traditions and democratic institutions. Mrs. Simpson's contribution to the prince's attitude to life and his role in the unstable, radical 1930s was to give form and direction to his long-suppressed aspirations. Held back by tradition and by his very conscientious but narrow father and mother, suddenly he saw in Nazi Germany a dynamic, no-nonsense system sweeping away nineteenth-century conventions. Here then was a man adored by his Empire, whose people hung on his every word, but who was in reality only an image of power, the embodiment of an idea. As head of the world's greatest empire, he could, paradoxically, exercise no power. There can be little doubt that he would have welcomed the chance to meet with the world's leaders, most of whom he already knew, but not as a figurehead—as an equal in the exercise of Britain's imperial power, which in the 1930s was at its zenith. By her very naiveté, Mrs. Simpson held out the promise of power to the prince as surely as Eve held out the promise of knowledge to Adam.

It seems almost certain that the danger to be feared from her was through her influence over Edward as king. In this regard there is a difference of opinion as to whether she was in any way concerned with politics, many people arguing that her interests were of a purely social kind, while others, such as Lord Beaverbrook, who knew her when Edward was on the throne, insist that she did display an interest in current affairs. But then she was an intelligent woman. What seems likely is that she was ambitious for the king and that her role was the feminine one of wishing to find a sphere of interest for her man. It is not impossible that she lured him to strike out for himself, to ignore the stupidities of the politicians, to play an active part in saving the world from war, and not improbable that she admired the regimes that made trains run on time and had swept away hidebound conventions.

By 1936 Hitler was developing another line of communication to the royal family, employing one of their German relatives, Karl Eduard, Duke of Saxe-Coburg-Gotha, a first cousin once-removed to Edward, Prince of Wales. Coburg, then aged forty-five, had been an Etonian with Edward. During the First World War he had been a general in both the Prussian infantry and the Saxon cavalry. By the 1930s, however, he had wholly embraced Hitler's doctrines and was, indeed, a great admirer of the Führer, who made him a senior officer in the Nazi Stormtroopers, the infamous SA; he was also president of the German Red Cross.

During these momentous years Coburg had, nevertheless, remained a close friend of his British relatives, and whenever he visited London he stayed at Kensington Palace, the home of his sister Princess Alice, the Countess of Athlone. Early in January 1935, when in Germany final preparations were being made for the move into the Rhineland, Coburg visited Britain once more. He arrived in London with the intention of visiting King George V, who was at Sandringham, the king's private estate in Norfolk, "to discuss certain events" with him. By then, however, the old king was ailing, and unfortunately he died before they could meet. The king's death was a tragedy not just because he was a well-loved monarch who had encouraged his hard-pressed people through the terrible traumas of the First World War but also because, in spite of his words to Hoesch in 1934, he seems to have been sensible of the threat posed by the upstart German dictator. He was aware, nonetheless, that his heir was regrettably by no means opposed to the Nazis and was very susceptible to their influence. When, in June 1935, the Prince of Wales had made a speech at a British Legion function calling for a new friendship with Germany and declaring that German exservicemen would be welcomed in Britain, the king had been very angry and immediately warned his son in no uncertain terms that he should not make such public declarations; it was, he insisted, unconstitutional. To what degree the king was angered by the public acclaim the speech brought from Dr. Goebbels in Germany rather than by the sentiment, we cannot tell. Certainly his warning to Edward was not to meddle publicly in politics rather than to change his views of the Germans.

When the announcement was posted that the old king had "slipped quietly away," Coburg lost no time in calling on the new king, Edward VIII, at Fort Belvedere. He reported that he had his first conversation on the day after the death of King George V on the occasion of carrying out the Führer's commission, "a little more than half an hour (with pipe at fireside). Following this I accompanied him on his journey to Buckingham Palace." In fact, Coburg was Edward's sole companion when he motored to Buckingham Palace to take up his new duties and was a close friend of the king during the next busy days. He had two more conversations with the new king, the first during his visits to Queen Mary for tea and again between a state dinner and reception at Buckingham Palace.

We do not know what the "certain events" were that King George had wanted to discuss with Coburg, and in any case the discussions never took place; presumably they were connected with the Rhineland, for while Hitler's timing was a surprise, it was assumed that at some time in the near future he would do so, and the timing of the visit suggests this.

Thanks to the report made by Coburg on his return to Hitler, we know something of what took place between himself and King Edward VIII. Coburg had asked him whether a discussion between British Prime Minister Stanley Baldwin and Hitler might be desirable—again, one assumes about the Rhineland. But, Coburg reported to Hitler, the new king had loftily retorted: "Who is King here, Baldwin or I? I myself wish to talk to Hitler, and will do so here or in Germany. Tell him that, please."

Coburg was able to assure the Führer that "King Edward was determined to concentrate the business of government on himself, although he admitted this was not too easy in England. The general political situation, though, especially the situation of England herself, will perhaps give him a chance. His sincere resolve to bring Germany and England together," Coburg cautioned, "would be made more difficult if it were made public too early." For this reason, he went on, "I regard it as most important to respect the King's wish that the non-official policy of Germany towards England should be firmly concentrated in one hand and at the same time brought into relations of confidence with the official policy. The peculiar mentality of the Englishman must be taken into account if we want to achieve success—which undoubtedly is attainable." Hitler was evidently pursuing his own "non-official foreign policy," apart from the declared Foreign Ministry one, a point worth remembering in relation to the subsequent events in Portugal.

Coburg concluded on a hopeful note. "The King," he said, "asked me to visit him frequently in order that confidential matters might be more speedily clarified in this way, and to fly to London at any time he wishes."[10]

Skeptics may well deride this report and claim it is exaggerated, but the proposed emissaries, flying to meet the prince, the careful choosing of the right time and stressing of caution lest the connection become public too soon, all suggest intrigue, even some decisive prearranged action in due course. The fact is, though, that this method is virtually a prototype for what happened in Portugal just four years later, and those events will clearly reveal Edward's willing hand.

The conversation reported by Coburg indicates that the king was impatient with his ponderous prime minister, Stanley Baldwin, and was anxious to take a much more positive role in the government of Britain than was customary or even constitutional. Eventually Edward would meet Hitler and discuss with him all the matters he had so wanted to in 1936.

It is significant to this story that a carbon copy of this document was found together with a covering letter from the Duke of Coburg's chief of staff, Herr Nord, to Goering's private secretary, Herr Gritzbach, which includes this passage: "The Duke gathered from the conversation he had the day before yesterday that there was a certain interest on the part of the Colonel-General (Goering) for his mission in England. On the Duke's instruction I enclose herewith the January report to the Führer, which is perhaps somewhat revealing concerning a number of persons."

Meanwhile, Leopold von Hoesch, the German ambassador in London, too, had sent a dispatch on January 21 confirming the king's ". . . warm sympathy for Germany. I have become convinced," he cabled, "during frequent, often lengthy, talks with him that these sympathies are deep-rooted and strong enough to withstand the contrary influences to which they are not seldom exposed. . . ." Later in the same cable he says: "King Edward will naturally have imposed restrictions on himself at first, especially in questions of foreign policy, which are so very delicate. But I am convinced that his friendly attitude towards

Germany might in time come to exercise a certain amount of influence in the shaping of British foreign policy. At any rate, we should be able to rely upon having on the British throne a ruler who is not lacking in understanding for Germany and in the desire to see good relations established between Germany and Britain." Hoesch was at pains to point out as well that the king was no pacifist and wanted a strong Britain, although he saw war as no way to settle international disputes because he believed any new war would ruin Europe and see its submergence by Bolshevism.[11]

The communications did not end there either, for later in January 1936, as Winterbotham recalls, de Ropp was ordered to go to Britain to see the Duke of Kent again. His directive was to explain to the duke the aims and objectives of the Nazis, presumably to reinforce Coburg's connection. As became apparent in Portugal, Hitler was always reluctant to employ the same "secret emissary" too often and interchanged them frequently, although always using people known to the duke. De Ropp said that "the request had originally come from King Edward VIII" but it was thought advisable to make the contact through his brother, thus forging another link in the communication chain between Crown and Swastika. Edward was by then under fairly careful surveillance by the security services, although many people have assumed it was because of his association with Mrs. Simpson. De Ropp almost certainly knew of this since he worked closely with Winterbotham, who was himself a top man in the Secret Intelligence Service.

This development, however, presents an intriguing question: who ordered de Ropp to go? If, as seems likely, de Ropp's visit stemmed from Coburg's contact, which had been reported directly to Hitler, and as we have already seen, de Ropp was regarded by Hitler as his personal contact with the British, it seems likely that the order originated with the Führer. So the Führer sent de Ropp to London. When I asked Winterbotham about this possibility, he accepted it as a straightforward fact that Hitler would have been the one who sent de Ropp. That being so, then obviously the king had sent a request for information about Nazi aims by the highest possible channel, Coburg, direct to the Führer. Hoesch is also on record, though, as having paid extremely surreptitious visits to the king's retreat, Fort Belvedere, even changing from his official car to a less noticeable vehicle to do so. By this time, evidently, King Edward VIII had several direct Nazi links to Hitler.

What Baron de Ropp told the Duke of Kent in his late-night visit in January 1936 and how he characterized the Nazi leaders, can well be imagined without recourse to a transcript of this nocturnal conversation. As Rosenberg fortunately recorded in his diary, written at the time: "R[opp] gave the Duke the benefit of his knowledge based on his personal experience of many years." The captured German records do not make clear how far this direct contact was developed, although the Duke of Kent does crop up in documents and signals up to 1940. It must be kept in mind, though, that he was, in 1935 and 1936 and also in the later connections, very much a go-between, the less obvious way of contacting his eldest brother. Although Farrago makes the point that he (Kent) "neither sought nor had any access to the corridors of power . . . and was not an ideal partner for such a game," this is not entirely accurate. The king certainly had access to the most important state papers, and every night several red dispatch boxes of such papers would be delivered for his perusal. A number of visitors to Fort Belvedere during Edward's short reign have concurred that he had no sense of their confidential nature and would inevitably leave opened dispatch boxes lying about while he went off to his gardening, of which he was very fond. Edward was also a great talker and would discuss the most intimate state matters with whoever happened to be present. This is not to suggest that Kent deliberately sought access to state secrets, but in the company of his brother it was hard not to become privy to those secrets. Once again this trait of Edward's will be seen to have had ominous repercussions by the time war had broken out.

"One of the strangest aspects of Edward's reign is that he spent much of it under the surveillance of security officers," writes Donaldson. "Mrs. Simpson was the primary source of these attentions, but, they were so often together, it was impossible to take this kind of interest in one of them without extending it to the other."[12]

The possibility that Mrs. Simpson had connections with Germans in Britain, which made her suspect, arose originally from her social acquaintances. This rumor had persisted despite the total lack of evidence to substantiate it, both then and in examinations of German records since the war.

It was widely believed that Ribbentrop had tried to establish an association with her, but again there is no firm evidence that she met him more than a few times at a luncheon or dinner party. The German Embassy certainly attempted to curry favor with the Prince of Wales by asking her to a reception on July 10, 1935, but given their well-known friendship by then, it was a normally shrewd diplomatic move to win the support of the heir to the throne. Why then did this malicious story originate? If one discounts social backbiting, then it seems more likely to have been a useful ruse by the security services acting for the government to keep an eye on Edward, whose meetings with Germans cannot have been ignored. It was, too, a clever way of discrediting Mrs. Simpson and thereby maneuvering the king into a position from which his eventual removal from the throne could be effected with the least embarrassment to the royal family. It would also imbue the tedious affair with a romantic overtone—a king who abdicated for love of a mischievous woman rather than a sinister figure who might have threatened his country's democracy. Anthony Eden, the foreign secretary, is said to have remarked about the king's increasing intervention in foreign affairs that if he went on like that, there were ways and means of making him abdicate.[13]

There is also a considerable body of evidence that the king differed with his ministers in many respects with regard to foreign policy and allowed himself a freedom of expression that was completely unconstitutional, creating in Germany an impression of warm sympathy and an exaggerated idea of his power and influence, as shown by Hoesch's cable on January 21. As early as 1935 Hoesch reported to the Reich Chancellery that the then prince had inquired in great detail about the progress of the Anglo-German conversations then taking place in Berlin and was critical of the "too-one-sided attitude of the Foreign Office," while he had once again showed his "complete understanding of Germany's position and aspirations." During this conversation he was reported also to have said that he had long foreseen that, if there were no general disarmament, Germany would one day take it upon herself to decide the scale of her armaments; but, in speaking of the German demand for the return of colonies, he had advised that "in the interests of retaining Britain's sympathies," Germany should not put forward a formal demand with regard to the British mandated territories. However, Hoesch says this: "He fully understood that Germany wished to face the other nations squarely, her head high, relying on her strength and conscious that Germany's word counted as much in the world as that of other nations."[14]

His attitude was summed up succinctly by Channon: "The King is insane about Wallis. He, too, is going the dictator way, and is pro-German, against Russia and against too much slipshod democracy. I shouldn't be surprised if he aimed at making himself a mild dictator, a difficult enough task for an English King."[15]

In his defiance of Baldwin and determination to talk to Hitler, the new king was casting himself in the mold of his grandfather, Edward VII, who had personally intervened on occasion with both kaiser and czar. They had been relatives, though, and his actions a part of the accepted old-world diplomacy along the family grapevine. Edward VIII wanted to talk with a German dictator, a man who had already shown himself as a ruthless, cunning political leader of utter unscrupulousness. Of even greater significance was the king's regard for the Nazis and his attitude to European problems, which was contrary to that of his prime minister. Nevertheless, the king was in tune with an important enough group of people, the so-called Cliveden Set.[13]

The Cliveden Set in the years before the Second World War was persistently regarded by Hitler as a significant source of British foreign policy. This was just as persistently denied in Britain. But Hitler was getting the advice of his embassy staff in London, as we have seen by the 1933 memorandum from Hoesch, and Hoesch was a very well-informed non-Nazi who moved in London society. Later, when Ribbentrop was appointed ambassador to London, he was supposed to have influenced Hitler in his belief that the British were effete and would not fight. He may well have voiced these opinions in 1936 and 1937, but he certainly *did* advise Hitler that he should regard Britain as his most important enemy who *would* fight, in a memo in 1938, as we shall see. Ribbentrop was certainly haughty and obtuse in his relationships with foreign diplomats, and afterward persisted in coupling offers of peace with an alternative threat of force, so that he could hardly be taken seriously. But he was certainly not so dense as to misread the evidence that the British would, if pushed far enough, turn and fight. Perhaps his legendary denseness was a convenient way of protecting the reputations of those in important places in Britain who, had the decision been theirs, *would* have preferred to stand aside while the Nazis built their European empire. In the mid 1930s the Germans were listening to people who were more alarmed by Russian Bolshevism than by the new German Nazism.

The ramifications of the Cliveden Set were many, and the people linked through communion in the great country house were important and influential, including Geoffrey Dawson, the editor of the *Times*, who had been so sympathetic to Rosenberg. Among others were Lord Rothermere whose *Daily Mail* was threatened by its Jewish advertisers with the loss of their business if the paper did not tone down its approval of the Nazis. Another figure was Lord Lothian, formerly Philip Keer, who saw Hitler twice, in February 1935 and May 1937. On his return in 1937 he wrote to Nancy Astor: "I hope the British government will go and have a real talk in Germany as to how Europe is to be pacified. Hitler is a prophet—not a politician or an intriguer. Quite straight, full of queer ideas, but quite honestly wanting no war." It was written of Lothian, "Of the Cliveden Set. The most wrong-headed of them was Philip Lothian, yet his was not the wrong-headedness of an original mind. Most of his political ideas at that time were the commonplace of the thirties in England."[16] In 1939 he was appointed British ambassador in Washington.

This, then, was the environment in which Edward moved as Prince of Wales and then as king. What was said of Lothian's ideas was also true of his, but they were infinitely more dangerous for the influence they carried at home and abroad. Curiously, the subtle censorship that works so well in Britain, which was evinced by the total lack of public knowledge about Mrs. Simpson until the very last weeks, meant that his views and his potential as a leader for peace were much more widely appreciated in Germany.

Is it surprising that he should have fallen under the spell of the dynamic dictator who was doing for Germany all the things that Edward saw should be done in Britain? Edward could visit the depressed areas of Britain and do nothing but make promises that were beyond his power to implement, but Hitler had got eight million unemployed working again. Edward's great fear was of Bolshevism, and this theme runs through his actions for years and is to recur many times in this story.

So, in relation to the Rhineland, Hitler had bided his time during the winter of 1935 to 1936. France and Britain were preoccupied at that time with Italy's aggression in Abyssinia, and the fact that Mussolini seemed to be getting away with his invasion must have appeared encouraging to the Führer. Meanwhile the French government was still dragging its feet over ratifying the pact with the Soviet Union, mainly because the French right wing was opposed to Communism, but this was not good news for Hitler, who was looking for an excuse to occupy the Rhineland. If the French chamber actually rejected the Moscow alliance, he would then have to seek another pretext for *Schulung*—the reoccupation of the Rhineland. But his luck held, and the French played into his hands. On February 27 the pact was approved by a vote of 353 to 164. Hitler thereupon seized the opportunity to justify his action, and two days later, on March 1, he gave orders for the operation to take place.

The French nation was already unnerved by internal strife, and defeatism was much in evidence; nevertheless, if the French had known of Blomberg's apprehension, they might have acted differently. The French Army was weak in both equipment and morale. The French government was certainly aware that Hitler was going to send his troops into the Rhineland, although without knowing exactly when. Their apprehension is borne out by a cable of March 4 from the British representative in Geneva, Mr. Edmunds, to the Foreign Office. It detailed a statement from M. Pierre Flandin, the French foreign minister, that the "French Government will not proceed to any isolated action. It will only act in agreement with co-signatories of Locarno." This statement did not imply that the French would not act at all but that they would do so only through the correct machinery of the Locarno Pact, which meant principally in alliance with Britain. That the French were actually preparing to act is shown by the telegram from Sir G. Clerk, Britain's ambassador in Paris, on March 8, the day after the reoccupation. At 8:40 that evening he cabled: "All leave stopped in sixth, twentieth and seventh regions. Fortified works Montredy southward occupied and mobile formation complete with artillery concentrated in accordance with normal concentration plans for defense of frontier limited to Anti-Aircraft defense. . . ."[17]

Although the situation grew tense as the world waited to see if the French would attack, the German press, under Dr. Goebbels's capable control, ensured that the German people got only the best of the propaganda. Phipps, the British ambassador to Berlin, evidently read the papers early the next day, March 9, for soon after 10 A.M. he was cabling Anthony Eden: "This morning's Berlin press conveys the impression that Germany's entry into the demilitarized zone is welcomed with enthusiasm by the London Sunday newspapers. Tribute is paid to British calm and sense of reality which are compared unfavorably with French excitability and unreason."[18]

Behind the scenes Germany's ambassador to Britain was doing all he could to insure the success of Hitler's plans. Late on the night of March 11, Hoesch paid another secret visit to the highest level of Britain's government. It is not known how long his visit took, but by three minutes past ten o'clock that night he was signaling Berlin:

> Most Urgent,
> No. 40 of March 11, 1936. London, 10:03 P.M.
> With reference to our written communication [not found!]. Today I got into direct touch with the Court. The view prevailing in the authoritative quarter is that our proposals could well constitute a basis on which to construct a lasting peace system; in other respects, too, there is understanding there for the German point of view. The directive given to the Government from there is to the effect that, no matter how the details of the affair are dealt with, complications of a serious nature are in no circumstances to be allowed to develop. Hoesch.[19]

Adolf Hitler had developed the habit of staying up until the early hours of the morning, and so one can imagine the immense relief it brought the Führer when Neurath hastened from the Foreign Ministry to the Chancellery with that signal. From then on he must have realized that the chance of military intervention by the West was minimal. France would not attack without Britain, and Britain was virtually certain to do nothing "of a serious nature." All his planning and intriguing were going to pay off.

There is further evidence, too, that Hitler was perhaps indulging more in playacting than cliff-hanging as he established his reputation for intuition. Albert Speer relates how on the evening of March 7—while his forces were consolidating in the Rhineland—the Führer and his entourage were traveling by special train to Munich. The atmosphere, Speer related, was tense until at one station a message was handed to Hitler, who sighed with relief: "At last! The King of England will not intervene. He is keeping his promise. That means it can all go well." Does that message relate to Hoesch's reference in his March 11 cable to "our written communication," which was never found? Again it substantiates the central role that Hitler at least believed that Edward was taking in his action to recover control of the Rhineland.[20]

Despite Hitler's confidence in success, his generals were still having to make their decisions on the evidence of their military assessments. By March 12 Blomberg had lost his nerve and actually gave orders for the troops to withdraw from the Rhineland if the French moved to oppose them. Clearly then, Hitler's optimism was based on diplomatic advice and not military.

Francois-Poncet had already asked his government what it would do in case he was proved correct and had been told they would take the matter up only with the League of Nations. Despite the alert ambassador's timely warnings the previous autumn, Germany's reoccupation still found the French and British governments and their general staff with no plans to oppose Germany. Once the French government had recovered from the initial shock, however, it wanted to act, but it was held back by its own general staff. "General Gamelin," the French commander in chief, says Francois-Poncet "advised that a war operation, however limited, entailed unpredictable risks and could not be undertaken without decreeing a general mobilization."[21] Such an action would have assuredly scared the Germans stiff, but unfortunately it would also have rocked the unstable French political scene. All the French did, therefore, was to concentrate forces in thirteen divisions to reinforce the Maginot Line along the German frontier. This was evidently only a defensive reaction while they awaited Britain's intentions, but it was enough to throw a panic into the German high command. Blomberg, supported by Jodl and most of the senior officers, insisted on withdrawing the three battalions, for as Jodl testified at Nuremberg, "Considering the situation we were in, the French covering army could have blown us to pieces."[22]

Had Gamelin ordered his numerically vastly superior French divisions into the Rhineland, that would have certainly been the end of Hitler. "The forty-eight hours after the march into the Rhineland," Paul Schmidt, his interpreter, heard him say later, "were the most nerve-racking of my life. If the French had then marched into the Rhineland, we would have had to withdraw with our tails between our legs, for the military resources at our disposal would have been wholly inadequate for even a moderate resistance."[23] The German dictator could never have survived such a fiasco. Hitler himself concluded later: "A retreat on our part would have spelled collapse." That he survived at all has been attributed to his iron nerves, which alone saved the situation. But it is clear from the evidence that the crafty arch schemer had laid his plans with Machiavellian precision and had really left very little to chance. He knew that Britain's reaction would be hamstrung by its pro-German king, who if opposed could have precipitated a constitutional crisis of the first order.

Hitler was confident that the French would not march without British support, which he had blunted, so he brusquely turned down all the appeals from his wavering high command to pull back. General Beck, the chief of the general staff, implored the Führer at least to soften the blow by declaring that he would not fortify the Rhineland. The Führer turned that down flat, for he was already planning the West Wall to secure his western frontier from French intervention when he turned east.

All the same, if the French high command was loath to

precipitate military counteraction, the government was not. Its problem, though, was to create circumstances in which the sluggish generals would be bolstered into action, and their one hope was to get active British support. Pierre Flandin flew to London on March 11 and begged the British government to back France in a military counteraction in the Rhineland. But his eloquent pleas were fruitless. Britain, he was firmly told, would not risk war even though Allied superiority over the Germans was absolute. Lord Lothian remarked: "The Germans, after all, are only going into their own back garden." And even before the French arrived in London, Anthony Eden told the House of Commons on March 9: "Occupation of the Rhineland by the Reichwehr deals a heavy blow to the principle of the sanctity of treaties. Fortunately," he added, in eloquent complacency, "we have no reason to suppose that Germany's present actions threaten hostilities."[24]

Hitler's successful Rhineland gamble was more staggering and fatal to the West in its consequences than was comprehended at the time. It fortified Hitler's popularity at home and consolidated his power in a way that no previous German ruler had ever enjoyed. Of greater importance by far, though, was the ascendancy it gave him over his generals. They had hesitated at a moment of crisis when the Führer's will had held firm. They were until then the last hope of stopping the Nazi party's rampage to power, but instead they had been taught the humiliating lesson that in foreign policies and even in military affairs, his judgment was superior to theirs. They had warned him that the French would fight, but he had known better.

France's failure to repel the three Wehrmacht battalions, and Britain's failure to support her in a comparatively simple police action, was the disaster from which sprang all the later German aggressions of infinitely greater magnitude. In March 1936 the two Western democracies were given their last opportunity to slam the door on the rise of a virulent, militarized German dictatorship and bring tumbling down Hitler and his regime. The Rhineland occupation, though small in itself as a military operation, opened the way to vast new opportunities in Europe. Only Hitler and Churchill saw that the strategic situation in Europe had been irrevocably changed by just three battalions goose-stepping across the Rhine bridges.

The Rhineland occupation irrevocably signaled France's demise. Her Eastern Allies, Russia, Poland, Czechoslovakia, Romania, and Yugoslavia, were all suddenly faced with the dire reality that France had backed down against a German aggression that threatened the security system that France herself had so laboriously constructed. Worse still, it dawned on those Eastern Allies that even if in the future France did make a stand against German aggression, she was now cut off and would not be able to offer them more than token support. Germany was feverishly building an impregnable *Westwall* along the Franco-German border. This fortress line was clearly changing the strategic map of Europe, for it would prevent France's planned response to German aggression in the east, which had been to invade the Rhineland and attack the Ruhr. A France that with one hundred divisions did not repel three German battalions was not going to have her youth slaughtered against the impregnable German West Wall fortifications; memories of the 300,000 French men lost in just four days in August 1914 against the German Metz fortifications would see to that. Henceforth the French could do no more than tie down in the west only a small part of the growing German Army while the remainder was hurled against Germany's eastern neighbors. It was, in effect, the reverse of Germany's First World War Schlieffen Plan—the Germans had learned their lesson well.

4

The King's Downfall

S IR JOHN Reith said, "This is Windsor Castle. His Royal Highness, Prince Edward."

Looking grave and seated uneasily behind a period desk incongruously occupied by an ungainly BBC microphone, Edward began his abdication broadcast. His usually steady, measured voice wavered as he started anxiously:

"At long last I am able to say a few words of my own.

"I have never wanted to withhold anything, but until now it has not been constitutionally possible for me to speak.

"A few hours ago I discharged my last duty as King and Emperor, and now that I have been succeeded by my brother, the Duke of York, my first words must be to declare my allegiance to him. This I do with all my heart."

He went on to explain the reasons that had impelled him to renounce the throne, that he had found it impossible to carry his heavy burden of responsibility "without the help and support of the woman I love." He stressed that the decision was his alone.

"This decision," he continued, "has been made less difficult to me by the sure knowledge that my brother, with his long training in the public affairs of this country and with his fine qualities, will be able to take my place forthwith, without interruption or injury to the life and progress of the Empire. And he has one matchless blessing, enjoyed by so many of you and not bestowed on me—a happy home with his wife and children."

He talked on and, nearing the end of his broadcast, his voice gained confidence: "I now quit altogether public affairs, and I lay down my burden. It may be some time before I return to my native land, but I shall always follow the fortunes of the British race and Empire with profound interest, and if at any time in the future I can be found of service to His Majesty in a private station, I shall not fail. And now we have a new King. I wish him, and you, his people, happiness and prosperity with all my heart. God bless you all. God Save the King."[1] He finished with an exclamation that was almost a shout.

Within a few hasty hours of making his abdication speech, Edward, then the Duke of Windsor, had departed from Britain, leaving the aptly named Farewell Jetty at Portsmouth Naval Docks aboard the new destroyer HMS *Fury* on his way into exile.

With Edward's departure from Britain it seemed that a unique chapter in Britain's history had been closed. The unthinkable had happened. The youthful, charming, and immensely popular Prince of Wales had gone after reigning as uncrowned king for less than a year.

Careful, self-imposed constraints by the British press over the years had ensured that his subjects in Britain had, in the main, been oblivious to the growing ignominy that had increasingly surrounded his affairs and made headline news in the United States and Canada; no one suggested that censorship had prevailed, but then in Britain it remains a subtle art. Nevertheless, trans-Atlantic travelers, seamen, and visitors to Britain were gradually disseminating tidbits that aroused public curiosity and incredulity. Even among Edward's closer acquaintances, few, it seems, ever seriously believed he would actually marry Mrs. Simpson. Walter Monckton, his friend since Oxford days and a barrister of formidable repute who advised the king before and during the crisis, noted that he had underestimated the strength of the king's devotion and "of their united will." He thought that ". . . they would in the end each make the sacrifice, devastating though it would be."[2]

According to Ralph G. Martin, who interviewed one of Mrs. Simpson's former household staff, she had gathered them all together, with her friends the Herman Rogerses, to listen to the abdication speech. One of them insisted that she had said while listening, "The fool, the stupid fool." Did this imply that she, too, never thought he would do it?

The story of the abdication has been explained and expounded by many authors. Briefly put, the king's friendship with Mrs. Simpson had begun to look more discreditable as the spring of 1936 lazed into summer. As Europe settled uncomfortably in the aftermath of Hitler's march into the Rhineland, the king continued to make faux pas. At the beginning of May he had talked with Count Grandi, the Italian ambassador, and by May 8 an account of that meeting was with Neurath in Berlin. "About a week ago an exhaustive conversation took place between the King of England and the Italian Ambassador . . . Grandi, at the house of a mutual friend." The report described how Grandi had tried to explain Italian ambitions in Abyssinia and how the Italians wished to respect British interests. "In reply the King allegedly expressed profound regret that such serious tension should have developed in Anglo-Italian relations." He went on to tell Grandi that he ". . . could not say how much he had already done in this sense as Prince of Wales or what he intended to do in this sense in the future. Although under the parliamentary system the government was not in the king's hands, he would continue to do what appeared to him to be possible and necessary." He finished by opining that, "The League of Nations . . . must in his judgment, be considered dead."[3]

By the end of June Monckton says he became seriously disturbed "not by the prospect of the king marrying Mrs. Simpson if and when she got her freedom, but about the damage which would be done to the king if he continued to make his friendship with her ever more conspicuous." But Monckton was to be worried further, for in late summer the king blithely made his holiday arrangements by deciding to forgo his customary vacation in France, which was beset by strikes and was in any case too near the civil war by then raging in Spain, and to charter the yacht *Nahlin* to sail away with Mrs. Simpson and some close friends. Although he attempted the childish subterfuge of calling himself by one of his lesser titles, the Duke of Lancaster, this fooled no one, and the incognito was soon dropped. The presence of Mrs. Simpson ensured the focus of the world's press as they carelessly flaunted themselves from the French Riviera through the Mediterranean to Turkey. The king further inflamed his family and government at home by stripping down to his shorts whenever the mood took him; in the still prudish world of the 1930s this was calculated to offend.

On his return to Britain the king paid a brief visit to London, where he dined with Queen Mary and announced his intention of taking two weeks' holiday at Balmoral. The queen's pleasure at what she took for his return to staid royal convention turned sour, though, when instead of inviting the usual dignitaries, he chose Mrs. Simpson and her friends Mr. and Mrs. Herman Rogers. As well as his friends, his brothers and their families also stayed in the area, and further offense was given when Mrs. Simpson quite unnecessarily acted as hostess to receive the Duchess of York, the future Queen Elizabeth. It was probably no more than Mrs. Simpson's gauche unawareness of custom and an American woman's innate hospitality for a bachelor friend, but it did offend.

By October the lid could not be kept on the simmering scandal much longer. Prime Minister Baldwin went to see the king after returning from his own holidays to find a great assortment of protesting letters about the king and Mrs. Simpson from British residents abroad who had access to foreign newspapers. To add extra seasoning to this already unwholesome brew, Mrs. Simpson was by then petitioning for a divorce from her husband, citing an arranged adultery on Mr. Simpson's part. As early as 1934 there is evidence that Mr. Simpson was angry at the attention Edward was giving his wife but that he had been advised that under English law he could not sue the king in Britain. Meantime, Monckton and Mr. Allen, the king's solicitor, had been to Buckingham Palace to persuade the king to see that the divorce was going to make headline news. They accordingly got the king to telephone press baron Lord Beaverbrook to solicit his help in playing down the event. Beaverbrook went to see the king two days later, having pleaded dental trouble as the reason for the delay; his appointment book, however, indicates that during those two days the wily Beaverbrook saw Ernest Simpson. Nevertheless, after some discussion Beaverbrook agreed to limit reporting to the actual proceedings alone and got the Press Association to cooperate.

Stanley Baldwin was a shrewd politician, although many would have preferred the epithet "crafty." He was a solid, rather old-fashioned, and, most people agreed, kindly man, who was genuinely fond of the king. He had a reputation for laziness, however, although it was rather a deliberate, almost rural manner that avoided precipitate action; he liked to ruminate a problem—to the frustration of his more hasty colleagues. So, when he eventually met the king that October, he behaved very correctly, although according to the king he was clearly very nervous and asked for a drink. In his fatherly way he tried gently to apprise the starry-eyed king of the trouble that was bound to arise from Mrs. Simpson's divorce and his association with her. He pointed out that news of the affair had already spread widely in the dominions and would soon reach Britain; it could not be hidden forever.

Winston Churchill suggested that the king was being advised by his ministers to abdicate, and if one telescopes the whole lengthy procedure, there is an element of truth in the assertion. Baldwin first advised the king that Mrs. Simpson would not be acceptable as queen, implying that, if the king was determined to make her his queen, he and his government would resign. The king's response was to declare that he did intend to marry Mrs. Simpson and that he was prepared to abdicate rather than compel Baldwin's disapproving government to resign. While Baldwin went away to think this over, the king, in a last desperate effort to find a solution to the impasse, sent word to him proposing a compromise. One short sentence from Baldwin's own speech of December 10 confirms this. When Baldwin addressed the House of Commons about the events of that fateful week beginning on November 16, he said, "For the rest of the week, so far as I know, he was considering that point."

The king had suggested to Baldwin that he could marry Mrs. Simpson as the Duke of Lancaster, one of his other titles. This had the advantage that she could then become only Her Highness the Duchess of Lancaster, not her Royal Highness, and therefore would rank below the three royal duchesses, as the king's wife but not his queen. Rumors of this suggestion were circulating around London that week, and Mrs. Simpson's close friend Herman Rogers wrote to an acquaintaince in Cannes telling him of the king's suggestion, which was never officially contradicted.

On Wednesday, November 25, the king anxiously sent for Baldwin again and asked whether he had considered his proposition, which would require Parliament to pass an act enabling Mrs. Simpson to be the king's wife without becoming queen. Baldwin warily replied that, "I can give you no considered opinion," according to his own account. Then Edward, in his worry to behave with the strictest constitutional correctness, unintentionally handed Baldwin the chance for an extra turn of the screw, because there was no necessity for Parliament to pass such an act. A precedent had been set by George IV, when he refused to have his wife Caroline crowned. Baldwin replied, according to his account, by merely saying that Parliament would never pass such an act. This was in fact a scarcely veiled threat that the prime minister would use his full authority to see that the government opposed the bill. He then blandly asked the king if he wished him to examine the proposition formally, to which the king agreed. Baldwin ponderously weighted the problem by explaining at length that it would mean putting the suggestion before the whole Cabinet and seeking the views of all the dominions' prime ministers too. Did His Majesty wish him to do this? The king again agreed.

On December 10, the day before the abdication, Baldwin stood at the bar of a crowded house. He was insistent that the only occasion on which he asked for an interview was on October 20, but he had also seen the king on Friday, November 27, in a surreptitious visit to Buckingham Palace; this he omitted to mention. Why then in his speech did he proceed straight from the November 25 interview to the one on December 2? Can the explanation be that Baldwin had asked him for that interview November 27 and that it was the most crucial of all the interviews in the ultimate development of the situation? Was he protecting himself from a charge of forcing the king's hand? The minutes of the Cabinet meeting held on Friday, November 27 would confirm this, but they may never be made available to historians. Notwithstanding the customary secrecy of the Cabinet, often somebody will leak a story to the press, as we have seen in recent years, and on that occasion the press in

Fleet Street believed it knew what had taken place in that Friday cabinet meeting. An account was written that, late on the evening of the cabinet meeting, which was supposedly dealing with the question of nonintervention in Spain, Baldwin went to Buckingham Palace and was admitted "through a little used door and was taken through the long corridors to the King"—like a character in a Dumas novel. Mention of the audience never appeared in the *Court Circular*, and to cover his secret movements Baldwin was said to be "staying in town that night to attend a private dinner." But according to journalists Frank Owen and R. J. Thompson:

> Mr. Baldwin had been asked to go to the King again and to say definitely that the Cabinet would give up office if the King persisted on his action. . . . The interview lasted, so it was said, two hours, and it was a frank one on both sides.
> The King had said that he was determined to go on with his project, that he had as much right as anyone to a private life. Mr. Baldwin replied that in that event the Cabinet had authorized him to say that they could not continue as the King's advisers. Then he took his leave without any definite reply from the King.[4]

This account makes a complete mockery of those consultations with the dominion prime ministers, for it is clear that Baldwin was determined on the outcome. Baldwin had made himself responsible for handling the king, and it was generally accepted that the editor of the *Times* made himself responsible for handling the people. In Fleet Street it was widely believed that a leading article was already in type that amounted to an ultimatum to the king. It was to be published at the decisive moment, thereby ensuring that he would not get his way. Once the government had decided to oppose the king's marriage, it was clear that, although he would appear to be the prime mover on the matter, with complete freedom of choice, at the same time, to put it crudely, he was being given enough rope to hang himself.

In his own account of the abdication, the Duke of Windsor implies that from the first he saw Baldwin as his enemy. It has been suggested that this attitude was nothing more than sour grapes resulting from the duke brooding over his treatment in exile, but was it? We have only two accounts of the meetings, Baldwin's and the king's. Baldwin's account was derived from his own notes, which he made afterward, and from what he said to Parliament. The official records of these events are secreted away. So what is being hidden?

While no one can doubt that the prime minister went to see the king about Mrs. Simpson, did he perhaps also maneuver the headstrong, stubborn, and gullible king into a corner from which he could not escape abdication? Other suggestions as to how Edward could remain king and still marry, or at least associate with, Mrs. Simpson were made by various people, including Winston Churchill. One alternative was that of a morganatic marriage by which their issue would have no claims as heirs to the throne. All suggestions were subsequently rejected, although the king believed that a morganatic marriage was possible, albeit it would have created powerful tensions in the court and might not have worked for long.

We have seen that the king's political views and ambitions were far from Baldwin's, and there can be little doubt that Britain's political response to the Rhineland reoccupation had been hamstrung by the king's influence. Baldwin was, by 1936, a tired old man worn out by responsibility who wanted to retire and would do so the following year. But he must have seen that once the king was crowned on May 12, 1937, his position and stature would be much stronger and he would be virtually unassailable in his office. It was also impossible to know what would happen if an attempt was made to remove the monarch, should he then try to take matters into his own hands, especially after the pomp and ceremonial of a coronation. Indeed, no one has ever said how it could have been done without the appalling prospect of a political crisis of the first magnitude, perhaps even civil war. Remember, civil war was then raging in Spain, whose monarch had been deposed; there had been a Nazi revolution in Germany, and few doubted where that was leading the German people; only nineteen years before, the Bolshevik revolution had swept away the Russian imperial family. Who could have positively foretold it could not happen in Britain in the volatile 1930s? At the very least it would have shaken the Empire and alienated the dominions, perhaps destroying the roots of the imperial power that would be needed shortly to face up to Germany and Italy.

On that dark winter's night when the ex-king, now the Duke of Windsor, sailed on a choppy sea from Britain, he had only the vaguest idea where he was going. Few plans had been made, an indication that Edward had never really contemplated leaving Britain; certainly it did not occur to him that he would never be welcomed back again. Coincidentally, it was exactly 248 years to the very day since James II had fled from England, and Edward was about to become another "king across the water." He had wanted to go to France to be near Mrs. Simpson, but his lawyers had hastened to point out that he should, in the interests of her pending divorce, keep a frontier between them until it became absolute.

Two days before the abdication a cable had been hurriedly sent to Baron Eugene de Rothschild, of the international banking family, asking in a simple commercial code if "David" (as the Duke was known to his family and friends) could go to his house near Vienna, Schloss Enzesfeld. Rothschild consulted the head of his family and agreed. On abdication night, therefore, HMS *Fury* and an accompanying warship hove to in the Channel and the following morning landed the duke in France. From there he took the train for Austria. When he said goodbye to the few friends whom he had allowed to accompany him thus far, he made a remark that characterized the tragedy: "I always thought I could get away with a morganatic marriage."

He stayed at the impressive Schloss Enzesfeld for just over three months, leaving at the end of March 1937, when he moved to a small hotel near Ischl. At the watering-place resort of the former Habsburg ruler of Austria-Hungary, he waited impatiently and anxiously for confirmation of Mrs. Simpson's divorce.

During his months in Austria he was comforted by the companionship of his old friend Major "Fruity" Metcalfe, a former Indian Army officer, who would be his aide off and on until 1940. Metcalfe's value to history lies in his rare gift for letter writing. In the months he was with the duke, Metcalfe wrote frequently to his wife, whom he missed but whom the duke would not have near, and told her of the duke's moods and activities. The duke threw himself enthusiastically into recreation, frequently skiing all day and dancing until the early hours. But he was only killing time, ticking off each day on a calendar and remarking every night, "One more day nearly over." "It's very pathetic," Metcalfe commented.[5]

Notwithstanding his abdication and exile, though, the duke was still a center of attention, and far from being the royal family's outcast, he was visited by his sister Princess Mary and her husband, Lord Harewood, and by his faithful brother Prince George, the Duke of Kent; Kent's wife, though, refused to meet the Duke of Windsor. He was also frequently in the company of diplomats, especially Sir Walford Selby, the British ambassador to Austria, who was to be ambassador to Lisbon when the duke and duchess reached there in 1940. All the while he was in Austria, Metcalfe tells us the duke spoke only German.

On February 4, 1937, the duke had a significantly long and friendly talk with Franz von Papen, Hitler's ambassador to Vienna. Papen had been sent to Austria in 1934 to smooth over the mess left by the Nazi murder of Chancellor Dollfuss. By the time he met the duke, the dapper former German chancellor, whose slippery intrigues had backfired and given power to Hitler, was busily undermining Austrian independence for the coming *Anschluss*, barely a year away.

The duke had at this time evidently still not realized the full impact of his abdication, to the point of not accepting the irrevocable. Edward even spoke to his cousin Lord Louis Mountbatten of returning home and of the kind of work he would like to do. In his mesmeric obtuseness about the realities of life, he bore an uncanny resemblance to Hitler's April 1945 dreaming of returning to Linz to build an art gallery. Mountbatten tried in vain to persuade his cousin of the changed feeling in Britain about him since the abdication, but Edward blithely prattled about a royal wedding at which his two youngest brothers would be his supporters. It was in this insistence on his continuing popularity in Britain, bolstered in the coming years by his duchess, that lay the seeds of the duke's fervent belief that he should return home to lead his country out of the war. Among his family, too, his exile seems to have appeared a temporary rebuff that time would heal. It was only after his bitter intriguing in the early war years that attitudes publically hardened, and by then his closest family supporter, Kent, had died in mysterious circumstances.

In February 1937 the duke's dreams were to suffer an immediate check, however, when Walter Monckton arrived by air in Austria and hurried to Schloss Enzesfeld on extremely delicate matters. One of the duke's fantasies since abdicating was the notion that in some way his brother had taken his place as a sort of caretaker-king. The duke had telephoned the new king, George VI, almost daily to offer advice and unwanted guidance, until the king had firmly told him to cease the calls. His interference was upsetting the new king, who was bravely overcoming his own shyness as he struggled with his enormous responsibilities, but apart from that there was a security risk in these calls, and we know from an examination of German records that the ubiquitous Nazi were tapping the duke's calls whenever possible. Monckton had to deal with this ticklish problem and also to reassure the duke about the settlement for which he was relying upon the king's generosity. The duke was not likely to live in penury, however; he had been left the royal residences of Balmoral and Sandringham, which the new king had agreed to buy from him, besides which he had his personal fortune and was said to have transferred huge sums from the country when he left. It was, all the same, a rather pathetic situation for a man who, after a lifetime of power and total material satisfaction, was to be faced with the prospect of only his own few millions on which to exist. As will become apparent, the duke had a reputation for parsimony, as did the duchess, in due course; perhaps both needed the added security of wealth to replace the image of power. Certainly in spring 1937 the duke was feeling the onward creep of isolation and impotence.

The months at the Schloss and then at Ischl were hectic with forced activity and gaiety, but under the surface there must have been stirring a bitter realization of what he had relinquished and a gnawing desire to claw back at least the semblance of power and position. Then, at the beginning of May, when his frustration and impatience were nearing breaking point, the news was telephoned to him that Mrs. Simpson's divorce was absolute. That very same day he left Austria and flew to her.

5

The Mysterious Man at the Wedding

ACCORDING TO the duke's biographer Donaldson, "King George VI was finally responsible for the choice of the Château of Candé for his brother's wedding." There were the usual protocols to be observed in this "unroyal" wedding, and circumspection had to be maintained, if only to keep at bay the world's press hordes and ensure that no hint of unseemliness should tarnish the royal image. La Croë, a villa in the south of France, was one possibility but was rejected because of the Riviera's reputation as the rich man's playground. The duke chose instead the other final option, the large, beautiful Château de Candé near Tours, which had elegance and privacy. It was, in retrospect, an unfortunate choice.

It is doubtful if King George VI knew the full facts about the choice of the château, for it had originally been offered to Mrs. Simpson as a refuge at the time of her flight to France in November. The owner of the château was a man named Charles Eugene Bedaux, who had made the offer through Mrs. Simpson's friend Herman Rogers. For the next few years the names of Bedaux and Rogers are going to run through the Windsors' story like the silver thread in an old five pound note, unobtrusive but vital to its verity. The paths of Bedaux and Windsor entwine like threads in a tapestry of intrigue. No one at the time, though, seemed to think it odd that an apparent stranger should volunteer his home to the couple for the wedding, especially since, according to Donaldson, "only the most cursory inquiries had been made." In the end, Bedaux, like some Tolstoyian character, would bring reputations tumbling down, and it would cost him his life.

To understand this strange and treacherous relationship, we again have to go back, this time to the First World War. The following account is drawn from Military Intelligence and FBI sources in the United States.

The known story of Charles Eugene Bedaux begins on October 5, 1917, in the small American city of Grand Rapids, Michigan. On that late autumn day when the surrounding hills were flushing scarlet and gold, George F. Weinhard, an American Intelligence operative, made a report to his superior, William S. Fitch, about the affairs of a locally based efficiency expert and production engineer, Charles Eugene Bedaux. Bedaux was gaining quite a reputation in the Grand Rapids area by applying the teachings of the management pioneer F. W. Taylor to the need for greater efficiency in America's wartime industrial output. Taylor had very much identified man with the machine and endeavored to manipulate the worker in the same way as the machine. (Bedaux'a vigor in applying this principle was in time to make him very unpopular among America's trade unionists.) Fitch's report eventually reached the desk of Colonel R. H. Van Deeman, the chief of Military Intelligence in the War Department in Washington. Van Deeman read the report and then took a thick crayon and underlined the words "whose occupation enables him to go through the factories of various concerns by whom he is employed, and make plans and drawings and to list their equipment." Van Deeman also noted that Bedaux was thus enabled to obtain full and accurate information about every plant he could get on his list. The colonel read on, scribbling notes about points of particular interest, that are still visible on the photocopies in my possession of Fitch's six-page report.[1]

Bedaux had been in Grand Rapids since early in the European war, having arrived in late September 1914. Many people were, it seemed, suspicious of him and did not believe his claims to have served briefly in the French Army, from which he had been discharged wounded. The operative who filed the report, Van Deeman noted, believed that Bedaux's income, which according to his wife was $10,000 a year, was not entirely derived from his efficiency work alone: "The operative feels he is looking after other interests. . . ."

In the autumn of 1916, it was reported, Mrs. Bedaux had made a hastily arranged trip to Japan, accompanied by her son and a woman companion—a trip which, Bedaux commented to an informant, albeit risky, was one in which "a woman was not so likely to be suspected as a man," although he did not reveal of what she would be suspected. Mrs. Bedaux had then returned in January 1917 and promptly obtained a divorce, although whether this resulted from her trip to Japan or not is not known. Nevertheless, Bedaux had a reputation, the report asserted, as a womanizer, so it seems probable that on her return his wife found he had been carrying on with someone else. This is substantiated by the fact that soon after, on July 3, 1917, he married a local girl, a Miss Fern Lombard.

According to the *Grand Rapids Herald*, Bedaux and Fern Lombard had been driving along when they had had a puncture. While they were fixing this, another car pulled up and its driver asked, "May I assist you?"

"If you are a minister, you may," replied Bedaux, who just happened to have a marriage license tucked away in his pocket.

"I am," replied the driver to their great surprise, and the ceremony was performed there and then at the roadside, with a peach orchard as a background. The bride, the reporter added, was the daughter of a prominent Grand Rapids businessman, and she was herself a favorite in local society and music circles.[2]

After reading the report, it was clear to Van Deeman that more information was needed about Bedaux. "Operative 68" suggested investigating Bedaux's records to discover if he had ever served in the French Army and, if so, why he had left it. They would investigate, too, whether he was receiving money from other sources because a chance remark by his first wife had revealed that Bedaux was not unduly concerned by rumors that he might be doing secret work for the enemy. As events in 1939 reveal, Bedaux's egoism about his nefarious activities did not change with the years. His first wife was a source of other information, too, and one wonders if her trip to Japan with her young son in the autumn of 1916 was not triggered by

suspicion that she was being watched. In the summer of 1916 a
Department of Intelligence operative reported that during a
journey by train from Chicago to Richmond, Virginia, he met
Mrs. Bedaux, whom he described as "young and pretty, very
clever, and spoke French, Spanish and German. She had a
little boy with her about six years old. She told me her husband
was a mechanical and electrical engineer whose business took
him all over the world; that they had both just returned from
Spain and France and that he was now getting ready to go to
Japan and that she perhaps would go with him." Obviously she
went "hurriedly" in his place. Mrs. Bedaux told the operative
that she was hoping to visit the Panama Canal Zone but more
significantly that, "her parents were German; that they lived in
St. Louis; that she spent most of her time with them while her
husband was traveling."

Van Deeman's inquiries went on, and a search by the Military Intelligence Department of Bedaux's records produced
the registration card that he had completed on arrival in
Grand Rapids, under the Selective Conscription Act. It recorded: "Age 30; Home address, 306, Eureka Avenue, Grand
Rapids; Date of Birth, October 10, 1886; Has declared his
intention to become a citizen of the United States; Born in
Paris, France; Occupation, Consulting Engineer; Married,
with wife and child; Served as corporal for six months in the
infantry branch of the Foreign Legion."

Once these details had been unearthed, Van Deeman sent
Intelligence operative E. Berkey Jones to investigate, and in
due course he submitted his report. He had interviewed a Mrs.
Lucie Margantin who owned the house in which Bedaux lived.
She confirmed Bedaux's story that he had served in the French
Army but added that he always got depressed at reports of
French victories. One day, she told Jones, he had come down-
stairs in bare feet to answer the telephone, and she had noticed
that there was no sign of the wound in his foot that he had
claimed had been so bad as to be the reason for his discharge
from the French Army and that supposedly was the reason for
the limp he affected.

On one occasion, Mrs. Margantin continued, Bedaux had
borrowed her camera for about six months. She had discovered
he had used it to photograph documents, although she was

never allowed to see the finished prints. At that time the only person with whom he regularly kept company was a Carl Andersch, a German music teacher. From Bedaux's landlady, Jones was directed to see a local chiropodist, Mr. Labouselier.

Labouselier confirmed that he had attended two lectures that Bedaux had given at the public library. They had been so flagrantly pro-German that he never went again. Another contact was Professor Massenge, an instructor in the local school. He said that he regarded Bedaux as so pro-German that he had written to the French Legation saying he believed him to be a spy. Massenge also said that he had earlier met Bedaux at a meeting when he explained again how he had been wounded, to account for his discharge from the French Army. Massenge agreed, too, that Bedaux did always walk with a pronounced limp, although after that meeting, he explained, he had walked some way home with Bedaux (during which he had been pumped by him for information about local women), and "then a street car passed and, despite his 'wounds,' Bedaux ran like a rabbit with no trace of a limp." Massenge said he had next encountered Bedaux a few weeks later giving an art lecture. On that occasion, he recalled, Bedaux had become extremely agitated, claiming that the French alone were responsible for the German destruction of artworks in Belgium and France and calling the French soldiers "swine." The professor, according to others whom Jones contacted, had become so enraged that there and then he called Bedaux a German spy, before the other guests. At that Bedaux had collected his hat and swept out of the school in anger.

From other people who knew Bedaux, Jones learned that a particular friend of both him and Carl Andersch was a Mrs. William Rowe and that it was at her house that Bedaux had raised his glass with the words, "If I must drink French wine, it is *Prosit* to the Kaiser!" There could be little doubt about his very strong pro-German sentiments.

Van Deeman's initial investigations revealed that during some three years of consultancy Bedaux had surveyed most of the factories in the area and taken away drawings. He had paid particular attention to Muskegon Harbor, the docks, and munitions plants. He had also spent a great deal of time going hunting, as he called it, although later it was discovered that he had been snooping with his binoculars around the airplane plant at Ludington, Michigan.

On December 4, 1917, almost two months after first reading Weinard's report, Van Deeman received another report, this time from the Intelligence Section of headquarters, 85th Infantry Division, at Battle Creek, Michigan. This report provided a great deal more information of a general nature and confirmed that Bedaux did speak fluent German, despite persistent denials to acquaintances that he had any knowledge of the language, albeit his wife had German parents and spoke the language fluently. To confuse matters further, he had with equal persistence claimed to have lived for two years in Alsace, that province of France where German is widely spoken and that had been German since 1871. This report concluded, "His associates at private dinners are all persons under suspicion by the Government."

With this information in hand, Van Deeman decided to extend his investigation and wrote to a number of agencies. To the Office of War Trade Intelligence in Washington, he wrote on December 7, 1917, asking if they had information about Bedaux, concluding his letter, "This man is strongly suspected of espionage."

Van Deeman also wrote, on December 22, to General Vignal, military attaché at the French Embassy, to which the general replied on February 19, 1918, confirming the general facts of birth etc., and giving extra details of Bedaux's military service. But in the latter he explained that the records showed that "Bedaux has never fought on the French front and has never been wounded." So what were the intelligence authorities to believe about the urbane and mysterious Charles Bedaux? Strangely enough, library records in Grand Rapids state that Bedaux arrived in the United States in 1906, although no one seems to know where he was between 1906 and 1914, when he reappeared in Grand Rapids.

Inquiries went on until August 1918, by which time the department intelligence officer at the War Department in Washington had gathered quite a dossier on Bedaux. Among these papers it was clearly stated that he was "in positions to get full and accurate information at all plants . . . believed German spy; actions under suspicion; wife, Mrs. Bedaux suspected...." Perhaps the most interesting comments were in another report from the Intelligence Section of the 85th Division that stated, "associates with low types of persons, apparently enemy born, possible impostor...." There were other intelligence reports about Bedaux that pointed to connections in Japan and Spain.

Of all these statements, two stand out. First there is the evidence that in spite of his claims to have been invalided from the French Army as a wounded soldier and his apparent limping, there is no evidence at all that he did have a wound, and according to French records he had never been wounded or even served on the French front. Then, one asks, what was a French corporal doing in the United States by late September 1914? The war had only begun in early August, and he would have had to have been trained, fought, been wounded, been treated in hospital, been invalided out, and traveled by sea to America in that time; it is not possible. Neither does this square with his apparent arrival in America in 1906, his marriage and activities. His wife, too, made no mention of his military service, although she seemed willing to talk about anything else. It may be that she finally divorced him after finding out that he was, indeed, a spy, in order to protect herself and her parents. This we will probably never know. The other point to bear in mind is his undoubted pro-German activities and his ability to speak German, which was attested to by several people who knew him, although he always denied this. The intelligence reports suggested he was an impostor, and perhaps he was. The details certainly do not add up to a bona fide French ex-soldier turned production engineer.

At the end of the First World War inquiries into Bedaux's activities in America seem to have been set aside—except for the records in the Intelligence files—in the general euphoria of peace. He continued to operate his consultancy business, although increasingly unpopular with American labor organizations, who knew him as the "speed-up king"; his system was considered inhuman even by many managers. In the next decade he prospered and spread his business interests to Europe, including Germany. When Hitler came to power in 1933, however, he suffered a setback, for the new masters of Germany suppressed his firm along with many others that did not fit into the Third Reich's system. But Bedaux was not the type to give up easily, and he spent the next four years cultivating friendships with top Nazis in order to get his business going again, and his eventual success was to derive from his newfound friend the duke of Windsor.

Bedaux, as I have already said, runs like a thread through Nazi intrigues, and by 1941 he was to be an agent of the Nazis in France, where he was their front man in a strange Vichy-Nazi organization.

Bedaux was a peculiarly manic character, very determined in all he attempted. He was short and stockily built, with a boldly battered face dominated by dark eyes. He dressed with taste and always had a discreetly arranged handkerchief in his breast pocket; a shy, slightly derisive smile played on his wide, rather tightly closed lips when he talked, belying the alert watchfulness of his eyes. Bedaux missed nothing, and his undoubted natural charm was enhanced by that fine balance of culture and bad language that makes for amusing conversation. He was, too, a superbly discreet man, with an innate ability of never intruding, a man whose presence could easily be forgotten, which is a valuable accomplishment for a spy.

It was always assumed that he was a complete stranger to the Windsors' circle when he offered his château, and although one source suggests he was in fact an earlier acquaintance of Mrs. Simpson, there does not appear to be any evidence of this, although he was evidently known to Herman Rogers, who with his wife, was a longtime friend of Mrs. Simpson. There is a possible connection in the fact that Bedaux had connections in the Far East, where Mrs. Simpson had first met the Herman Rogerses; Mrs. Simpson and Bedaux's wife, Fern, certainly got on well together, though that was only natural for two Americans in France.

Charles Bedaux had bought the Château de Candé in 1927 from a Cuban family, Drake des Casillo. It stood in a thousand acres of gorgeous meadowland and soft woods, from which its impressive bulk rose in a series of spires and turrets. Inside the château were more than fifty splendidly proportioned rooms, high-ceilinged and beautifully paneled. When Mrs. Simpson visited it with Herman Rogers, she was delighted with all she saw. Fern Bedaux, her hostess, was tall, with an aristocratic bearing far removed from the secretarial days in Grand Rapids. She graciously showed them around, walking the long corridors lined with huge bins full of logs for the innumerable open fireplaces. It was a romantic setting, straight from the reign of Louis the Sun King, for in the spacious and secluded grounds there roamed wild boar and deer. Inside, Bedaux had lavished money in his efforts to make it a comfortable and convenient home; it was said that over sixty tons of piping had gone into modernizing the plumbing, while tennis courts, badminton courts, archery butts, golf course, and swimming pool were available for the occupants' leisure.

Mrs. Simpson moved to Candé just as soon as she was able to complete her arrangements and spent most of April there with just the Rogerses for company, although from time to time friends visited her. During one of those afternoons her little dog, Slipper, was fatally bitten by a viper in the garden, but this upsetting experience was soon put aside by the news on May 3 that her divorce was final. The duke arrived the day after.

The wedding was a much quieter affair than the duke had envisaged, and far from it being the royal occasion he had planned, his family did not even accept his invitation to attend. (A telegram eventually arrived from the king and queen and his mother on June 4.) This obvious and public snub greatly upset the duke, but, as his wife wrote: ". . . the unspoken order had gone out. Buckingham Palace would ignore our wedding. There would be no reconciliation, no gesture of recognition."[3] Ostracized by his family, the duke found that many of his friends, too, stayed away in deference to royal pleasure. There was even difficulty in finding a clergyman to perform the ceremony since the Church of England refused to countenance the marriage of a divorced person. In the end a Reverend R. A. Jardine offered to marry them although he fell afoul of the Church for performing this service.

In consequence the wedding was attended by only a few close friends of the bride and groom, including, of course, Mr. and Mrs. Herman Rogers and Major Metcalfe and his wife, Lady Alexandra Metcalfe, who kept a diary of events. She wrote rather condescendingly of the Bedaux: "Infinitely better than expected. She is like a borzoi & is not at all common & he is brilliant & very astute, but unattractive. They are very retiring and might be guests," which suggests she did not think they were guests. Although Fern Bedaux does appear in some wedding photographs, her husband does not and, indeed, seems to have kept well out of any photographs. Lady Alexandra apparently warmed to Bedaux later, however, and wrote of a luncheon they both went to in Sembeacy: "I like the Bedaux more & more, they have done fascinating trips & are very interesting." Bedaux was in truth a great raconteur, and this was an important part of his attraction to the duke, who also loved to talk.

Another cause of the duke's bitterness resulted from an unexpected event on the evening before the wedding. Walter Monckton arrived at teatime, the bearer of harsh news. He had brought a letter from King George VI notifying that he was by letters patent able "to declare that the Duke of Windsor shall, notwithstanding his act of Abdication . . . be entitled to hold and enjoy for himself only the title, style or attribute of Royal Highness, so however that his wife and descendants, if any, shall not hold the said title or attribute."[4] The king hoped this decision would not be taken as "an insult."

Monckton had written to the home secretary, Sir John Simon, cautioning of the bitterness this would arouse in the duke, and that it did.

On June 3 Lady Alexandra noted, "The bitterness is there alright. He had an outburst to Fruity while dressing for dinner. The family he is through with. The friends, staff and Perry (Brownlow) have also been awful. He intends to fight the HRH business as legally the King has no right to stop the courtesy title being assumed by his wife. Monckton and Allen agree but let's hope he does nothing." She continued, "She (the Duchess) said it didn't matter to her but she minds a great deal really & says Monckton has made her sign just Wallis on the documents today. She said that she realized there was no insult they hadn't tried to heap on her. . . ."[5]

There was indeed a great deal of acrimony generated among various authoritative people declaring that the duke could not in any event be denied his rightful titles, and some argued that the duchess, too, should have been afforded that honor, but it was counterargued that the dominions especially were against her having a royal title. Whatever the arguments for or against, it did drive home to the duke and his wife like nothing else up till that time that they were out in the cold. Much of what followed can be attributed to the deep sense of grievance that stemmed from that untimely wedding-eve snub, which made it plain to the world that the duke's wife was not acceptable to the court and dominions, nor was he any longer. It sheared him of the last vestiges of royal authority and power so that from then on, he would have to procure such authority by other means. He did so from regimes that delighted in the embarrassment that such attention gave to Britain and her empire. They were not to find either the duke or the duchess unreceptive to their overtures.

According to French law there were two wedding ceremonies, the first a civil wedding followed by a religious one. By 3:30 P.M. it was over. There was more than a touch of pathos in the subdued gathering in the château as the guests toasted the couple. Lady Alexandra wrote: "We shook hands with them in the salon. I realized I should have kissed her but I just couldn't, in fact I was bad the whole of yesterday. . . . If she occasionally showed a glimmer of softness, took his arm, looked at him as though she loved him one would warm towards her, but her attitude is so correct. The effect is of a woman unmoved by the infatuated love of a younger man. Let's hope she lets up in private with him otherwise it must be grim."[6] Lady Alexandra was more reflective about the opinion of the duchess attributed to Baldwin: ". . . as a schemer and intriguer she is unsurpassed." Her own opinion was that Mrs. Simpson had hoped to be either queen or morganatic wife. Bitterly she wrote in her diary, ". . . although I loathe her for what she has done, I am unable to dislike her when I see her."[7]

One may conjecture that Baldwin had known the king too well. Edward was, despite his anxiety to appear a modern, twentieth-century man, a product of Victorian tradition. That he was an honorable man, few could doubt. But there was a slightly comic-opera quality to his honor—the prince who romantically gave up all for the woman he loved, which is precisely what Baldwin knew he would do.

Baldwin's intrigues and the duke's unbending resolve to stand honorably by Mrs. Simpson set the path of his future course. The bitter resentment they both felt at being blown aside amid the public censure of their romance was to ferment in the coming years, fed by the ever-attentive Germans, until by the spring of 1940 it needed only the torrid Spanish heat to come to the boil.

On the evening after the wedding, the duke and duchess left the Château de Candé. They departed for Wasserleonburg, the German home of Count Münster, where they would remain in covert isolation for most of the summer of 1937. When they did leave that autumn on their travels, it was to cause another storm of gossip and recrimination as they were paraded through the new and martial Third Reich.

6

The Duke's German Visit

A LTHOUGH AT the time of his abdication, Edward had given no great thought to his future career, he never doubted that after a short period abroad he would return to some post that would make use of his talents and training. It has already been noted that he seemed to look upon his brother George VI as a temporary monarch who would step aside in due course. All Walter Monckton's qualities were once more fully employed therefore when he visited the Windsors at Wasserleonburg.

The duke's anxiety and resentment about financial matters had diminished somewhat, but added to the permanent bitterness about the title, there were new difficulties because he was already worrying about his eventual return to Britain and what work would be found for him there. Monckton records that he became uneasily aware of the duke's boredom and eagerness to return and also of his wife's discontent at the ambiguity of his position. He wrote: "She, I think, was in some sense beating against the bars. She wanted him to have his cake & eat it. She could not easily reconcile herself to the fact that by marrying her he had become a less important person."[1]

While they were at Wasserleonburg there occurred an incident that further opened the duke's eyes to the feelings of his family. The Duke and Duchess of Kent were in Austria on a short holiday. Realizing that he would be somewhere close to the Windsors, the Duke of Kent had wanted advice as to what he ought to do, and Monckton had told him that it would cause trouble if he visited the Windsors without taking his wife with him. When the time came, the Duke of Kent, nevertheless, proposed to visit his brother on a day when his wife would be away. "By all means," Windsor replied to his suggestion, "and bring Marina with you." Kent said that she would be visiting her family that day, and to this Windsor replied; "Well, put off your visit for a day or two and bring her with you." The Duchess of Kent absolutely refused to go, and so Kent referred his difficulties to the king, who on Monckton's advice directed both him and his wife to call on the Windsors. However, the duchess still refused.[2]

At about the same time the Windsors were invited for a short visit to the Hungarian home of their new friends the Bedaux, at a castle called Borsodivanka. The duke had got on well with Bedaux at Candé, where they had spent hours talking together. According to an article in the *New Yorker* in 1946, Bedaux and the duke were deeply interested in labor conditions and the working man, a subject on which Bedaux said that the duke was "insatiable."[3] From their conversations at Borsodivanka, the duke was persuaded by Bedaux to make a tour first of Germany and then the United States, ostensibly to study labor conditions.

After three months of sitting in a silent castle, the duchess was indeed tired of being out of the limelight and wanted a change. Her political naiveté matched the duke's, and she, too, saw no harm in such a trip. So the duke instructed Bedaux to go ahead with his plans, and while he was making the arrangements, the Windsors went back to Paris. There they took a nine-room suite in the Hotel Meurice, overlooking the Tuileries Gardens—the same suite he had occupied as Prince of Wales. Thus comfortably installed, they began to look for a house of their own.

In the meantime Bedaux had been continuing his wrangling with the obdurate Nazi Party over his efforts to have the suspension of his business annulled. He had used all the angles he could and must have been wondering if he would ever succeed, when in the early summer of 1937, he got the breakthrough that he had stubbornly sought. Some said it was because of the considerable publicity he got by hosting the Windsors' wedding at his Château de Candé, but in view of subsequent events and his close involvement with the Nazis, anyway, it seems much more likely that his offer of Candé was the price for getting into business again. We have already seen how the Nazis had established channels of contact to Edward when he was in Britain, but for those to be reopened to the exile in France would have been too obvious. His abdication had taken them completely by surprise, for in spite of all the publicity the crisis had received in the last weeks of his reign, particularly in foreign newspapers, the Nazis had not expected him actually to go. In fact, Ribbentrop claimed that he had been instrumental in getting Hitler to keep the Simpson affair out of the German press.

Ribbentrop had later explained to a disappointed and baffled Führer that the real reasons for the recent crisis were not those constitutional and moral considerations that had been publicly declared. Baldwin's real motive had been to defeat those Germanophile forces that had been working through Mrs. Simpson and the former king with the object of reversing the present British policy and bringing about an Anglo-German entente. The Führer had been very distressed to hear how the crisis had resolved, as he had looked upon "the King as a man after his own heart and one who understood the *Führerprinzip*, and was ready to introduce it into his country."[4]

It had indeed been a disappointing blow to the Nazis' long-term plans, so they were naturally anxious to open a new contact with the Duke of Windsor. Then, from nowhere, Bedaux had made his offer through Mrs. Simpson's friend Herman Rogers, and amazingly it had been accepted. With the wedding over and Bedaux firmly established as a friend of the ex-king, the rest of the arrangements began to fall into place.

Bedaux persuaded Count Joseph von Lederbur to act as his intermediary, and through him the door was opened to a meeting with the Nazi economic and financial genius Dr. Hjalmar Schacht, another of those erratically brilliant men who were the pillars upon which the Third Reich was balanced. William L. Shirer says of Schacht: ". . . the fact remains that no single person was as responsible as Schacht for Germany's economic preparations for the war which Hitler provoked in 1939." In

January 1937, on his sixtieth birthday, the army's publication *Militär Wochenblatt* had even hailed him as "the man who made the reconstruction of the Wehrmacht economically possible." Schacht was indeed a financial wizard who had used every economic trick to pay for the Reich's expansion, including the wholesale printing of bank notes and even special bills called Mefo with which the Reich paid armament manufacturers.

As a result of Bedaux's interview with Schacht, it was arranged that he would pay $20,000 in what the Nazi double-talk called re-investment money and $30,000 in so-called penetration money—crudely put, it meant that for $50,000 in cash, of which $30,000 went directly into the Nazi party's slush fund, Bedaux could begin operating again. But there was another condition: He could do so only in partnership with the notorious Dr. Robert Ley.

Robert Ley was a thickset, aggressive Nazi, an alcoholic, too, who spoke with such a naturally slurred speech that it was said to have been difficult to tell whether he was drunk or not. A staunch Nazi from the early days of the party, Ley instigated many wild schemes, such as concentrating all German fashion into one giant enterprise to be run by his wife. He rose to be one of the very top seven or eight Nazi leaders, although, like Martin Bormann, whom he resembled, Ley shunned the limelight. Nevertheless, this evil man, who was Nazi gauleiter of Cologne and headed the German Labor Front for twelve years, after ruthlessly suppressing the trade unions, remained, with just Goebbels and Bormann, the only Nazi leader to be trusted by Hitler until the very end. Ley was a violent man, too, who constantly advocated the use of poison gas and who in 1945 was vaingloriously proclaiming that the Nazis had the "deathray." This then was the man with whom Bedaux was to associate closely in the 1930s in the working of his efficiency business, a useful asset to Ley, who was obsessed with uniformity in all things, design, seating, fashion, working conditions, leisure, and so forth. Albert Speer (Hitler's architect), who would later work closely with Ley in running the Reich's armaments industry, knew Bedaux by sight and recalled him accompanying Ley to a meeting with Hitler at Berchtesgaden in 1938. Ley would eventually hang himself to escape trial as a war criminal at Nuremberg, thus outliving his dubious partner, Bedaux, by some two and a half years.

But the links between Bedaux and the Nazis were several, and that between Bedaux and Schacht, for instance, had other important ramifications for the future. Bedaux was, it seems clear, the new main link between the Nazis and the recalcitrant duke and would in this way become decisive in 1939. His connection with Schacht, though, was to lead to his direct involvement in the Nazis' industrial warfare in Europe, for which, with his business contacts in so many countries and his past espionage in America in the First World War, he was admirably suited. Paul Winkler, a lonely voice in wartime France warning against German intentions, summed up their aims: "German economic agencies follow closely on the heels of armies of occupation and endeavor to transform the temporary hold on conquered countries into a permanent economic control."[5] Bedaux's contact with Schacht was leading him into just that role.

Schacht was involved with leading German bankers in planning the economic penetration of French industry. Foremost among the bankers, after Schacht, was the powerful Cologne banker Baron Kurt von Schroeder, who was later going to play an important role in Vichy France and North Africa. Schroeder's representative in France was the Paris company Worms et Cie. "The Worms Bank and its members," say J. and S. Pool, authors of *Who Financed Hitler?*, "appeared in the financing of all prewar activities hostile to the Third Republic, notably the Cagoulard plot, and . . . it was the center of the transfer of France's businesses to German ownership." With the collapse of France and the establishment of the Vichy government, virtually the entire board of the Worms Bank turned up as ministers in Vichy president Pétain's cabinet. "The Banque Worms was the leading spirit in the plundering of France for Germany's benefit, and gradually, the conviction grew in the minds of those who studied this process that it was M. Lemargue-Durbreil who represented the Banque Worms with the Bank of France, and this made its activities possible."[4]

Although these events occurred generally after the years with which we are specifically concerned in this book, they are important in determining the extent of the network of intrigue into which the Duke of Windsor was being drawn by his involvement with the nefarious Charles Bedaux, considering the latter's connection with Lemargue-Dubreil.

The Cagoulard plot just mentioned had occurred in January 1937, when a group of right-wing organizations led by Lemargue-Dubreil attempted to overthrow the French government. The Gaullists later charged that Lemargue-Dubreil financed Fascist organizations and publications, was involved in the February 6, 1934, attempt to install a totalitarian regime in France, and was instrumental in a similar attempted military coup in 1937. A thorough police investigation at the time came to nothing, for the trails led to such high officials that it was feared any action might lead to civil war. Instead the dossiers which listed top businessmen, generals, and marshals were classified and secreted in the Ministry of Justice. Pétain's government went to great lengths to hide the incriminating evidence. Many of the Cagoule members who had fled abroad returned to join Pétain's Vichy government after the fall of France. The incriminating documents might never have been found but for the wife of the concierge at the Bordeaux tribunal who showed Free French officers where they were hidden behind a secret partition, after which a parliamentary inquiry revealed the truth.

I have spent a few paragraphs detailing the activities of Lemargue-Dubreil because of his connection through von Schroeder with Schacht and the Nazi plan to take over most of French industry. But it was through Lemargue-Dubreil's activities that Bedaux's wartime role also came to light. By 1942 very large transfers of capital were taking place between France and North Africa, in particular by the two largest Franco-African companies, one a chemical concern owned by a Franco-German combine and the other the Trans-Afrika Company which was under majority control of the Deutsche Bank and several German industrial firms. But the operational control of the Trans-Afrika Company was in the hands of two men especially, Lemargue-Dubreil and his associate, Charles Eugene Bedaux.

Soon after the Windsors' visit to Germany, Bedaux was indeed on intimate terms with many of the Nazi leaders, and his widely dispersed efficiency offices gave him the entrée to industrial plants all over the world, so he was in an ideal position to undertake industrial espionage. From the autumn of 1937 Bedaux would never be seen again in the United States until in 1943 he was flown from El Biar in North Africa to Miami, under arrest and in military custody. There he was turned over to the Department of Justice. At the time of his arrest he had been engaged in a scheme to lay a pipeline through the African desert with the object of bringing peanut oil to the Nazis. On his person he carried many incriminating documents, including an *Ausweis*—an exit visa—from Vichy France on which he was described as "attached to the German Military Occupation High Command."

General Dwight D. Eisenhower's naval aide Harry C. Butcher wrote in his diary on December 8, 1942: "Items I've failed to record: Charles Bedaux, the stretch-out promoter with whom American labor leaders raised hell when he was discovered as the advance man for the Duke and Duchess of Windsor's visit to U.S. has been arrested here by the French on charges of being a Nazi agent. They have photostats of certain letters appointing him as an industrial agent by the Germans. . . ."[6]

Now, when Bedaux was arrested, he was carrying an attaché case full of documents. These documents were, according to American Military Intelligence, taken by British Intelligence and *have not been seen since*. Group Captain F. W. Winterbotham, who had played so large a role in the 1930s in establishing de Ropp in Germany, was in North Africa at that time as chief of air intelligence of the Secret Intelligence Service. When I asked him about Bedaux and the documents, he claimed to remember something about the incident but no more. What these documents contained no one has discovered, but it was enough to make them disappear. It has always been suggested, hitherto, that Bedaux was an opportunist who used his wedding venue connection with the duke to get his company reopened and subsequently fell into bad Nazi company. From what I now know of his First World War activities and the veritable matrix of connections he had with the Nazis, I do not believe that one can see him as anything but a German spy who was instructed to establish a close relationship with the ex-king and his ambitious wife, both well-meaning but not very astute people. Later we shall see just what disasters were inherent in this strange relationship.

On September 3, 1937, a statement was made by T. H. Carter (formerly the duke's clerk), who was on a visit to the Windsors, that "In accordance with the Duke of Windsor's message to the World Press last June that he would release any information of interest regarding his plans or movements, His Royal Highness makes it known that he and the Duchess of Windsor are visiting Germany and the United States in the near future for the purpose of studying housing and working conditions in these two countries."[7]

The announcement took many of the duke's friends by surprise, and few thought the visit to Germany a good idea. But the headstrong duke did not see the need to discuss the trip with the king or the British government, and indeed, considering the depths of his feelings toward them at that time, it would have been surprising had he done so. Nevertheless, he did meet Lord Beaverbrook, who flew specially to Paris to try to talk the duke out of going. Beaverbrook was appalled at the idea of his dealing with the Nazis, which, he emphasized, would only further their cause. He urged the duke to go only to the United States, but this the duke stubbornly refused to consider, for he still heeded only advice that confirmed his own views.

In her own autobiographical account the duchess says that Bedaux assured the duke that the visit would be under the auspices of private citizens and there would be no question of their being involved in Nazi propaganda schemes. If they really believed that, the Windsors were to be quickly disillusioned.

They traveled across Germany by train and arrived at Berlin's Friederichstrasse station on October 11. They alighted from the train to be met by Mr. Harrison, the third secretary of the British Embassy, who handed them a letter from the chargé d'affaires, Sir George Ogilvie-Forbes, which informed them that the ambassador, Sir Neville Henderson, had unexpectedly left Berlin and that he himself had been directed to take no official cognizance of their visit.

Also lined up on the platform was an important delegation of German officials, headed by Dr. Robert Ley, as the Windsors' visit was officially only as guests of the German Labor Front. Despite Bedaux's assurances about the privacy of their visit, however, the welcoming delegation included Ribbentrop, the foreign minister, Gorlitzer, the deputy political leader of Berlin, Captain Wedgemann, one of Hitler's adjutants, Schneer, from the Office of the Four Year Plan, and Walter Hewel, whose presence is interesting because he was Hitler's personal liaison officer to Ribbentrop and constantly pops up in this story coordinating the work of numerous Nazi contacts and agents who were to feed information to the Führer.

The Windsors were then driven away to the Kaiserhof Hotel, where Ogilvie-Forbes called unobtrusively to see them. According to the duchess, Sir George, who had known the duke as Prince of Wales, offered his unofficial help "behind the scenes," although there is no record of anything he did. Nevertheless, his recognition of their presence is interesting because it meant that the British government must have been aware of the duke's actions while he was in Germany, many of which were dubious to say the least.

Their busy round of engagements began that afternoon when Ley whisked them off to a model factory where he delivered a speech welcoming the duke, taking the opportunity to ram home to the world's press how Hitler alone had cured unemployment. The euphoric atmosphere was whipped up with careful German planning as Ley requested the assembled workers to rise and give three heils in gratitude to the Führer. Then, with arms vigorously outstretched in Nazi salute, the happy band of National Socialist workers sang the British and German national anthems. When the Windsors left the factory and piled back into the open Mercedes-Benz, Ley squashed his black-uniformed bulk in between them—the duke looking harassed and sunk into his usual overlong topcoat and the duchess valiantly maintaining her chic in smartly formal black—and they raced away for tea at Ley's villa in the still leafy though chilly Grünewald.

From this time on, the traveling was something of a nightmare for the poor Windsors, for the duchess was a notoriously unhappy traveler. For the next two weeks she was driven about at breakneck speed through the cities and on the open road, always with Ley squashed between her husband and herself.

On their second morning, October 12, a German communiqué announced that Field Marshal Goering was to pay an official visit to Austria in return for a visit that Austria's assistant foreign minister, Dr. Guido Schmidt, had just made to Berlin. The Windsors were then politely informed of a slight change in their schedule. Instead of going to Essen on the 14th, as planned, they would be entertained by Goering himself at Karinhall. In the meantime there was plenty to do that day and the next when they were taken to visit the National Socialist Welfare Organization and had dinner with Ribbentrop in the evening. The *Times* reported: "His Royal Highness acknowledges with smiles and the National Socialist salute the greetings of the crowds gathered at his hotel and elsewhere during the day."

It has been tentatively mentioned in other accounts of the duke's visit that once or twice he gave "his version" of the Nazi salute, that martial, pseudo-Roman salute that would soon be a sign of servility throughout most of Europe—"something between a wave and a salute" as one writer put it. It is clear that in the enthusiasm of the trip he did often respond with the dreaded Nazi upthrust arm and was pleased by the response it got him.

October 14 was as crammed with appointments as all the other days of their "private" visit. In the morning their first stop was at the Pomeranian Training School of the elite Hitler bodyguard, the SS Regiment Leibstandarte Adolf Hitler. There they were treated to a tightly disciplined display by the immaculate, hand-picked, physically and ideologically perfect specimens of the Master Race, to which the duke responded with another, and this time well-recorded, Nazi salute.

It was then time for the Windsors to make their visit to have tea with Field Marshal Goering and his wife at Karinhall, their great mansion about forty miles from Berlin.

In her account of her husband, Emmy Goering recorded their conversation about their expected guests before they arrived. She said to her husband that an abdication seemed to her something like capitulation: "I don't understand this woman not giving up her marriage in view of everything that was involved." Goering, however, was firmly convinced that the marriage was simply a pretext to get rid of the king, "a man

who understood the signs of the times and knew how to interpret them." Goering did not conceal the fact that the German
government had earnestly hoped to see the duke as king. "The
natural opposition between British and German policy, which
the German government was doing everything to remove,
could," said Hermann, "easily be set aside with the aid of such a
man as the Duke."[8]

Goering made a big hit with the duchess. After the couple's
regal drive along nearly a mile of his private road through his
estate, there he was to greet them at the door of his baronial
country home, a great mountain of a man, vast in his white field
marshal's uniform. He greeted them effusively, the huge grin
and sparkling eyes of jovial "Fat Hermann," as he was popu-
larly known, contradicting the absolute ruthlessness of the
monster who originated the Gestapo and was the original Nazi
bullyboy.

"Emmy Goering played her part as hostess well," wrote Paul
Schmidt, Hitler's interpreter. "Quiet and modest, she created
an atmosphere of hospitality in the best sense of the word,
occasionally smiling deprecatingly when her Hermann got
carried away and used coarse language. She herself said very
little, just unobtrusively contributing to the pleasant family
atmosphere of those Anglo-German conversations at the
Schnorheide."[9]

Once the formalities were over, Goering took them on a tour
of his huge house, named after his late first wife. They were
shown Goering's magnificently equipped gymnasium where
the Reichsmarschal romped playfully with some of the appara-
tus. They even went to the attic to see his toys, and the chief of
the Luftwaffe demonstrated his favorite wire-controlled airplane, which dropped wooden bombs. Of greater significance,
though, was a map that the duke saw hanging in Goering's
study. On this map Austria had already been merged with the
Reich, a grim prophecy. In answer to the duke's inquiry,
though, Goering just laughed and said that he had needed a
new map, and since Austria would soon be a part of the Reich,
it would save him having a new map made later. Bearing in
mind Goering's imminent departure for Austria, one might
have expected the duke to have informed Britain's diplomats,
but there is no evidence that he did. Perhaps he was not sur-

prised, and considering the talks he had had with von Papen in Austria the year before, it is possible that he knew what was coming. In fairness, most political observers of Europe knew Hitler would eventually merge his homeland into the greater Reich; it was only a matter of time.

When they took their departure from Goering's magnificent home, they were rushed to the immense bathing resort for workers at Rügen for a brief stay, and then they were off again to Bielefeld on the start of their tour of the Rhineland.

While the Windsors were traipsing around the vast Krupp steelworks at Essen the following day, Hitler delivered another stentorian, emotionally charged oration about Germany's right to live and the Germans' demand for living space. And in England a German Luftwaffe delegation headed by General Milch, the air minister, with Lieutenant General Stumpff and Major General Udet, arrived at Croydon. They came in response to an invitation arranged by squadron leader F. W. Winterbotham and de Ropp. The Germans, who were rapidly modernizing their own air force with the Stuka and Dornier 17 bombers that were already proving in Spain to be war winners, were treated to a view of the RAF's obsolete junk, which must have greatly heartened their own plans.

The Windsors gallantly went on speeding in trains from one side of Germany back to Leipzig and Dresden. It was at Leipzig that the duke attended one of Ley's Labor Front meetings and told the audience: "I have traveled the world and my upbringing has made me familiar with the great achievements of mankind, but that which I have seen in Germany, I had hitherto believed to be impossible. It cannot be grasped, and is a miracle; one can only begin to understand it when one realizes that behind it all is one man and one will."[10]

It was in Dresden that the duke's relative, the Duke of Coburg, who had been Hitler's emissary in 1936, gave a dinner party at the Grand Hotel, in their honor. Coburg, who knew all about royal protocol, had a place card set for the duchess bearing the German equivalent of "HRH"; he thus became the first European royalty to recognize the duchess's claim to the title. The flattery she received as the only woman present at the dinner was further enhanced when an official of the Saxon State Chancery declared that Berlin had instructed all local

authorities to address the duchess as Your Royal Highness.
The Nazis were well aware that the way to gratify the duke
was through his wife. So, knowing of her special interest in fine
china, they included in her itinerary a visit to the world-famous
Meissen porcelain works. They also ensured that whenever the
ducal couple arrived at a railway station, guards of honor were
ready and well-rehearsed crowds chanted, "We want the
duchess!"

While the duke and duchess were being greeted by crowds
and endless demonstrations of Nazi bonhomie, nothing had
really changed in Germany, for while the duke smiled and
waved, banner headlines in the October 19 edition of *Volkischer Beobachter* screamed invective at the duke's own country: "British Policy in Palestine—Nazi Picture of Horror! . . .
numerous houses are razed to the ground—what a triumph for
democracy . . . the democratic Eden regards the mass
parades—he stages instead mass explosions. . . . When the
Union Jack flutters victorious over a picture of horror and
devastation, over the desolate homeland of punished Arabs,
enough has been done for the peace of the world!"

The press did not stop there either. The same paper carried a
ruthless attack on Czechoslovakia, winding up the hate in
readiness for that state's obliteration. "Lies, hate, murder and
terror," its pages howled, "attended the birth of the Czecho-
slovak state . . . the Sudeten Deutsche ought to know that the
whole German people stand behind them."

But the ducal tour went blithely into its second week, with
the Windsors being shown around the Nazi party parade
ground at Nuremberg before being rushed by train to Stutt-
gart for the afternoon. In the Württemberger capital they were
again welcomed by chanting crowds in the bright autumn
sunshine, although a chill wind was blowing from the Alps.

In Vienna, meanwhile, Reichsmarschal Goering's visit had
passed, but on that crisp autumn day the Austrian capital
experienced a distinct, almost tangible uneasiness at the
attacks on their country in the vitriolic German press. In yet
more scathing Nazi protestations, the German papers be-
moaned that "Objection is taken to Austrian Chancellor's refusal to contemplate the idea of an *Anschluss* between Austria
and Germany, and his declaration that Austria wished fer-

vently to maintain her independence. . . ." Hitler, who used habitually to hum the childish ditty "Who's afraid of the big bad wolf?" and fancied himself in that role, even calling his wartime headquarters the "wolf's lair"—could not understand why the Austrian lamb refused his invitation to the slaughter. The German press responded to their Führer's ire with outraged indignation.

The climax of the Windsors' tour was on the 22nd, when they were to take afternoon tea with the Führer at Berchtesgaden, his mountain retreat some seventy miles from Munich. Although it was supposed to have been a last-minute addition to the tour and it is claimed they were told only the day before that Hitler would see them, this is frankly unlikely in view of Hitler's years of courting the duke. But it would have been viewed with extreme distaste by the press had the arrangement been announced beforehand. Anyway, the duke and duchess obediently took the train for Hitler's retreat. Unfortunately, the train arrived an hour earlier than expected, and they were courteously informed that the Führer was taking his afternoon nap and could not be disturbed; they would have to wait. A car was provided, and they were politely shown the neighborhood sites before arriving back when Hitler was ready for them.

By the autumn of 1937 there was a small colony of top Nazis living in the immediate vicinity of Hitler's residence; Goering and Bormann had houses there, and when Hitler placed the house of his old friends the Bechsteins—of piano fame—at Speer's disposal, he became the fourth "Obersalzberger." By the time of the duke's visit it was a huge estate, largely acquired by Martin Bormann, who simply turned off the land anyone whose house was wanted, either for living in or for clearing the land. With a dismal insensitivity towards the glorious Alpine scenery, Bormann had driven concrete roads through the meadowland and laid paving stones over mountain paths where once delicate flowers had nodded. There was a barracks for the SS troops, a vast garage building for the fleet of cars, a hotel for special guests, and dormitories for the hundreds of workers. When Hitler had decided to enlarge his then-modest house in 1935, he set about drawing up the plans, which Speer then detailed. The result was a huge sprawl of a building. To quote Speer: "The resultant ground plan was most impractical for the reception of official visitors." The Windsors were ushered into this vast, semisunken room furnished in a motley assortment of styles, even with a grand piano covered by an antimacassar and a potted plant; its windows gave a fine view towards the Untsberg. Ominously, it was the room in which Hitler would receive Chamberlain only months later.

Hitler greeted them with a smile and then, with only his interpreter, Schmidt, he and the Windsors sat down to talk. Schmidt says that he was asked to interpret the Führer's words in spite of the fact that the duke spoke in German all the while, even sharply correcting him when his rendition did not meet exactly the duke's interpretation. The duchess listened carefully but only joined in when the subject had a particular interest for women.

According to Schmidt, the duke expressed his admiration for the industrial welfare arrangements he had seen, especially at the Krupp works at Essen, and he was also full of admiration for the workers' housing he had been shown by Ley. Social progress in Germany was said to be the principal subject of the conversation between himself and Hitler during that friendly afternoon discussion. Hitler made himself as amiable as he could to the duke.

The official German account of the meeting was, reputedly, never found in the files at the end of the war, but Schmidt's account of the talks implies that they were general in nature, and he says they did not talk of political matters, which is difficult to understand given the desire of both men to cooperate. It is apparent that Hitler thought he had great potential for leadership in Britain by the attention he paid the duke in the years ahead, culminating in Portugal in 1940. Hitler personally bade them farewell with that curious, half-shy smile of his that never touched the piercing blue eyes. When they had gone, he turned to Schmidt: "She would have made a good queen," he said simply.

The duchess was obviously impressed and wrote later, "I could not take my eyes off Hitler." She also remarked on his long slim hands and said that she "felt the impact of a great inner force." She was most affected by his eyes, though, like most people who met the Führer: "truly extraordinary—

intense, unblinking, magnetic, burning with the same peculiar fire I had earlier seen in the eyes of Kemal Ataturk."[11]

Schmidt's account does not tally with the duchess's, for she later explained that she had tried to learn from her husband what they had talked about. The duke told her little, she said, only that Hitler had discussed mostly what he'had done for Germany and how he hated Bolshevism. This seems more likely in view of the areas of agreement the two men had anyway, especially about Bolshevism. The duke also gave his account—much later though and with the inestimable value of a long hindsight after the war. He described, too, the Führer's eyes as piercing and to an extent excused his behavior by saying that Hitler frankly took him in. "I believed him," he wrote after the war, "when he implied he sought no war with England. . . . I acknowledge now that, along with many other well-meaning people, I let my admiration for the good side of the German character dim what was being done by the bad. I thought that . . . the immediate task . . . of my generation . . . was to prevent another conflict between Germany and the West that could bring down our civilization. Well, I was wrong about that."[12]

The duke and his wife boarded a special train at 5 P.M. and were rushed back to Munich, where they were welcomed by the former Grand Duke of Mecklenburg. Later that evening they were guests at a private dinner party given by Deputy Führer Rudolf Hess.

The couple's final whole day in Germany ended with what was later described as the duke's most enjoyable night. They went along that evening to a popular Munich beer hall, the Platzl. As usual it was filled with a cheerful crowd swinging mugs of foaming Bavarian beer. The duke heartily drank three pints of beer and then sprang onto his chair to make a speech in German, telling his happy audience how much he loved their city. The packed hall echoed to the roar of approval as the men, many in leather shorts, pounded their stone mugs and roared in delight as he put on a false mustache. According to the London *Daily Express*, the duke received "the kind of applause that only the old Kings of Bavaria could expect." The duchess, it was reported, took away fond memories of the "delightful little white sausages."

There was just time the next morning to cram in an official tour of the Brown House and other National Socialist buildings in Munich, including the Temple of Honor, which contained the bodies of the Nazis who had died in the 1923 putsch. Then they were off on their return journey to Paris, escorted as far as Kehl on the French frontier. The farewell cheers to the duke were, nevertheless, metaphorically drowning the sound of breaking glass that echoed frighteningly around Danzig where Nazi mobs went on an orgy of Jewish window breaking to the screams of "Jews must perish!"

In Britain the newspaper treated the visit very guardedly and only briefly reported the broad facts. In the Labor magazine *Forward*, however, Herbert Morrison echoed the views of many British people who impatiently felt that the duke would "not retire from public life." Morrison expressed the view that the duke had never realized that in a constitutional monarchy neither as heir to the throne nor as king could he publicly pronounce his opinions on controversial matters. He went on to criticize the duke and make remarks about Mrs. Simpson's (as he still called her) rumored political tendencies. "If the Duke wants to study social problems," he wrote, "he had far better quietly read books and get advice in private rather than put his foot in it in this way. . . . Although what he is going to do with this knowledge I do not know, for he cannot be permitted to reenter public life—in this country at any rate. . . ."

The American press was unfettered where the duke was concerned and therefore treated the visit thoroughly. *The New York Times* reported on October 23, 1937:

The Duke's decision to see for himself the Third Reich's industries and social institutions and his gestures and remarks during the last two weeks have demonstrated adequately that the Abdication did rob Germany of a firm friend, if not indeed a devoted admirer, on the British throne. He has lent himself, perhaps unconsciously, but easily to National Socialist propaganda. There can be no doubt that his tour has strengthened the regime's hold on the working classes. . . . The Duke is reported to have become very critical of English politics as he sees them and is reported as declaring that the British ministers of today and their possible successors are no match for the German and Italian dictators.

By the time the duke's German tour ended in late October 1937, German expansion had hardly begun—only propaganda threatened Austria, Czechoslovakia, and Danzig; a year later the situation would have greatly worsened, so that if one could excuse the duke his enthusiasm and naiveté in 1937, it would be less easy in 1939 and unforgivable in 1940.

While the German tour further sullied the duke's already tarnished reputation, Bedaux came off still worse. He had stayed out of sight during the tour, having made the arrangements, as was his way. But he had then begun to prepare for the duke to make a similar tour of the United States. It soon became clear, however, that the American press and public were against the tour, following as it did on the questionable German visit. The American unions, led by those of Baltimore, the duchess's hometown, announced they would use the occasion for an attack upon Bedaux. He was described as the archenemy of labor, and they declared they would not cooperate with the Windsors, "whether emissaries of a dictatorship, or uninformed sentimentalists."

Through a press release the duke denied he had engaged the services of an American agency to organize his forthcoming tour in the United States: "His Royal Highness's visit is of a purely private and unofficial character, and the itinerary in the industrial areas has been arranged through the instrumentality of Mr. Charles Bedaux." But the tour was canceled.

It was all too much for Bedaux; the hostility and the shock of finding himself in so much trouble prostrated him physically and mentally. During the next few weeks he was persuaded by the acting head of his American companies to sign an agreement not to interfere in their operation, and later he relinquished his voting rights. On November 10 he fled to Canada and from there to Europe. He was never willingly to set foot in the United States again.

7

War!

THE SECOND World War began with a lie.

Given Hitler's mendacious nature, it was inevitable that even the greatest holocaust yet to befall mankind had to be started with a deliberate and cruel falsehood. Right up to the final collapse of peace, Hitler struggled to maintain the "legality" of his policies by initiating a particularly detestable deception. Even before Munich, Reinhard Heydrich—who controlled the *Sicherheitsdienst*—internal security service of the SS, the dreaded SD—had evolved a plan by which the Wehrmacht would invade Czechoslovakia by faked frontier incidents. The Munich capitulation by the Western Powers obviated the need. The intended showdown with Poland then set Heydrich planning again, and by early August 1939 he had a scheme by which the world could be made to believe that Germany had been provoked into war by Poland.

Heydrich's plan was that on the night before the German attack, SD squads dressed in Polish uniforms would create incidents along the frontier. But, to add realism, Heydrich initiated a horrifying plan for real bloodshed. He wrote: "Actual proof of Polish attack is essential both for the foreign press and for German propaganda."[1] The bodies were to come from the concentration camps, prisoners who were to be given lethal injections on D-Day. ("D-Day" is used by *Der Spiegel* in reference to the German attack on Poland, although at the time the German Command used "Y-Day." In Gestapo parlance, they were referred to as "canned goods." The Führer was told of the plan and jumped at it. The plan was carried out on the night of August 31, 1939, when the pseudo-Poles occupied the German radio station at Gleiwitz and destroyed a German customs building at Hohenlinden. The concentration camp "soldiers" were shot. Next day, in a welter of indignation, Germany invaded Poland, and the war had started.

The pertinence of this account to this story is that it was carried out by the SD, and the leaders of this elite scourge of Europe, Reinhard Heydrich and Walter Schellenberg, became key figures in the intrigue in which the duke knowingly involved himself nine months later.

When war was declared on September 3, the day was, the duchess recalled, "hot and humid even for the Côte d'Azur at that season."

The Windsors were at La Croë, the beautiful white villa they leased in the spring of 1938. It stood on a small prominence overlooking the blue Mediterranean at Cap d'Antibes. The villa had been only partly furnished, and ever since moving there the duchess had been absorbed in decorating the house, as well as a house in Paris, which they leased in January 1939. By the outbreak of war neither had been completed to the satisfaction of the duchess's fastidious attention to detail.

As the Riviera summer of 1939 lazed almost imperceptibly toward autumn, noticeable more in the yellowed, parched lawns and the ripening fruit than in any chill air or golden leaf, the numerous British tourists and residents still thronged the terraces by day and casinos by night. The blazing colors of the gardens were only slightly muted by the passing season, and at night myriad lights winked into the placid waters, creased only by elegant yachts. Nevertheless, even the treasured distractions of these idyllic surroundings could not relieve the general depression that day after hearing from the French morning news broadcasts of the disintegration of Poland's forces before the German blitzkrieg. Already changes were threatening to impede the progress of pleasure along France's holiday coast, as waiters, gardeners, footmen, and hoteliers were called for mobilization as France prepared to fight.

Later that same Sunday morning the duke condescended to bid farewell to two of his French staff who had been ordered to report for military service. He stood solemnly on the outside steps, his usual bored expression reflecting the tedium of change in his well-ordered life, as the Frenchmen were graciously given leave to go. Major Metcalfe, who had been the duke's best man and had recently reattached himself to his retinue, recalled that with his duty done to the departing servants, the duke immediately began making arrangements for his entire party to fly back to Britain.

Relaxed in the vividly colored trousers he liked to sport with a casual shirt, the duke spent hours in the library trying to cope with the French telephone system, which was already jammed by a confusion of people all equally anxious to get to somewhere else. After a lifetime of aides and secretaries to undertake most of his mundane or tedious tasks, the duke got quickly impatient when the world about him did not instantly order itself to his needs. His exasperation finally won, and he gave up trying to telephone.

"There's nothing we can do from here right now," he told Metcalfe despondently. "I'm sure that I shall hear from my brother the moment any decision is taken."[2]

Outside, the sun blazed down on the whitened, flower-splashed rocks of the prominence, and gulls idled by. After a moment's thought the duke turned and gloomily suggested to the duchess that they all go for a swim. It took them a while to gather their bathing things, and it was just before noon when the duke and duchess, together with Metcalfe, were making their way down to their own swimming pool cut into the scorching, sun-bleached rocks of the point. They had not reached the pool, though, when a servant hastened after them from the house to call the duke to the telephone, telling him that the British ambassador, Sir Ronald Campbell, was on the line from Paris. The duke told the others to go on without him and then turned back up the winding, mimosa-scented path to the house.

It was ten minutes later, the duchess recalled, when the duke rejoined them at the sparkling blue pool. Walking straight to the edge of the pool, he said in a quiet voice, "Great Britain has just declared war on Germany, and I'm afraid in the end this may open the way for world communism."[3] Without another word, he plunged into the water, as if, metaphorically, cleansing himself of the catastrophe that had overtaken Europe.

He had lived for twenty years with a deep, father-instilled dread of Communism, and he perceived in this conflict that when Britain, France, and Germany had exhausted themselves again in the Flanders mud, the huge manpower resources of the Soviet Union would flood westward. According to his beliefs, he had done his best to steer his country away from the brink, however inexpert had been his discussions and conversation with the Nazi leaders. Certainly, his had not been a lone voice crying for peace, but his assertions had been muffled and cost him his throne. Moreover, the war that had just started would not only be strategically very different from the terrible war of his youth, it was also going to be a war in which there would be dissenting factions on both sides. Among these intriguing factions the duke would soon find himself a cat's-paw of power as both sides played him along.

When the bathing party had returned to the house and changed, the duke energetically tackled the travel problems once again. He had always intended to return to Britain, as we have seen, and the war had brought about the opportunity for him to do so with honor. Evidently he was keen to leave as soon as possible, and one cannot help but believe that while his wife had lavished so much time and wealth on their leased houses, he had just been biding his time. Now his impatience at what seemed to be permanent exile overflowed, and he busily made his arrangements, although it would inevitably be left to the long-suffering Metcalfe to implement the details.

No sooner had some results begun to emerge in the complicated travel arrangements than Walter Monckton telephoned from London. Metcalfe was reading a book in the drawing room, from where he could hear the heated exchange that took place between the duke and his adviser. The conversation suddenly ended, and the duke stalked from the library and tartly announced to his retinue that while arrangements had been made for them to fly home, he and the duchess would not be going with them. He petulantly declared, "I refuse to go unless we are invited to stay at Windsor Castle and the invitation and plane are sent personally by my brother."[4]

The simple truth that was so unpalatable as to be avoided by the duke was that he was just not welcome in Britain anymore.

The duke's German trip and the way he had fawned on his Nazi hosts, despite the hollow protestations of a private visit, had been ill-received in Britain. There is little evidence available cf formal government attitudes because the relevant Cabinet papers are not available, but from the utterances of individual ministers it is clear that he had been an embarrassment.

His German visit had ended in the third week of October 1937, and shortly afterward the Nazi path of conquest had begun. Within five months Austria had fallen to the usual ruthless Nazi combination of bullying and trickery. Chancellor Schuschnigg had been ordered to Berchtesgaden, where he was reduced to tears and impotence by Hitler's harsh, blatant, and uncompromising threats. He had resigned on his return to Vienna, and the Austrian Nazi party leader, Seys-Inquart, who took his place, immediately called for German aid to restore order—the Wehrmacht had then marched in, and Austria became the German province of the Ostmark. The year 1938 had seen Nazi demands on the Sudeten region of Czechoslovakia lead to the threat of war as the determined, well-armed Czechs prepared to fight behind their powerful fixed fortresses and defenses. But the West had been outsmarted, outmaneuvered and outthought by Germany, ably supported by Mussolini's aspirations to be a big power, too. At Munich the Czechs had been forced to relinquish the Sudetenland and their defenses. Returning from Munich, Chamberlain had proudly reported that his visit alone had prevented an imminent invasion, and the Duke of Windsor had been among those who approved publicly and applauded. But the Czechs had been stripped of their defenses, and they could do nothing a year later when Germany seized Bohemia and Moravia and expunged their state.

According to Winterbotham in the SIS, Chamberlain "sold Czechoslovakia down the river" in 1938, because he had "a growing conviction that morale in France was no longer to be relied upon." The fact that Winterbotham held this view, which was not believed by Francophiles in the Cabinet, may indicate that the SIS had a good idea of the way that French politicians and military commanders were moving, and almost certainly the SIS advised Chamberlain. The motives of the SIS, however, are less easy to determine. Carrying through this tale is the notion that they would have preferred Germany to turn east, for they had already identified where the real threat to Western democracy lay, and it was to be hoped that the two vicious dictators, Hitler and Stalin, would finish each other off.

Next it had been the turn of Poland, and the hatred in the Polish-controlled, predominantly German port of Danzig, which had begun while the duke was in Germany, ran amok. The Western Powers, Britain and France, had had enough and gave guarantees to Poland that were manifestly impossible to implement. Britain had no troops available, and France was securely boxed in by the German West Wall. Their bluff was called, Poland was invaded, and war began.

What brought about this sudden acceleration in Germany's aggressive policy, which they knew was bound to lead to a confrontation with Britain and France because it flew in the face of all the West's defensive alliances?

It has hitherto been assumed that Germany was surprised by the Allied declaration of war in September 1939, having been assured by her foreign relations experts that Britain would not fight and would thus restrain France; in other words, Germany invaded Poland as a logical next step in her declared aim of her *Drang nach Osten*—drive to the East, believing that war would not result. But is there another interpretation of these events?

Winterbotham maintained that Hitler's air force was incorrectly designed to fight an all-out war against Britain. It had been developed essentially as an air adjunct to the army, and indeed, its failure in the Battle of Britain was in large measure due to its lack of strategic bombers. Only later was an attempt made to introduce heavy bombers. The reason for this failure in the air, Winterbotham says, was that "right up to 1938 Hitler believed he could secure British neutrality." It was, in fact, then, after the abdication, that Hitler realized he would have to fight a total war, first in Europe and only after that in Russia.

The Luftwaffe, through, was apparently supreme in the air, for at the outbreak of war its order of battle totaled some 4,700 aircraft, against just over 800 obsolescent Polish aircraft; France had virtually no modern bombers, while the RAF's total of 3,600 aircraft contained a high proportion of obsolete types and was, in any case, committed to deploying many squadrons overseas. There is no doubt, however, that in the summer of 1939, Germany was absolutely stronger on land than Britain and France. In the field the German army had fifty-three first-line divisions fully supplied with modern arms and equipment. This was not the case with the twenty-eight French divisions recruited at the same time and assigned to the vital northeast front. The German army did have a certain lack of artillery, but this was offset by their airborne artillery, the Stukas. In the French army, moreover, matters were much worse, particularly in the "Category B" reserve divisions, which had been mobilized with grave deficiencies in every sphere. In armored forces both Britain and France were hopelessly outclassed in equipment and experience. Only at sea therefore did the Allies have an advantage, in 616 warships compared to only 130 German.

The Germans knew that Britain was straining to rearm, especially in the RAF. Did Germany deliberately provoke war in 1939, therefore, in the belief that it would be a quick war in which her overwhelming strength on land and in the air would secure a decisive victory *before* Britain's traditional response of a naval blockade could have any effect? In any case, Germany's surprising coup in August 1939, of a pact with the Soviet Union, assured her of a supply route that negated the blockade threat altogether in the short term.

From 1932 onward, as we have seen, men like Rosenberg were straining to keep Britain neutral. Hoesch's report in 1934, after his dinner at Windsor, had assured Hitler that King George V "would do everything in his power to forestall every possibility of war."

With Ribbentrop's appointment as Germany's ambassador

to London, the process of ensuring Britain's benevolent neutrality was intensified. Ribbentrop had made every effort in particular to establish friendly connections with members of the Cliveden Set. His personal acquaintance with influential Englishmen had been stressed by Hitler to Goering, which prompted the cynical Reichsmarschal to reply, "Yes, but the trouble is that they know Ribbentrop."

Harold Nicolson, in an unpublished essay written for Michael Astor, wrote: "Clandestine meetings between Herr von R., some Cabinet Ministers and others were certainly arranged at St. James's Square or at Lady Astor's sea-side residence at Sandwich; from these meetings the German Ambassador did acquire the idea that there existed an influential minority in England prepared, if only the British Empire were left undisturbed, to accord Nazi Germany a free hand against Russia, and the resultant mastery of Europe. This was a disastrous impression to have conveyed to so ill-judging a man as Herr von Ribbentrop, and Lady Astor must certainly bear her part of the blame."[5]

But Ribbentrop had established other connections, too, and had introduced numerous influential Britons to Hitler, who were only revealed in 1945, when American troops captured the interview transcripts—Beaverbrook, Nov. 22, 1935; T. E. Jones, Baldwin's private secretary, May 17, 1936; Sir Thomas Beecham, November 13, 1936. But the documents of these and other interviews have since mysteriously and unaccountably disappeared. Even if Ribbentrop had been getting assurances from these contacts that Britain would stand aside while Germany drove east, it is clear that they had been incidental to the really important pledges from Edward. But by late 1937 Ribbentrop had revised his prediction: *He was then warning Hitler that Britain would fight.*

In late December 1937 he submitted a summary to Hitler, declaring that Britain "regarded Germany as her most deadly potential enemy, as Hitler alone could threaten the heart of the British Empire, Britain herself."[6] Even more pertinent, though, was Ribbentrop's memorandum to the Führer sent on January 1, 1938. It was a long memorandum, but the essential paragraphs make its warning unmistakable: ". . . French intervention on behalf of her eastern allies is likely, or at any

rate is always *possible* and so, as a consequence, is war between
Germany and England." Ribbentrop's answer to the French
threat was to keep Britain out by a "superior concentration of
powers," i.e., an alliance between Germany, Italy, and Japan.
With Britain's limited resources being dissipated in Africa
and Asia to contain Italy and Japan, it was more probable that
she would be neutralized in Europe.

It is evident from various documents that Germany did not
consider France alone much of a threat. All French military
thinking since the 1920s was defensive and based on the Maginot Line, although there was a contingency for a Franco-
British army to attack through Belgium and Holland toward
the Ruhr. However, the Germans knew full well that, through
the machinations of the Cagoulards and especially men like
Lemargue-Dubreil and the many other influential business
and military men, it was already agreed that France would put
up only a nominal resistance to any German onslaught. They
wanted to preserve France intact even at the cost of liberty,
which they in any case scorned with bitter memories of the
1920s Paris communes.

Ribbentrop's New Year's Day memorandum continued:

> This is my evaluation of the situation after having carefully
> weighed all the circumstances. I have worked for friendship
> with England for years, and nothing would make me happier
> than the possibility of this achievement. When I asked the
> Führer to send me to London I was skeptical about the likeli-
> hood of success, but, *because of Edward VIII, it seemed that a
> final attempt should be made. Today, I no longer have faith in
> any understanding.* [My italics.] England does not desire in
> close proximity a paramount Germany, which could be a con-
> stant menace to the British. . . .
>
> Henceforth—regardless of what tactical interludes of concil-
> iation may be attempted with regard to us—every day that our
> political calculations are not actuated by the fundamental idea
> that England is our most dangerous enemy, would be a gain for
> our enemies. R.[7]

Such a strong, unequivocal warning as that makes nonsense
of the myth established at Nuremberg in 1946, that Ribben-

trop wrongly judged British intentions and encouraged Hitler
to go to war. Ribbentrop, like Rosenberg and his own predeces-
sor, Leo von Hoesch, met and talked with many prominent
political and social personages who welcomed an understanding with Germany whereby Britain and Germany would leave
one another alone. The most important single figure, though, in
Germany's reckoning of whether or not Britain would fight
was Edward, and once he abdicated, Ribbentrop definitely
realized that the political balance had shifted against British
neutrality.

On Sunday, September 3, 1939, Britain was momentarily
stunned by the awful and final reality of war. It brought back
to the generation that had suffered so appallingly in the First
World War all the dormant nightmares of unending slaughter
for a few miles of shell-pocked, wire-entangled slime. There
was also the new terror of bombing that might reduce London
to rubble, perhaps within days. The reality would be six years
long and quite different. Germany had learned the futility of
static warfare based on trenches and the fortress and, drawing
on the brilliance of the British armored warfare exponents
such as Liddell-Hart, was prepared for swift-moving, total
warfare combining the infantry, the tank, and the airplane,
against which the seemingly invincible Polish cavalry simply
broke their lances.

At La Croë the Duke of Windsor was already beginning to
experience the inconvenience of war and the reality of life
stripped of its glamour. He wanted to go home, just like the
hundreds of other Britons on the Riviera that early autumn.
Yet so simple a matter as returning to Britain to offer his
services to his country at war was complicated by the cleavage
with his family since the abdication. In the end it was the
duke's long-suffering friend and chief camp-follower, the
debonair Metcalfe, who offered the Windsors the hospitality of
his own home, Hartfield House, in Sussex. The Metcalfes' home
would accommodate the Windsors in fitting style and was close
enough to London for the duke to commute by car to conduct
his official business.

The duke informed Monckton that he was returning to Britain to stay at Hartfield House, which prompted Monckton to write: "The decision about the Duke's immediate future was therefore added to the Prime Minister's other anxieties." Since Chamberlain had been in Baldwin's Cabinet in November 1936 when the abdication was discussed, one supposes he knew the underlying reasons for the abdication and what Windsor's return would mean. Clearly the duke's return to Britain would be acutely embarrassing to the royal family and government, for the Windsors had shown little circumspection in their public utterances and had all too often criticized the royal family and government.

When the king learned that his elder brother was returning to Britain, he consulted his prime minister, and as a result the duke's return was made conditional on his accepting one of two posts that would be offered him. The first was that of deputy regional commissioner for Wales, nominally in charge of such things as civil defense in the principality; the alternative post he could accept was with the British Military Mission to General Maurice Gamelin, the French commander in chief. That job involved acting as a liaison officer between Gamelin's headquarters and the British Expeditionary Force under General Lord Gort, a post requiring more diplomatic than military skill. It was confidently assumed in London that since the Windsors were resident in France anyway, he would accept the French posting so long as he was not offered any aid in getting home. They quite forgot his mercurial contrariness.

Once it had been settled that the duke would stay at Metcalfe's home, his next problem was transportation. He fully expected no less than the king's personal attention, which was not forthcoming. However, a solution was found. At the outbreak of war Winston Churchill had been appointed First Lord of the Admiralty, the post he had held at the outbreak of war in 1914. He immediately bent his profound intellect to the weighty consideration of the stranded duke. On September 11, he sent a signal to the duke's cousin, Captain Lord Louis Mountbatten, whose biographer recorded that "On September 11, Mountbatten got a hurry call to Whitehall. Orders so secret they could not be telegraphed were handed to him at the Admiralty, and as he read them Mountbatten must have smiled. The

First Lord had a great sense of humor."[5] The written orders
directed Mountbatten to take his destroyer, HMS *Kelly*, to Le
Havre, to pick up the Windsors.

Meanwhile the duke was still in the south of France, where
the majority of wealthy British residents were content to stay
in the sunshine remote from likely battle zones. It was there
that he received a melodramatic telephone call from the British ambassador in Paris telling him of the arrangements for
them to be transported across the Channel. The ambassador
told him to head for the embassy, where they would receive
"further instructions."

Plainly the duke was in a great hurry to get back to Britain
and reestablish himself in an important job. With the destroyer
Kelly on its way to Le Havre to collect them, there was clearly a
need for all haste. The trouble was that the duchess would not
be parted from the embellishments of her position and insisted
on taking with them "certain valuable possessions, mostly David's." The duchess was most particular in domestic matters,
and the packaging of possessions had to be done just right; they
were carefully wrapped in "brown butcher's paper" and put
into cardboard boxes. Only when the duchess was satisfied that
all was ready did they depart La Croë. The expedition set out in
two cars, loaded with boxes, baggage, and their three cairn
terriers, Preezi, Detto, and Pookie. It was a long, hot and tiring
drive, and the chauffeurs must have been hard pushed. The
couple stopped briefly in Paris, where they were given secret
and complicated instructions before departing for the Channel
coast, which they reached late on September 12.

In the meantime, Mountbatten had carried out his instructions and taken his destroyer across the dark English Channel,
first to Cherbourg, where he collected Winston Churchill's son,
Major Randolph Churchill, before racing along the Normandy
coast to the ancient port of Le Havre at the Mouth of the Seine.
Although Mountbatten only then informed his crew of their
task, he was surprised to discover that most of them already
knew their destination; somehow or other the *Daily Mirror*
had learned of the voyage and published an account in that
morning's edition. This was alarming, as the Germans were
known to have large numbers of U-boats at sea, and it was
possible they would try to intercept *Kelly*. Late that night the

destroyer nudged its way cautiously alongside the jetty at Le Havre.

"At Le Havre," the record shows, "Major Churchill jumped onto the heavily guarded dock." At this point Mountbatten's account politely omits a bit about the duchess's indecorous obsession with her butcher's paper parcels and boxes, which by then were untidily stacked on the front lawn of the house occupied by the British admiral-commandant of the port because he had refused to have his house cluttered with them. It was there that Randolph Churchill met the Windsors. Mountbatten's biographer's account continues: "Under the shaded lights Mountbatten saw him [Churchill] returning with his passengers. The crew stood at attention and the boatswain's squealing pipes echoed among the wharf sheds as Lord Mountbatten at the gangway welcomed his former King aboard."[8]

The duke looked rakishly disheveled, with his fair hair awry and his now near-habitual hunted look. He wore a long, loose overcoat over the inevitable checked suit—many of these suits, according to the duchess, had belonged to his father, which evinced the duke's oft-remarked-upon parsimony. The duchess, however, doggedly maintained her chic appearance in the customary close-fitting felt hat, while fussing over the dogs and boxes, most of which were being carried by Metcalfe and the chauffeurs. Mountbatten also protested the amount of luggage, but in the end the duchess had her way and stubbornly refused to be parted from anything. Eventually all was stowed, and the Windsors' party went below.

As soon as all was ready, the destroyer cast off and edged warily back into the cold waters of the Channel. Commander Evans took the bridge, and with her crew all closed up to action stations, *Kelly* bounded at high speed into open water and headed for England. While the crew stood to and kept careful watch for the U-boats, the duke and duchess, with Churchill, were in the captain's quarters. As Mountbatten recalled, "It was a gay party. The duke, alight with enthusiasm and the hope of being able to serve his country once more, seemed years younger than the last time I had seen him."

It was very early on a cold and dark morning, September 13, by the time Mountbatten brought his ship alongside Farewell

Jetty at Portsmouth, ironically the one from which the duke
had sailed into exile almost three years before. As the hawsers
were made fast, a few subdued lights broke the blackout and
feebly glinted on the fixed bayonets of a khaki-clad squad of
honor. A Royal Marine band rendered the national anthem
against a background of sea and wind. "Edward shook his
cousin's hand with an extra hard grip, and went quickly down
the gangway with Wallis. They paused to wave goodbye to the
cheering crew and the duke said, 'God bless you and keep you
safe.'"

After a brief hesitation the duke went on down the gangway
and stepped onto the grimy cobbles. The wartime security, the
very absence of ceremony, pitched emotion high as the former
king stepped onto England. There he was welcomed by the C in
C, Portsmouth, Admiral Sir William James. There may indeed
have been a certain shady melodrama in the duke's wartime
arrival on that lonely, cloudy morning, but he could not fail to
recognize a deliberate slight as well. In fact the occasion was
strained more by the intentional and evident royal snub than
the strictures of wartime. Monckton, who was by then adviser
to King George VI, had indeed approached the Palace for
someone to welcome the duke home, but no one was forthcoming; the Palace even refused a request for an official car. If the
duke needed further reminding of his now-invidious position in
Britain, that was it. Apart from the admiral only Walter
Monckton and Lady Alexandra Metcalfe met the returning
exiles.

No arrangements had been made for the Windsors' overnight stay, and since the local hotels were considered unsuita-
ble, they were invited to stay with Admiral James and his wife
at Admiralty House. After refreshment there, they chatted
politely, as the duchess recollected, before they went up to bed.
Here, as elsewhere, though, she sought the limelight and
insists it was she in whom the Jameses were most interested,
not the duke. This need for attention and to be at the center of
conversation, often at the expense of the duke, was recognized
by many who knew them as a feature of their relationship.

They did not remain long in Portsmouth and were soon on
their way to Metcalfe's home in Surrey, where they settled in.
The duke was full of restless energy and the next morning,

September 14, went to London, anxious to play his part in the war. Monckton, however, insists that he had arranged the meeting and then only after "long and rather boring discussions"—for which, albeit, there does not seem to have been time.

At the Palace the duke was reunited with his brother and offered his services in "any capacity," although preferably as deputy regional commissioner in Wales. King George had by then been able to think over the matter of his elder brother's appointment for several days and discreetly suggested that the duke could be employed most usefully as a member of the military mission to France. However, the king continued in his slightly impedimented soft voice, if he agreed to this suggestion, he would have to relinquish his rank of field marshal, which he still retained as a former sovereign. He would have to revert to the rank of major general for the duration of the war. It was evidently a fraught moment and very difficult for the king. The duke received this suggestion with grim reserve and finally muttered that he would think about it.

Windsor gave the whole matter considerable thought overnight, and the more he thought of the king's suggestion, the less he liked it. Apparently he had no objection to going back to France, but he did resent giving up his field marshal's baton, which was a totally unique demotion in the British Army. Besides, he pondered, he certainly did not want to embark for France again without the opportunity of making a tour of the various army commands in Britain, so that he "could be in contact with the soldiers again." With these ideas firmly in mind, the duke went to see the war minister, Leslie Hore-Belisha, on September 15.

London must have seemed a very different place from the city the duke had left in 1937. Now there were antiaircraft guns in the royal parks and great knobbly sandbag walls in front of public buildings. Windows were crisscrossed with endless miles of sticky brown tape, and people carried the ubiquitous cardboard boxes containing their gas masks.

The duke called at the War Office unofficially and in secret. He arrived in civilian clothes and hurried through the Ministry door carrying his own cardboard-boxed gas mask strung over his shoulder.

Horer-Belisha, then in his middle forties, had been at Oxford with him and as minister of transport in the thirties had often seen the duke, who had taken a lively interest in his campaign to reduce road accidents. After the duke's exile, he had been the first British cabinet minister to pay an informal call upon the Windsors in Paris. The two men were, therefore, well disposed to each other, and Hore-Belisha would very much have liked to help the duke. But, as the details of the duke's proposals were made known to him, Hore-Belisha "began to see difficulties." Carefully and with great tact the war minister explained the importance of his mission in France, of the difficulties of rank when the head of the mission, Howard Vyse, was only a major general. There was also the problem of the status of the French high command, it was explained; Britain was sending only two corps to France, which would be actually subordinate to the French Army group commander, and thence to Gamelin. When it was made clear to him that to cede the right would be a unique sacrifice, the dejected duke with considerable reluctance abandoned his insistence on remaining a field marshal. Notwithstanding his capitulation in the matter of his rank, however, the duke still had other demands. He explained that the duchess, who intended to convert their villa in the south of France to a convalescent home for British officers, must accompany him to Paris, and furthermore, he wanted her to go with him on his preceding tour of the commands in Britain. This Hore-Belisha was not prepared for. He feared that the king would be very much opposed to any suggestion of the duchess touring all over the British Isles with the duke. The matter was left temporarily in the air while Hore-Belisha sought further advice.

The following morning Hore-Belisha was summoned to the Palace, where he found his fears fully justified. The king "seemed very disturbed and walked up and down the room ... in a distressed state. . . . He said the Duke had never had any discipline in his life. . . . He thought that if the Duchess went to the commands she might have a hostile reception, particularly in Scotland. He did not want the Duke to go to the commands in England at all."

One wonders how much this aversion was motivated by fears that the Windsors would catalyze emotions for or against themselves and how much the taint of Nazi contact was still lingering. In any event, Hore-Belisha promised that he would try to arrange the matter satisfactorily without bringing the king's name into it. He then had to take leave of the king to attend a meeting of the War Cabinet before managing to allay the king's anxiety completely. The king pressed him to return to Buckingham Palace that afternoon when the War Cabinet had ended.

At 2:30 P.M. Hore-Belisha returned to Buckingham Palace, this time accompanied by Field Marshal Sir Edmund Ironside, the chief of the Imperial General Staff. They found the king extremely agitated and clearly worried by Windsor's return. He protested that all his ancestors had succeeded to the throne only after their predecessors had died. "Mine," he complained, "is not only alive, but very much so." He repeated his anxiety about the Windsors traveling about the country and asked Hore-Belisha and Ironside to do their utmost to persuade his brother to go back to Paris immediately.

Thirty minutes later Hore-Belisha had been driven the short distance back to Whitehall and was in the War Office. The duke, who had never been disposed to taking no for an answer, or even expecting that he would be refused, was already waiting there. He "expressed his pleasure at going to the commands in England and making contact with the soldiers," but Hore-Belisha exercised great diplomacy as he carefully pointed out that when a soldier was given an appointment, he invariably accepted it without delay. So far as visiting the commands was concerned, he explained that "the troops were moving about, the secrecy involved, and that the Duke's presence would attract attention" (to the troops' location). "It would create an excellent impression," he advised, "if the Duke showed readiness to take up his appointment [in Paris] at once." Windsor had listened to the rejection of all his plans and hopes to figure again prominently in Britain and in response stoically said that he appreciated all the arguments and expressed his agreement; he must have realized that he had lost his gamble on being accepted back into the royal circle. And so, Hore-Belisha thought, the difficulty of his going to the commands had been resolved.

But the duke was nothing if not resilient, and he opened up

other topics with Hore-Belisha. He persisted in his questioning: What about his younger brother, the Duke of Gloucester, who was being paid as chief liaison officer with the British Expeditionary Force? He himself had come back voluntarily to offer his services and did not want any payment at all. He added that he would like this point to be announced in the press. Also, he wanted to know, could he wear his decorations on his battle dress, and could Fruity Metcalfe be appointed as his equerry? Hore-Belisha tactfully assured the duke that everything would be done to make things easy for him and that his chauffeur would be enlisted as a soldier. No doubt to the war minister's ineffable relief, the troublesome duke finally left after about an hour.

Outside, as the duke hastened to his car, a small crowd gathered to cheer him as he drove away. This pleased the duke, who smiled and raised his hat.

Hore-Belisha was mistaken in his belief that the duke was reconciled to his new role. Once in the privacy of his temporary home, it was different. The public sangfroid, practiced over forty years, was quickly shed in private, and for once, the duchess records, the duke's "face set itself into a mask barely concealing his deep-smouldering anger." So although the appointment in France had quickly and conveniently removed the tiresome Windsor from England once more, it had left a renewed and penetrating sense of grievance.

By then the duchess should have realized that she had no future in a Britain under the current leadership. She had evidently looked forward to being welcomed back to Britain as the duke's respected wife at some time; instead they had stolen ashore in the dark without a single note of welcome from his family, and she had been totally excluded from his discussions in London. The duke's rejection in Britain must have driven the truth rudely home to her that by marrying Edward, she had ironically destroyed all chance of helping him achieve his goals. For his part the duke was furious that his offer of service to his country had unbelievably been manipulated by Palace and government in a way that to him smelled of complicity. But how much, one must conjecture, did his fury derive from an unwilling realization that his wife was not just unacceptable herself in Britain but, moreover, was still barring him from the positions of authority and prestige that he coveted? How much blame did he attach to her? Behind the still-boyish facade there was a selfishness that was often ill-concealed. What then were his true feelings for her, feelings that obstinacy and pride would forbid revealing? His last dreams of restoration in Britain had been ruthlessly dashed, but did his bitterness, frustration, and vanity now begin unwittingly to guide him along an alternative path to power? The duke had long been childishly petulant when thwarted, and that characteristic was now reinforced with bitter resentment and an abiding sense of grievance that his own country had been so debased that it had rejected him. This was a dangerous combination in his new wartime role, for the Nazi enemy had applauded him and treated his wife with the respect his heritage demanded.

8

The Man Who Knew Too Much

ONE OF the riddles of the Second World War was why Hitler suddenly abandoned his long-laid plan to attack the Western powers in November 1939. In this chapter we will see that Hitler's Western strategy was closely connected to his intimate and intriguing contacts with the Duke of Windsor—a contact that spelled disaster for France and Britain.

The Polish campaign took Germany just eighteen days to complete. By the time it was over, the German armies had largely overrun the demarcation line agreed between Stalin and Ribbentrop on August 23, and Poland, invaded by Russians and Germans together, ceased to exist.

Meanwhile, on the Western Front the French had launched Operation Saar, which had been detailed in the French Army instruction of July 24, 1939, and was to be the first of General Maurice Gamelin's "limited offensives," the feeble remains of plans to attack Germany's rear should she attack France's Eastern Allies. The attack was launched on September 7, under the command of General Gaston Prételat, who commanded the French Second Army Group against German positions along the frontier between the Rhine and the Moselle.

It was a complete fiasco. That section of the frontier had been expressly defined by the victors of Waterloo as a barrier to future French aggression, for it had given Germany the high ground. The full French push was in any case "pulled" by Prételat, who attacked with only nine of the thirty-one divisions at his disposal. French heavy artillery was directed at the Siegfried Line but did minimal damage, as the lower-caliber shells were too light and the heavy were of First World War vintage and most failed to explode. The German front was held by General von Witzleben's First Army, of whose seventeen divisions ten were freshly recruited. Nevertheless, they held the French, who managed to advance only seven miles in a week's fighting when the bulk of the German Army was engaged in Poland.

On September 13 General Georges, commander of the Northeast Front, against which the imminent German onslaught was expected to fall, issued a cautious and frankly superfluous warning to Prételat "not to advance beyond the objectives attained." So ended Operation Saar, in which the timidly led French Army had lost twenty-seven killed, twenty-two wounded, and twenty-eight missing amid the sunny, rolling birchwoods and vineyards above the sparkling Moselle River.

Theoretically the French could have fought their way to the Rhine in about two weeks had they been allowed to seize the initiative, for the German Army opposing the Western Allies had been stripped to a minimum for the Polish campaign. The reality is more difficult to determine, for the Germans who were left were dug in along the Siegfried Line. Although commentators in 1939 were declaring the line to be unfinished, this was not the case. The Siegfried Line (West Wall) was never a "Maginot Line" construction but an artfully designed use of terrain and existing structures reinforced with concrete casements and minefields. British and American forces discovered the terrible reality of the Germans' *Westwall* in 1945. Nevertheless, the French high command had shown itself timid and imbued with the turgid Maginot Line concept of warfare; it boded ill for that time when Germany would attack in full force.

The Duke and Duchess of Windsor had returned to France in late September 1939, by which time the French attacks had petered out and the phony war had begun. They went to Paris but did not open their house on the Boulevard Suchet, going instead to a hotel in Versailles. The duke then assumed his post with the British Military Mission, which was attached to the French general staff at Vincennes, near Paris, taking up his military duties with the much-resented rank of major general.

As the warm autumn of 1939 passed into a bitterly cold winter, the relationship between the British and French commands also grew colder, and there emerged a frigid atmosphere of distrust that never really thawed before the two national armies were disastrously separated at Dunkirk the following May. In spite of the raising of the Free French by de Gaulle and the support they received from, and also gave to, Britain, the entente was never so cordiale again. There were seeds of mistrust sown by both sides during the phony war, and as Winterbotham summed up 1939–40, "It was not easy for British personnel to visit areas under purely French control."

It might be assumed that the duke's post with the British Military Mission (BMM) was created just with a view to getting him out of Britain. Be that as it may, it was also a job in which the duke was engaged in traveling about the front, inspecting different sectors and visiting Maginot Line forts. The Maginot Line was a massive construction guarding the French frontier and containing enormous underground magazines, barracks, messes, cinemas, and communications, all connected by subterranean railways. Its mighty works and great gun emplacements absorbed a third of the French Army as well as several British formations, which, had they been available along the undefended Franco-Belgian border in 1940, could well have stopped the Germans, instead of which they were bottled up and bypassed in the Maginot Line itself.

The duke's peripetetic visits were not always welcome— among British units in particular—for he still imagined he was making royal tours. Immaculately dressed in unblemished riding breeches, mirror-bright riding boots and polished Sam Browne crossbelt, as was then fashionable for staff officers, he wore his red-banded general's cap at a jaunty angle and insisted on using his own cars and private chauffeurs. His was a royal progress, anyway, as he would not be parted from his own bits and pieces of superfluous luggage, which even included his own teakettle, which he always referred to by the childish name of "kettly." Thus accoutred, he conducted his official business as he might have done a grouse-shooting party at Balmoral, stopping when the mood took him and waiting happily while his staff made his tea. His visits to formations were an added irritation to staff officers already out of their depth and bored by the needless occupation of keeping busy in the phony war. The duke would carry out his duty in sublime ignorance of the irritation he was causing, and occasionally he received polite reprimands from embarrassed and frankly exasperated senior officers for some infringement of military regulations to which he was unaccustomed to paying any attention. Meanwhile, British troops along the Franco-Belgian border were digging, digging, and still digging, although the staff knew that once Germany violated Belgium, they would abandon these defenses and advance to the River Dyle at Liège.

While the duke bustled discontentedly about the front, his wife had been adapting to her new and unsettling lifestyle. For the first time in many years, she found herself adrift from her usual social circle. She was in a foreign city where the people were at war; she hardly knew the language and was alone with her resentment at being ousted from Britain. It is evident from those who knew them at that time that she never let the duke forget his anomalous position. In the opening stages of a war that was threatening to reach new measures of savagery, she constantly asserted her preoccupation with "the little cold war with the Palace, in which no quarter was given."[1] Clearly she was obsessed with what she believed to be the waste of her husband's talent and was convinced it was only because he might outshine his younger brother, King George VI, who had rapidly won the deserved affection of the British people. She knew only too well how Edward's almost nightly telephone calls to advise his brother had been politely and firmly stopped, which had neatly severed his lingering connection with the throne.

Early in October the duchess met an old friend from her first days in London, Lady Mendl, wife of the British press attaché in Paris. Through Lady Mendl, the duchess was introduced to war charity work, including the distribution of woolen comforts for the troops. In his time off, the duke, too, made his contributions, for he was a keen knitter and made gloves that for the sake of appearances, the duchess submitted as hers.

For a while the duchess found a degree of contentment in her work, but this could not be said of the duke, who felt he was nothing but decoration for the mission. During the first week of October he made a tour of inspection of the French First Army. From this tour he collected enough information on the short-comings of the French to write a report about them. Major General Howard Vyse, the head of the Mission, referred to this report in a letter to the War Office in London: "He (the Duke of Windsor)," Vyse wrote, "has produced a valuable report on the defence, of which three copies are coming over today...." The most important points which he detailed in his letter were that there was little attempt at concealment; antitank ditches were weak and inadequate; the location of antitank and antiperson-nel obstacles were too close together; the antitank crews he thought insufficiently trained; and he thought that too little work was being carried out and too few troops were to be seen. In short, the duke produced a detailed and apparently sound appreciation of French discrepancies. Vyse concluded his report, however, by writing: "It will be realized that to give the French any inkling of the source of this information would compromize the value of any missions which I may ask HRH to undertake subsequently."[2] So the report was shelved and care taken not to let the French know of the duke's interests in their defenses. But, significantly, the duke produced a second report of far greater importance, in which he was one of the first to express doubts about the French high command itself. Although this report has been confirmed several times, no trace of it can now be found at the Ministry of Defense or Public Records; it is missing. When I approached the Imperial War Museum for information about the duke's role with the mission, I was told that nothing at all is available for examination.

And so it was that the duke became increasingly baffled at the anomaly of his post with the British Military Mission. He was in a subordinate role for which his life had left him quite unsuited, liaising with the French, who clearly resented Brit-ain—with so few troops in the field—demanding too large a say in the planning, and producing reports that got nowhere. On top of this the bewildered duke was subjected to his wife's persistent admonitions to remember his princely training. He began, therefore, publicly to express even more candidly his criticisms of the way things were being handled. His biographer Ralph G. Martin states, "The duke was later accused of having babbled carelessly or deliberately in Paris . . . and on at least one occasion he babbled on about urgent plans. The duke denied everything."[3]

To all this talk the Germans were listening intently, as is apparent from an especially interesting report sent in January 1940, that, although it means jumping forward a few months in the narrative, is important at this stage because it confirms the importance still attached to the duke by the Germans. This report was sent to State Secretary Baron Ernst von Weizsäcker by the German ambassador to the Hague, Count Julius von Zech-Burkersroda. On January 27, 1940, he wrote

Personal,
Dear Weizsäcker,

Through personal relationships I might have the opportunity to establish certain lines leading to the Duke of Windsor.

As of course you know, W is a member of the British Military Mission with the French Army Command. He does not, however, feel entirely satisfied with this position and seeks a field of activities in which he would not have merely a representative character and which would permit him a more active role. In order to attain this objective he was recently in London. There, however, he achieved nothing and is supposed to be most disgruntled over it. He has expressed himself in especially uncomplimentary terms about Chamberlain, whom he particularly dislikes and, as he thinks, is responsible for his being frozen out. Also there seems to be something of a *Fronde* forming around W which for the moment of course still has nothing to say, but which at some time under favorable circumstances might acquire a certain significance. I do not know whether you are interested in the doings and activities of W. I recall, however, having formerly heard from English friends that W had had especially good connections with the Reich Foreign Minister (Ribbentrop) in London. I might have the opportunity to hear something from the group around Windsor and also incidentally to get something through to him. Thus when he was just recently in London, I had explained to him through an intermediary why it is completely utopian for England to effect a change of regime in Germany, and the statements of my intermediaries are believed to have made a certain impression on him. . . .[4]

A scribbled marginal note from Ribbentrop asked Weizsäcker to discuss the report with him.

This report reveals a number of Nazi connections that like spreading branches, lead on elsewhere into a veritable labyrinth of intrigues. That the Germans should know of Windsor's appointment to the BMM is not remarkable since it was the responsibility of their own Military Intelligence—the Abwehr —to find out such things. Neither is it too curious that the German ambassador in the Netherlands should be passing back this information since the still-neutral Netherlands were an important source of information for both sides. The real interest in this report lies in its intimate narration of the duke's feelings and attitudes. Zech said he might have the opportunity "to get something through to him," and he also wrote of the futility of England dreaming of effecting a "change of regime." All these points assume a special significance in the context of Windsor and the Netherlands, and the link is once again Charles Bedaux. But first let us set the scene in Paris once more.

Major Metcalfe had accompanied Windsor back to France as his unofficial aide-de-camp, and throughout this period he stayed at the Ritz Hotel. It is apparent from his many letters that although devoted to the duke, he was by no means happy at the way things were going with the Windsors in France. He was extremely discomforted by the fact that the duke was frequently entertaining Charles Bedaux as a houseguest.

On October 3 Metcalfe wrote: "I've had a few interesting talks with Mr. B[edaux]. He is like a will-o-the-wisp. He is never in the same place, town or *country* for more than 6 hours at a time. I can't make him out. He knows too much."[5]

By this time the immediate threat of air raids on Paris had passed, the Polish campaign had finished, all activity had ceased in the phony war, and the wealthy had returned to Paris. Maurice Chevalier was performing in *Paris, Resté*

Paris, while the Seine flowed peacefully on, carrying the falling leaves to the sea.

The duchess had, in the meantime, tired of hotel life and saw that with Parisian society in full swing once more, it was time to reopen their luxurious house—complete with golden bath—in the Boulevard Suchet. It was a time of furiously false hopes and fiercely effervescent enjoyment, although not a hundred miles away bored and depressed troops wearily occupied the Maginot Line and the inadequate trenches. The duchess had busily rejoined the Red Cross, as had most of her society friends, but as Fabre-Luce wrote irritably, "Twenty thousand nurses and more were demanding the wounded. Some of them gave the impression of believing that the military authority was failing in its duties by not providing them."[6]

When Metcalfe wrote again, on October 4, he sounded decidedly testy: "I am afraid it is going to be extremely difficult to work. HRH is, I see, getting gradually more and more dug in at Suchet. . . ." He went on to explain that servants were being called to Suchet from La Croë so that the house could be opened up. But, as he pointed out, the duke was forever getting involved with mundane domestic matters, "suddenly getting up to notice a door has jammed . . . the water does not run hot, or that Mrs. Bedford is to pay a bill for 7½ yards of linoleum for the back stairs. . . ." He continued: "Last night I fixed a dinner in a private room here (the Ritz) for Charles B[edaux] to meet them. He, Charles, had much to say. He knows too much—about *every* country in Europe & also our Colonies. It is *terrifying* & he is right a great deal." He then unwittingly wrote a couple of significant sentences: "He (Bedaux) has left at dawn for an unknown destination this morning. He hinted at Berlin being one of those places—He beats me but he is my pal!! . . ."[7]

What did Metcalfe and Windsor make of Bedaux's hint that he was going to Berlin? Supposing it had been taken as a joke, it would have been in bad taste to say the least, but in view of what subsequently happened, either the duke or Metcalfe should have been alerted. That Metcalfe apparently did nothing might be explained by his deference to Windsor, but the duke did nothing either, despite his important military post, and he continued to meet Bedaux. In fact, Bedaux was undoubtedly passing on secret information that the duke prattled out.

In July 1939, about ten weeks before, there had been some sharp exchanges between France and Germany over Herr Otto Abetz's activities in Paris. Abetz, who was a staunch Nazi of long standing, was the Paris representative of the *Dienstelle Ribbentrop* (Ribbentrop's special foreign affairs bureau established in 1935 as a kind of unofficial Foreign Office, nominally under Rudolf Hess; it would eventually have a staff of some three hundred). Abetz had left France on July 2, following an expulsion order issued by French Minister President Daladier, because of his political activities; it was said that he had been making sensational statements to various prominent French persons about an imminent German coup in Danzig, which contravened the latest decrees forbidding such propaganda. He may have done so, but he had been up to more sinister activities, too. When Ribbentrop cabled his ambassador to Paris on July 9, he pressed him to see the French foreign minister urgently: "I have no intention whatever of accepting this action by the French Government and intended to send Herr Abetz back to France in the near future." Ribbentrop continued in his habitually arrogant vein, telling his ambassador to get permission for Abetz to reenter France immediately. He explained his anxiety: "Herr Abetz was, as you know, a friend of the Reich Foreign Minister and had been for many years his collaborateur in his tenacious pursuit of understanding between Germany and France," Nazi parlance for subversion. "As a private individual, Abetz had always striven completely selflessly for that ideal of understanding, had helped in difficult situations, and had contributed to setting Franco-German relations on an even keel. Abetz was known to many personages in France for these activities of his."[8]

What Abetz had really been up to was conspiring with leading French industrialists and financiers, including Lemargue-Dubreil, whose purpose was to ensure that, when war broke out, France would put up only a token resistance and then establish terms with Germany, whereby France's industry would be phased in with Germany's to establish a superpower bloc in Europe to defeat Europe's real enemy, Soviet Communism. Unfortunately for the would-be French collaborators, the Germans had no intention of being equal partners. We have already learned that Bedaux would, after France's capitulation, become a close partner of Lemargue-Dubreil, who in the summer of 1939 was working with Abetz. But, according to American Military Intelligence sources, Charles Bedaux *was also a close friend of Otto Abetz!* Abetz was, as confirmed above, a friend of the Reich foreign minister, Ribbentrop, and again according to American sources, on the night that the German-Russian non-aggression pact was signed, August 23, 1939, Charles Bedaux was actually staying in Ribbentrop's house when Ribbentrop flew to Moscow!

Bedaux's involvements with the Nazis could not have been more intimate. In his cable from the Hague, Zech-Burkersroda referred to his connections with the duke. American intelligence sources, in 1941, say that Bedaux, through a Captain Joseph von Lederbur (who, it will be recalled, had introduced Bedaux to Schacht in 1937), obtained the transfer of technical files in his office in Amsterdam where the Germans released them to his brother. Through Abetz, Bedaux had obtained Lederbur's transfer from combat duty on the Russian front to occupational forces. By then, Abetz was an important man and gauleiter in Paris, a post to which he had immediately been appointed on Germany's occupation of France and in which capacity he was to establish a direct and friendly contact with the duke of Windsor when he was in Portugal, as we shall see.

So the connection that excited Zech in early 1940 was almost certainly Bedaux acting from his Amsterdam office and visiting the duke from time to time. Clearly Bedaux was meeting regularly with Windsor in Paris when the duke was a serving major general in the British Army, on the staff of the British Military Mission to the French high command. As all who knew Windsor agreed, he was a compulsive talker who had never learned to, or even had to, speak with caution, and as reported by Martin, he was said to have deliberately babbled about secret plans. Bedaux was a skilled raconteur, a flatterer, and in particular a good listener, a perfect companion and foil for the frustrated, embittered duke.

Zech sent another, even more revealing cable on February 19, 1940, which, as we will see, discloses that he had a most dangerous line established direct to Windsor. This must again have been via Bedaux.

What was really going on behind the scenes of Britain's

half-hearted war effort? Anyone who studies these opening months of the war must be aware of the reticence of both sides to come to grips with one another. While France was abysmally short of bombers—for which she looked to Britain—she had a big army, which, although woefully short in many aspects of equipment, was certainly capable of overrunning the Rhineland while the main German Army was engaged in Poland. Britain had a small standing army but was adequately equipped with bombers to disillusion the German people about their security from air attack. Apart from desultory raids on shipping in German North Sea ports and a number of quite pointless leaflet-dropping operations, no advantage was taken of Germany's total commitment in Poland. Why? There was a forlorn hope that so long as Britain did not bomb German cities, the war would be spared that horror despite the razing of Warsaw.

The connections with Windsor were not the only ones being exploited by the Nazis. Baron de Ropp had lost no time in reasserting his contacts with the Nazis. On September 25, 1939, an unsigned memorandum, believed to have originated with Rosenberg, was sent to the Reich foreign minister. It referred to

> ... his note of 16th August to the Führer. De Ropp was intended in case of war to act as advisor to the British Air Ministry on German problems. Believed it necessary to maintain contact to avoid long war as in 1914–18.
>
> On Saturday September 23, I received by the roundabout channel of a private address a card from Switzerland from Baronet de Ropp in which he asked whether at the end of September . . . a meeting could be arranged in Switzerland.
>
> I might add in this connection that the personalities who are especially close to Chamberlain are fellow club members of Baron de Ropp.

The memo concluded with a request for instructions from the Führer.[9]

The reference to the air ministry really hides the fact that de Ropp was acting for the Secret Intelligence Service (SIS), and this makes the memo particularly interesting because of the stress on maintaining contact *to avoid a long war* and, because it reflects the French intention to come to an arrangement. But the card from Switzerland is worth remembering because it explains many of the sources of information by which the Nazis were kept up-to-date with events close to the duke. De Ropp was a double agent with important connections, and obviously the Germans were anxious to exploit them. Another unsigned note (probably from Rosenberg) on October 5 confirmed that "in accordance with instructions a member of the *Aussenpolitisches Amt* [foreign policy department] of the NSDAP went to Montreux to invite Baron W. de Ropp to Berlin."

It is apparent from the memo that the swift and positive Nazi response took de Ropp by surprise, for he prevaricated by insisting he had to inquire of his minister; in reality, he was referring the matter to Winterbotham. Winterbotham told me that he never let de Ropp get involved with any other agents and so maintained his secrecy throughout the war. According to Rosenberg, de Ropp told him that it was not believed to be the right moment, as

> Because of the war psychology prevailing in England and the weak position of Chamberlain it was beyond the power of the Ministry at the moment to make use of the desired directions of a termination of hostilities, of the opportunity which had thus been offered. It requested, however, that the opportunity be postponed for a more suitable time. It considered that this moment would only come about through considerable losses on the part of the British air forces and the related effects on the unity of the Empire. It believed that then the views represented by the Air Ministry would have to be taken into account, since the Empire could not permit its air strength to be reduced beyond a certain point. For these reasons the gentlemen in the Air Ministry believe that it would be then that they could make use of our authoritative statement on Germany's intentions. . . .[10]

From Winterbotham's own writings it is evident that he certainly recognized the threat posed by international Communism, and clearly the SIS generally was cognizant of it; it may be that that was the reason why it was so well infiltrated by Communist spies such as Philby, Maclean, and Burgess. Was the SIS acting in accordance with the views of powerful people in the Cliveden Set and others who also saw the greater threat to Europe? The Nazi connection with Edward—as Prince of Wales—seems to have begun with Winterbotham and de Ropp, and the latter's presence is going to be the unseen hand pulling strings right through Windsor's intrigues in Portugal. Was this powerful SIS backing and influence the basis of the so-called *Fronde* that the Germans were so sure really existed? There is a devastatingly frank admission to the Germans in the advice to de Ropp that the destruction of the RAF would be a prerequisite of coming to terms, and that sounds dangerously similar to French belief that their forces needed a quick defeat to ensure that acceptance of what they believed would be honorable terms. If this is so, then it is not beyond possibility that in France Windsor was indeed passing information through Bedaux to the Germans, in order to avoid the protracted war that both he and others wanted to avoid because it would open the way for the Communists to take over Western Europe. By his conversations in France and by what he told the high-ranking Germans with whom he negotiated in Portugal, Windsor substantiates this possibility.

By October 10, 1939, Rosenberg's latest round of contacts with the Swiss-based de Ropp had developed further, and he was confirming to the Führer de Ropp's view that ". . . the outbreak of war between England and Germany was inevitable because of the chauvinistic attitude of the English people." For the moment, they agreed, not much more could be done to bring about a conclusion of the war, certainly not so long as Britain believed herself capable of winning, or at least holding Germany at bay along the Franco-German or Franco-Belgian frontier, perhaps until the Führer's dictatorship was toppled and that "change of regime" of which Zech was to write early in 1940 occurred. At the end of the Montreux meeting they came to a further arrangement: "It was arranged that if B.d.R [de Ropp] considered a new discussion of the situation expedient, he should write to the previously used address about 'excursions' [*Ausflugen*]. If Fred [Winterbotham?] wired him, however, that the Air Ministry now felt strong enough to be justified in hoping that it would prevail and the conditions were therefore created for his going to Berlin, he would write about 'snow.'" He concluded with the helpful advice "that German propaganda should hit England in her weakest spot. . . ."[11]

Once again the use of the term "Air Ministry" conceals the fact that it is the SIS with whom the Germans are really dealing, an inexactitude that was to snowball by May 1941 into one of the war's great blunders, the details of which have remained secret hitherto. But it is evident that certain people in the SIS and in Britain generally were anxious to end the war with Germany quickly and so enable Germany to destroy the base of Soviet Communism.

The eventual brilliant success of Germany's new strategy, which was to force France to surrender in six weeks and drive the British Expeditionary Force off the Continent at Dunkirk, has gone down in history as the Manstein Plan, after General Fritz Erich von Manstein. Manstein certainly elaborated the plan in all the staff detail of which Hitler was incapable, but this strategy, nevertheless, convinced Germany of Hitler's own military genius, thereby reinforcing the success of his Rhineland campaign. There is evidence, too, that Hitler first conceived this victorious strategy in late 1939. A postcard written by Colonel Nicolaus von Below, Hitler's Luftwaffe adjutant, to his uncle on May 14, 1940, records that "I hinted at it to you at Christmas."

At the end of January 1940 Hitler sent his chief military adjutant, Colonel Rudolf Schmundt, on a flying tour of the Western Front, and on his return on February 1 Schmundt was bursting to report what he had found at Field Marshal Gerd von Rundstedt's army group headquarters at Koblenz. Rundstedt's former chief of staff, Manstein, was as adamantly opposed to the existing *Oberkommando der Wehrmacht's* (OKW), the Armed Forces High Command, offensive plan as was Hitler, and moreover, he was advocating a radical alternative very similar to that which Hitler had been debating with his closest staff since November.

The radical plan, which had occurred to Hitler in November, was nothing less than to breach the French lines at Sedan after making a surprise crossing of the heavily wooded, difficult terrain of the Ardennes region of southern Belgium. That was the basic concept of Hitler's idea, crude and without a definite objective. It was to this basic notion that Manstein added the goal of pushing a powerful armored force straight to the Channel to cut off the elite British and French forces who, as the Germans evidently knew, would advance into Belgium as far as the Dyle River, Albert Canal, and Scheldt River as soon as Germany invaded that country. It was in effect a trap.

Manstein almost certainly conceived the idea for this war-winning strategy from Hitler, as is evident from the private diaries of Frau Schmundt. Colonel Gerhardt Engel, Hitler's army adjutant, also noted, "Schmundt was very excited and told me he had found M[anstein] expressing precisely the same opinion . . . as the Führer is constantly expressing." Hitler thereupon instructed Schmundt to send for Manstein secretly, without informing either Brauchitsch or Halder in advance. Afterward Manstein scribbled in his diary, "What an extraordinary conformity with my views." According to Colonel General Walther Warlimont, Hitler saw the general (Manstein) off with the words, "Manstein is the only person to see what I'm getting at."[12]

The French High Command, in the meantime, firmly believed that the heavily wooded hills of the Ardennes were impassable to armor—a mistake the Americans would repeat in 1944—and had, therefore, stationed their weakest forces, the largely reserve troops of General Corap's Ninth Army, at Sedan, opposite the Ardennes. Under their Plan D, which, says Sir Basil Liddell-Hart, had been finalized only in August 1939, the rest of their forces (apart from those manning the Maginot Line) and the BEF were going to advance into Belgium as soon as the Germans invaded that country. It was at this precise and vital weak point in the Allied defenses that the Germans struck with unerring tactical accuracy. To quote Liddell-Hart again: "It was the French High Command, however, which contributed most to Hitler's success. The shattering effect of the Ardennes stroke owed much to the design of the French plan—which fitted perfectly, from the German point of view, their own remodeled plan that every step forward that the Allies took made them more susceptible to Rundstedt's flanking drive through the Ardennes, *which had been foreseen when the scheme was drafted*." As Rundstedt himself told Liddell-Hart after the war: "We expected that the Allies would try to advance through Belgium and southern Holland against the Ruhr—and our offensive would thus have the advantage of a counter-stroke, with the natural advantages this carries."[13] Lieutenant Colonel Eddy Baur explained that "Although there is no record of Schmundt's report to Hitler, there is no doubt that he passed on Manstein's idea to Hitler and that the latter received it with delight, as a specialist opinion which justified the prompting of his 'intuition.'" But Manstein's involvement was brief, for in early February he was transferred to Stettin on the Baltic; his "job" had been done and could not detract from the Führer's glorious "intuition."

It may be a coincidence, but it is a fact that in the third week of October 1939, Hitler did suddenly abandon Case Yellow, the plan to invade the West as produced by General Franz Halder, chief of staff in the West. Hitler told General Wilhelm Keitel, the chief of OKW *(Oberkommando der Wehrmacht)*, and General Alfred Jodl, chief of operations at OKW, "You cannot get away with an operation like that twice." Halder's plan was based upon the Schlieffen Plan, first used in 1914, for a great wheeling movement through Belgium. Halder and his staff had brought it up to date and modified it as necessary to outflank France's strong Maginot Line. With the Maginot Line guarding their frontier between Switzerland and Belgium, the French high command had already assumed that the Germans would, indeed, violate Belgium's neutrality and made their dispositions accordingly. But, Hitler was then gleefully telling his army chiefs, "I have something different in mind. I will tell you about it in the next few days, and then discuss it with the army." On October 25, he explained his new plan to the generals. Field Marshal Fedor von Bock, who was there, wrote, ". . . Brauchitsch and Halder are obviously taken completely by surprise. . . ." David Irving, a leading authority on the German war plans, wrote, "This was the germ of the campaign plan that was to bring about France's defeat." Note that he says "germ." Hitler had conceived only the broad strategy and, at that particular date, was still awaiting further information from which the detailed plans could be arranged by someone else.

On October 4, 1939, Metcalfe had written that Bedaux had left Paris, hinting at Berlin "being one of those places. . . ." Once again Albert Speer was helpful on this point, for although he could not remember the dates, he confirmed that Bedaux was with Ley not long *after* the outbreak of war.

Following Bedaux's departure in the first week in October, there is no record of his being in the West again until he returned to Paris and the duke's home at Boulevard Suchet on November 20. In the meantime the atmosphere at Suchet was worrying Metcalfe, who wrote of the Windsors, "Their selfishness and self-concentration is terrifying." On October 22, he again wrote to his wife, "I can't figger things out. She (Duchess) and he know every d——m thing. She will know whom I dined or lunched with or have spoken to and even seen. I believe she had spies out and they work well. Anyhow, it's terrifying. . . ." He concluded his letter thus: "I don't like my job and I never feel secure and safe when working for HRH [His Royal Highness]," whom he frequently referred to as "the little man."[14]

What was really worrying Metcalfe? Did he possibly suspect that something odd was going on and that the duchess, especially, was very concerned to know exactly whom Metcalfe was meeting, or was the intelligence service watching Metcalfe on Windsor's behalf and reporting back, for as we have seen, they had their own penetrating feelers reaching out into Nazi Germany, and their objectives in ending the war quickly were very similar to the duke's. Indeed, by the time that he reached Portugal in July, there is a very close affinity between the duke's declarations and remarks and what de Ropp is communicating to the Germans through Switzerland.

November 9 was an important day in the Nazi calendar, and in 1939 it had a very special significance. It was the anniversary of the Nazis' abortive putsch in 1923 that had ended with Hitler, Hess, and others in jail and a handy group of Nazi martyrs who gave a nice touch of *Volk*-lore to the Germans. It was such an important event for the Nazis that even in the face of German catastrophes in the later years of the war, in the desert, at Stalingrad, in Italy and France in 1944, Hitler never missed the celebration, even if it meant that vital instructions to distraught field commanders were delayed.

In 1939 Hitler finished his tirade a minute or so after 9 P.M. The cavernous, swastika-bedecked beer hall, the *Burgerbräu-*

keller in Munich, was crowded with senior party members and local Nazi dignitaries, many pressed along the bow-shaped balconies to get a better view of their beloved Führer, their polished boots poking through the wooden banisters. His speech that night was shorter than his usual ninety minutes of invective, but even so, while Hitler ranted and abused Britain, his factotum, Julius Schaub, had passed him a note and then a series of cards on which he had scrawled increasingly urgent admonitions: "Ten minutes," then "five minutes," and finally "Stop." The train to Berlin was waiting.

What was the desperate urgency for the Führer to get his train back to Berlin that evening, when in the worst moments of the war he could not be dragged away? French author André Brissaud, in writing of that night's traumatic events, brings into the picture Emmy Goering, wife of the Reichsmarshal, who had entertained the duke and duchess in 1937. That night she was in Berlin with her husband, Hermann.

Back in Munich, meanwhile, Hitler was winding up his speech: "Party members, comrades of our National, Socialist movement, our German people, and above all our victorious Wehrmacht, *Siegheil!*" Hitler concluded and stepped into the throng of jubilant party officials. A harassed Schaub finally got the Führer out of the hall at 9:12 P.M. They had seven minutes to get to the waiting express train that was hissing steam into the chill autumn night. They made it with only minutes to spare, and at precisely 9:19 P.M. the "Führer Special" steamed majestically out of Munich station.

At 9:27 P.M. the still-crowded beer hall was ripped apart by a powerful explosion!

The paneled pillar immediately behind the crested lectern from which the Führer had thundered was blown to bits by the bomb that had been secreted within it. General Erwin Rommel, the commandant of Hitler's headquarters, reported "Six feet of rubble cover the spot where the Führer spoke. . . ."

In Berlin the Goerings' evening at home had also been interrupted.

> That evening [Emmy Goering told Brissaud] of November 9, my husband told me that a German living abroad under a false name had come to bring him sensational news. The man had to leave by train on the following morning and had to see Adolf

Hitler before then. At that moment an aide-de-camp burst into the room to announce that a bomb had just exploded in the *Burgerbraukeller*. There were dead and injured. I was astonished at my husband's calm when the aide-de-camp added, "What can have happened to the Führer?"

"Nothing at all," answered Hermann. "He is at present on his way to Berlin."

We looked at him, bewildered. My husband then explained that he had telephoned the *Burgerbräukeller* while the Führer was making his speech to order a note to be put on the table in front of him which said, "Hermann Goering asks the Führer to shorten his speech and to return to Berlin as anticipated by the quickest means possible. It is a matter of real importance."[15]

So that was why Schaub had passed Hitler that note and why the Führer quite uniquely absented himself from the subsequent celebrations.

Hitler's mysterious visitor is not identified, for once again, this part of Goering's vast accumulation of records is missing. The man, whoever he was, did in fact leave Berlin by air at noon the next day, after having talked with Hitler for more than an hour in Goering's presence. But can we make an intelligent assumption of the subject of what took place?

World War II, chapter 3, on the subject of Manstein's fears for the attack in the West states.

Hitler, therefore, was unaware of Manstein's plan when, on *November 9*, [my italics] he announced that he considered the armour in the southern wing to be too weak, and on the 15th ordered the transfer to Army Group "A" of Guderian's XIX Panzer Corps—two Panzer divisions, one motorised division, the motorised SS regiment Grossdeutschland and the SS Regiment Leibstandarte Adolf Hitler. Guderian's corps was to drive across the wooded terrain of the Ardennes through Arlon, Tintigny and Florenville and "secure a bridgehead across the Meuse at *Sedan* which will create favorable conditions for the pursuit operations if the armoured units of 6th and 4th Armies should fail to break through."[16]

In 1959 it was claimed by General Liss, the former head of OKH (*Oberkommando des Heeres*, the army high command) Military Intelligence (Section West), that they had broken the

French radio codes in October, which enabled them to read French signals, and of course British Intelligence were to do the same throughout the war. One would be surprised if the Germans did not have such intelligence sources, but the fact remains that the initiative for the change in plans for the assault in the West emanated from Hitler, who early in October summarily had canceled the established plan; he only later discovered that Manstein had also deduced that Case Yellow would not suffice. It is also evident from OKW sources that despite Liss's assertions, none of Manstein's suggestions nor his memos of November 21, November 30, December 6 and December 18 were passed from OKH to OKW. Since Hitler's advisers originated with OKW, it does not seem likely that his change of plan was prompted by any source other than one outside the Wehrmacht or army commands. It was not until the end of January 1940 when Schmundt visited the army command in the West that he discovered Manstein's views to be the same as Hitler's, and by then it is clear that Hitler had already hit upon the basic outline of the new plan for the attack in the West. As at the time of the Rhineland reoccupation, the Führer claimed intuition as the origin of his brilliant strategies, but then, as in 1939, they were based on highly secret information from a very exclusive source in the West.

It is impossible not to draw certain conclusions from the events of those early months of the war. The Duke of Windsor had a unique post on the staff of the British Military Mission and was in a position to see all the Allied defenses, know the deployment of the Allied armies in the Maginot Line and the plans for the advance into Belgium when Germany invaded that country, and he was also in an excellent situation to know all about the poor morale of the French forces so deployed. Throughout this period he was entertaining Charles Bedaux, a man intimately involved with the Nazis and who made at least one return trip to Berlin during that time. It is unlikely, though not impossible, that anyone, the duke included, then knew of Bedaux's intimate contacts with Ribbentrop and Abetz; so Bedaux could not have had a better communication system. He had an office in Amsterdam, in neutral Holland, from which he carried on intrigues for the Germans, and it was from the Netherlands that German Ambassador Zech was, by early

1940, feeding back vital information about the duke to Ribbentrop and the Führer and from whom we have positive evidence that the duke was passing highly confidential information to the Germans, as will be clear in the next chapter.

There was another curious, almost bizarre, series of events that also sprang from the Beerhouse Bomb Plot. For some weeks past, Walter Schellenberg, the SS *Brigadeführer*, had been developing a contact with British Intelligence in Holland. Soon after the outbreak of war, a German secret agent, number F479, made contact with the British Secret Service operating from the Passport Control Office in the Hague. He was really an ex-Hamburg policeman named Mors who had fled Germany on the "Night of the Long Knives" in 1934, adopted the name of Dr. Franz Fischer, and been coerced into working for German Intelligence as a condition of being allowed back into Germany. Believing that there was resistance to Hitler in Germany, Major Sigismund Payne Best, who headed the British "Z" network, an offshoot of SIS MI6 operations, and Major Richard Stevens of MI6 decided to establish contact with opposition leaders in Germany, and Best met Franz, from whom he had been getting snippets of information. Franz later introduced Best in Venlo to his friend Major Solms, who said that a certain German general wanted to talk with them. This was arranged after Best had the BBC broadcast a specific message to convince Solms of their bona fides.

It was at this point that Schellenberg was brought into the intrigue. Schellenberg was sent to take charge of the Dutch operation by his boss, SS *Brigadeführer* Reinhardt Heydrich, who had found out that they had a contact with British Intelligence. Schellenberg disguised himself as a Major Schaemmel of the Transport Department of OKW and claimed a link with a powerful German general who would lead a putsch to overthrow Hitler. Considering the lengths to which the SS would go later in the war to overthrow Hitler and establish themselves as the rulers of Germany, it is possible that there was indeed such a scheme afoot. Anyway the contact was developed, and Schellenberg, as Schaemmel, was given a two-way radio by Best and the call sign 0-N-4, with which he operated from his flat in Düsseldorf.

There is some evidence that this Dutch contact had been

established by the *Dienstelle Ribbentrop*, for whom, it will be recalled, Abetz worked, and that Ribbentrop got angry when his great rivals for foreign-policy making, the SS, began to move in and take over. Be that as it may, this promising contact was smashed on the night of November 9. But there are documents in the Public Records Office that show that although the Venlo discussions were handled by the SIS (M16), they were authorized by the Foreign Office. However, certain files referring to the Venlo affair are classified until 2015.

When the Führer's train reached Augsburg, the rumors of an incident in Munich were confirmed. Hitler listened in silence as the details were recounted to him, finally remarking that his escape had been a miracle. Next moment the full impact of the outrage burst upon the Führer. He stormed at Himmler that it was a heinous attempt to assassinate himself; then he had a flash of intuition—the British Secret Service were behind the attempt, and he knew exactly whom to blame! In Holland, he raged, there were two British agents, and he demanded that Himmler's SS arrange their seizure. Himmler immediately dashed away along the steam-blown, ill-lit platform to the stationmaster's office, from which he telephoned Heydrich to set in motion the SS and Gestapo.

The following day, after Himmler personally instructed Schellenberg to grab the two British agents, Schellenberg left for Venlo to meet Best and Stevens. Behind them there followed two cars full of SS agents, commanded by Alfred Naujocks, a most unsavory young thug who had arranged the atrocities at Gleiwitz. The operation was carried out with ruthless efficiency. Best and Stevens arrived at the Café Backus in Venlo, where they were met by Schellenberg and another SS man. No sooner had they left their car than Naujocks's strong-arm squad burst across the adjacent German border, grabbed the two Britons, and fled back across the border once more.

It was altogether a strange incident that resulted in the elimination of the British Intelligence system in Holland and much of Western Europe for some time. This has elsewhere been connected with the Duke of Windsor, too, although without much evidence; nevertheless, there is the Bedaux connection in Holland. The ferocity of the Führer's anger destroyed the tenuous link that Ribbentrop had seemingly established, alienated the Führer's opinion of the German Foreign Office, and increased his esteem for the ruthless efficiency of the SS-SD. Did Hitler get an inkling of a planned putsch, a change of regime, as Zech put it in January 1940? Who was behind the simple local carpenter who actually planted the bomb and was sent to a concentration camp, where curiously enough, he remained alive until the very end of the war before being liquidated on Himmler's personal orders, almost as an after-thought to tidy up anyone who knew what the SS had been up to? In view of what was to take place in Portugal with the duke in 1940 and long after between Schellenberg and American Intelligence in Spain, it is possible that the SS had made a move that misfired because an agent from the West, very possibly Bedaux himself, arrived on that same night.

It is significant that in eight months' time when Hitler wanted contacts to be reopened with the Windsors in Spain, it was to the SS-SD and especially the Heydrich-Schellenberg combination that he turned, much to the chagrin of Ribbentrop.

9

The Fall of France

JANUARY 10, 1940, dawned bitterly cold, with ice on the polders and rime on the withered sedges. The sun was a pale glow behind misty, opaque sheets of thin, cold clouds. It was a day when the Belgian sentries' breath hung before their frozen faces.

At 11:30 A.M. a light aircraft wobbled uncertainly from the direction of Germany, lost height quickly, with a tearing crash smashed onto the frosty ground, and skidded along on its flattened undercarriage until its wings were torn away by trees. The engine bulleted forward from the impact and buried itself in a low hedge.

Belgian soldiers ran toward the crash from their frontier post. They could see through the mist a single man in a long gray coat fidgeting by the plane, and then from behind the hedge a thin spiral of smoke arose; another man appeared, and it was obvious that he had been burning papers. Instantly the Belgian soldiers fired and then flung themselves on the two Germans.

The Germans were taken to the command post where the papers that had been salvaged from the small fire were presented to the guard commander. While the Belgians talked over what should be done, one of the Germans grabbed the papers from the table where they lay and stuffed them into a stove in a final desperate attempt to destroy them. The papers were again rescued, and then the German struggled for the Belgian officer's revolver. There was a brief fight, and the German was knocked down. "I'm finished," he moaned in German. "I'll never be forgiven for what I've done. If I wanted your revolver, it was because I wanted to kill myself!"

The papers turned out to be the "General Order of Operations: Luftflotte II," highly secret documents that set out the Wehrmacht's intentions. They clearly revealed the German plans to drive through Luxembourg and Belgium; Dutch territory, too, was to be occupied. Despite the burns, enough remained to make Germany's intentions evident.

Hitler flew into one of his worst rages of the war when he heard of the crash, and no one, including Goering, escaped his wrath. Nevertheless, in spite of his most vital plans being revealed—in part at least—the only important alterations made were to airborne operations in Holland.

This was potentially a disaster for Hitler's plans, and yet his iron will would not permit any fundamental changes. He must have known that the matter would be passed on from the Belgians to their "allies" in France and the whole operation discussed by the Allied high command, who had been given a unique foresight of Germany's intent. Unfortunately, the Germans also knew what was said at the subsequent Allied conference, and this must have helped them decide their own deployments and reactions, for on February 19 their diligent ambassador to the Hague, Zech-Burkersroda, sent the cable that was hinted at in the last chapter:

Secret.

Dear Weizsäcker: The D. of Windsor, about whom I wrote you in my letter of the 27th of last month, has said that the Allied War Council devoted an exhaustive discussion at its last meeting to the situation that would arise if Germany invaded Belgium. Reference was made throughout to a German invasion plan said to have been found in an airplane that made a forced landing in Belgium. On the military side it was held that the best plan would be to make the main resistance effort in the line behind the Belgian-French border, even at the risk that Belgium should be occupied by us. The political authorities are said to have at first opposed this plan. After the humiliation suffered in Poland, it would be impossible to surrender Belgium and the Netherlands to the Germans. In the end, however, the political authorities became more yielding.[1]

This cable is irrefutable evidence that, whether or not the Duke of Windsor was aware of it, he was passing vital information directly to the Germans. From this, Hitler had adequate confirmation that the Allies would almost certainly advance into Belgium and so into the German trap that would catch the BEF at Dunkirk.

On February 1 Metcalfe had written to his wife: "H.R.H. came back from England in great shape, seemingly everything went as he wished. It was really delightful to see how pleased he and W[allis] were to get together again. It is very true & deep stuff."[2] Donaldson comments that this last sentence reveals without equivocation that "after her fashion the Duchess loved her husband"; this apparently rare demonstration of feeling by the duchess he saw as the cause of the duke's high spirits. But from other sources it is evident that the duke's trip to London had been anything but successful; he had gone hoping to find a more significant assignment but had again been rebuffed. "The Duke received no encouragement and returned to Paris more resentful than ever."[3] This does not tally with Metcalfe's usually reliable observations, and so one is forced to conclude that the duke's resentment in London was a bit of playacting. Did he travel to London for some other reason, for surely by then even he must have realized he would be spurned there? Zech's cable of January 27, reporting on the duke's London trip, made it clear that he had met with other people, including a German emissary, to whom he had made plain his extreme dissatisfaction. It seems much more likely that his London trip to change his job was a blind to enable him to meet someone else in London, perhaps arranged through Bedaux. On February 3, Metcalfe is again writing, "W, in great form ... H.R.H. very busy bee doing God knows what," which was not how the Windsors usually behaved after being spited by London. Then, on February 5, Metcalfe reported: "H.R.H. told me that he goes at the end of this week up to GHQ to stay for several days. ..."[4] That, one assumes, was the occasion on which the German plans found in the plane crash were discussed. Within two weeks Zech was reporting the result to Weizsäcker at the German Foreign Office, from where it went on to Hitler and OKW.

Wieszacker replied on March 2, acknowledging both of Zech's letters about the Duke of Windsor. But he added a curious comment: "I submitted both letters to the Foreign Minister; he even showed the second one to the Führer. (However, I had to add a marginal note to the last two lines of your letter of Feb. 19, 'Abandoning the Coast')."[5] The text of Zech's letter of February 19, Document 621, was only a copy, which does not contain this marginal note; the original was, apparently, never found. Weiszacker concluded by asking Zech if he could obtain further information. But what was the "Abandoning the coast" mention implying? Was it guidance for the Germans as to France's intentions in the event of a German breakthrough, either in the Low Countries or in France?

The storm finally broke in the West on May 10. Already, in April, German forces had overrun Denmark and Norway. Although the Norwegians did their best to resist and belated Franco-British forces had landed at Narvik in the north of the country to try to drive out the Germans, it had been a signal defeat for the French and British.

At dawn on the sparkling spring morning of May 10, it was the turn of Holland and Belgium. German airborne forces swept into Holland and took the defenses completely by surprise. The Belgian fortress of Eben Emael, guarding the approaches to Liège and regarded as the strongest fortress in the world, fell when eleven German gliders with just seventy-eight men suddenly swept silently from the sky and skidded to a halt atop the ferro-concrete monster; it was all over in a few hours.

Against the 136 German divisions that were assigned to the western attack, the Allies mustered 135. But, of this near parity, most of the Dutch and Belgian divisions were reserves hastily mobilized, and though they fought well, they just were not of the caliber to meet the Germans. The ten British divisions, on the other hand, were a homogeneous, well-trained, and disciplined force that stood up well under fire, but they were far too few to be able to influence the battle except on a local front. The French had mobilized ninety-four divisions, but it was very much a case of quantity at the expense of quality, and while individual French units fought as bravely as any, the majority were very poor. General Sir Alan Brooke, the commander of British I Corps, was with General Corap when he reviewed his French Ninth Army. "I can still see those troops now," Brooke wrote. "Seldom have I seen anything more slovenly and badly turned out. Men unshaven, horses ungroomed, clothes and saddlery that did not fit, and complete lack of pride in themselves or their units. What shook me most, however, was the look in the men's faces, disgruntled and insubordinate looks, and, although ordered to give 'Eyes Left,' hardly a man bothered to do so."[6] It was these same Ninth Army troops of Corap who were, by May 10, dug in along the vital front around Sedan and facing the Ardennes.

Spring had come early that year and, following a warm April, May was already bursting with flowers. The chestnut trees along the boulevards were heavy with blossom, and more flowers spangled the Bois de Boulogne, through which Parisians went about singing their current favorite song, "*J'attendrai.*" The duke was at home during the early days of May and, according to the duchess, he would only give her "tight-mouthed" admissions that the battle was becoming serious. Around about this time Diana Cooper, wife of Duff Cooper, visited the Windsors and was outraged when the duke allegedly said that the English must be mad not to see they were doomed: "Well, maybe we are, but I'd rather be mad than turned slave by fear or reason," she commented.[7]

But Paris still functioned gaily, and theater-going was preceded by champagne in the newly decorated Ritz bar. Jean Cocteau had a new comedy at the Bouffles, while crowds packed the Comédie-Francaise for the latest production of *Cyrano de Bergerac.* There was a brief reaction to the German offensive when the straight Avenue Foch and the Avenue de la Grande Armée were blocked every fifty yards by a green bus in case the Germans tried to land troop-carrying planes.

The duke finally left home for the front and was driven comfortably by his own chauffeur, Ladbroke. All through the spring the duchess had irritably continued to drop loud asides about the big "phony" war and the "little war with the Palace." When the news broke that German forces were pouring westward across the Low Countries into France, however, it became clear that the phony war was over and blitzkrieg had begun.

Within a few days, events along the Allied line in France and Belgium turned serious. The British were forced to withdraw from their advanced positions when the Belgians fell back exposing the British flank. Along the French border, though, things were much worse, for the Germans had massed four panzer divisions amid the woods and narrow, tree-sheltered roads of the Ardennes. According to Winterbotham, this German armored force was spotted by a Royal Air Force (RAF) reconnaissance aircraft, but no action was taken. This mighty armored force launched their attack on the 12th and drove straight for the River Meuse at Sedan. French artillery along the river did their very best and fought magnificently to hold up the German river crossing, but they were soon wiped out by the screaming plunge of the Stuka dive bombers. When the French fire lessened, assault troops of the SS Regiments *Leibstandarte* and *Grossdeutschland* hurled themselves across and in spite of serious losses were soon established on the French side of the river. Within hours a sixteen-ton bridge was in use, and the panzers of Field Marshal Ewart von Kleist were rattling and grinding into Corap's pitifully weak Ninth Army. It was a rout, and the poorly equipped French troops broke. The panzers began their relentless drive to the sea, which they were to reach in a mere two weeks, cutting off the British Expeditionary Force (BEF) and the French and Belgian troops in Belgium.

At 7:30 A.M. on May 15, Winston Churchill, who had taken over as prime minister on the 10th, was awakened by an urgent telephone call from the French premier Paul Reynaud. "We have been defeated," the message rang like a knell of doom. "...the front is broken near Sedan; they are pouring through in great numbers with tanks and armoured cars." Churchill's memoirs make it plain that in the confusion of that fatal May morning, he was later unable to recall Reynaud's precise words, but his own reply, while comforting, was nevertheless indicative that even he had not then grasped the sheer dynamism and brilliance of the German campaign: "All experience shows," Churchill intoned, "the offensive will come to an end after a while. I remember the 21st March 1918. After five or six days they have to halt for supplies, and the opportunity for counterattack is presented."[8]

This time Churchill was wrong, for the Germans' armored drive to the sea was checked only momentarily, by a brief but determined British armored counterattack at Arras that soon ran out of steam and was in turn savaged by the Germans.

American ambassador William Bullitt was with the French defense minister, Daladier, when the terrible news broke, with a telephone call from General Maurice Gamelin, the Allied supreme commander. Daladier listened for a moment, then exclaimed; "No! That's not possible! You are mistaken!"

But, Gamelin insisted, an armored column had smashed through every defense in its path and was running loose between Réthel and Laon. Shock showed in Daladier's ashen face as he panted. "You must attack," he shouted back.

"Attack? With what? I have no more reserves," was Gamelin's stunning answer.[9]

Bullitt recollected that the grim conversation ended somberly: "So this means the destruction of the French Army?" to which Gamelin heavily agreed. Bullitt was so impressed with this somber news that the next day he cabled Washington: "It seems clear that without a miracle like the Battle of the Marne, the French Army will be completely crushed."[10] That was wishful thinking on the American's part, for in 1914 the Germans had been advancing on foot for more than a month and had committed the tactical error of bypassing Paris to the east and exposing the flank of the already exhausted army. In 1940 they were roaring to battle in their thousands of tanks, armored cars, and trucks and after less than a week's travel were far from exhausted. Bullitt also added that there was dissension between the British and French, the former considering their French allies "defeatist," while American historian William L. Langer interpreted Bullitt's dispatch to imply that the British were showing reluctance to "risk their own fortunes in the common cause." There was indeed a reluctance on the part of Lord Gort, the BEF Commander, to throw his limited numbers of well-trained troops into the fray to no useful purpose, as when he was commanded to send his Fifth and Fiftieth Divisions to hold indefensible positions south of

Arras. Besides, there had been ugly incidents when Corap's Ninth Army had broken and hordes of panic-stricken French troops overran British positions, looting and killing in their headlong rampage back.

By then it was clear that the Ninth Army was "on the brink of catastrophe," as General Billotte, the Army group commander, said when he telephoned his superior, General Georges. He wanted General Henri Giraud to relieve Corap's command of the army in the hope that it would create the "psychological shock" that alone would stiffen the crumbling Ninth. By 4 P.M. that day, Giraud had struggled along refugee-choked *Luftwaffe*-strafed roads to Vervins, Ninth Army's headquarters, but with only a solitary aide-de-camp, whereas he had wanted to fling against the Germans all the motorized and armored elements of his previous command, which alone might have checked the panzers' onward sweep.

That day the duke abruptly decided it was time to go back to Paris, and he promptly absented himself from his post. It was late afternoon when he burst into the house in the Boulevard Suchet to which the duchess had only just returned from her Red Cross work. He seized her arm and said, "You're leaving Paris this evening. I'll give you two hours to pack, but not a second more."[11]

At that time the Germans were still fighting in Belgium and along the French border and, despite their breakthrough, were still well over a hundred miles from Paris; neither had there been any air raids on Paris. The duchess relates that she was at first very reluctant to flee across France again, recalling her flight from the press just before the abdication in 1936. She insists that she told the duke that because of her Red Cross job, she did not feel it would be seemly for her to take to her heels as soon as danger threatened. But the duke insisted they should go, and so finally she said she would, but only after seeking advice from her friend the American ambassador, Bullitt.

The duchess, however, cannot have consulted Bullitt earlier than very late afternoon, as the duke had not arrived home before then. By then, therefore, Bullitt knew that the French had suffered a major defeat at Sedan, which does not agree with the duchess's recollection of his reaction. Bullitt, she says

1 The Duke and Duchess of Windsor in Paris, 1937

2 8th March 1936; German troops crossing the Hohenzollern bridge into Cologne to reoccupy the Rhineland

3   (above left) Otto Abetz, German ambassador in Paris and later Nazi Gauleiter; a friend of Bedaux

4   (above) Joachim von Ribbentrop, German Foreign Minister

5   Major E. D. ('Fruity') Metcalfe, the Duke's companion

6   The Duke and Duchess of Windsor with Dr Robert Ley, their
official host in Germany

7   Windsor in deep conversation with Dr Joseph Goebbels, Nazi
propaganda Minister, at dinner, 12th October 1937

8   Rudolf Hess, Hitler's deputy, with General Professor Karl Haushofer who greatly influenced his thinking

9   (bottom left) Sir Samuel Hoare, Britain's wartime Ambassador in Madrid, arrives at 10 Downing Street, 12th September 1938

10   (bottom right) The sinister Reinhard Heydrich, known as 'C', who master–minded the SS/SD

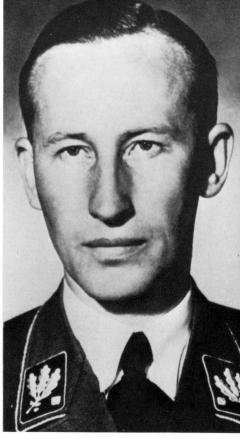

11   The Windsors are greeted by Hitler at Berchtesgaden

Please destroy this letter after reading it —
and destroy it most carefully. But perhaps
this is unfair: So I give you freedom
for your own discretion to show this letter
personally either to Lord H. or to his
Under-secretary Mr. B. — if you see fit
of course — under one condition: That
no notes should be taken, my name
never be mentioned, and the letter be
destroyed immediately afterwards. — As
a sign that you have received this
letter I only ask for some non-committal
picture-postcard to my normal adress)
telling me that you are well. If you
have seen fit to show the letter you
might add something about your family...
I do hope we may meet again ——
            Yours ever sincerely
                        A.

12   Albrecht Haushofer's earlier letter to the Duke of Hamilton, dated
16th July 1939

13   Hess sits with Hitler who has
just made his peace offer to Britain
in the Reichstag, 19th July 1940

14   SS–Brigadeführer Walter
Schellenberg who was sent to
Spain to 'kidnap' the Duke of
Windsor

R.A.F. ACE SCORES AGAIN—Page 2

Nazi Leader Flies To Scotland

Always Welcome

WILLIAM YOUNGERS BEER

Daily and Mail Record

ESTAB 1847—No. 29,624   TUESDAY, MAY 13, 1941   C   ONE PENNY

RUDOLF HESS IN GLASGOW -OFFICIAL

HERR HESS, HITLER'S RIGHT-HAND MAN, HAS RUN AWAY FROM GERMANY AND IS IN GLASGOW SUFFERING FROM A BROKEN ANKLE. HE BROUGHT PHOTOGRAPHS TO ESTABLISH HIS IDENTITY.

AN OFFICIAL STATEMENT ISSUED FROM 10 DOWNING STREET AT 11.20 LAST NIGHT SAID—

"Rudolf Hess, Deputy Fuhrer of Germany and Party Leader of the Nationalist Socialist Party, has landed in Scotland under the following circumstances:

"On the night of Saturday, the 10th, a Messerschmitt 110 was reported by our patrols to have crossed the coast of Scotland and be flying in the direction of Glasgow. Since a Messerschmitt 110 would not have the fuel to return to Germany this report was at first disbelieved.

THIS WAS HIS 'PLANE

Two pictures of the wreckage of Hess's Messerschmidt 110.

Later on a ME 110 crashed near Glasgow with its guns unloaded. Shortly afterwards a German officer who had baled out was found with his parachute in the neighbourhood suffering from a broken ankle.

"He was taken to a hospital in Glasgow where he at first gave his name as Horn, but later on he declared he was Rudolph Hess.

"He brought with him various photographs of himself at different ages, apparently in order to establish his identity. These photographs were deemed to be photographs of Hess by several people who knew him personally.

"Accordingly an officer of the Foreign Office who was closely acquainted with three before the war has been sent up to accompany to see him in hospital.

Benghazi Shelled

AN official Admiralty communique last night states During Saturday night powerful units of our light forces carried out an intense bombardment of Benghazi from point-blank range.

Damage was caused to shipping and military objectives.

Fire from the enemy shore batteries was ineffective, as were also repeated attacks by enemy dive-bombers. No casualties or damage were sustained to any of His Majesty's ships.

Danger to the record head wave of the last few days the British forces in the Western Desert are displaying an energetic aggressive spirit, according to military circles in Cairo.

Without waiting for the enemy to attack they are continually harassing the initiative and attacking with very little further results.

Rudolf Hess

"I Found German Lying In Field"

DAVID M'LEAN, A PLOUGHMAN, WAS THE MAN WHO FOUND RUDOLF HESS. HERE IS M'LEAN'S OWN STORY AS TOLD TO THE "DAILY RECORD." FIRST NEWSPAPER ON THE SCENE:—

"I was in the house and everyone else was in bed late at night when I heard the 'plane roaring overhead. As I ran out to the back of the farm, I heard a crash, and saw the 'plane burst into flames in a field about 200 yards away.

"I was amazed and a bit frightened when I saw a parachute dropping slowly earthwards through the gathering darkness. Peering upwards I could see a man swinging from the harness.

Continued on Back Page, Col. 1

HOW GERMANY BUILT UP THE HESS ALIBI.

See Back Page.

RADIO Page 6

Good Morning! Another Day Nearer Victory!

15   The *Daily Record* reports Hess's arrival in Britain

in her memoirs, was "confidence personified" and was adamant that nothing could defeat the great French Army. It would turn and fight, he is supposed to have told her, as it had on the Marne in 1914: "Remember the taxi cabs that turned the tide," he implored her. However, the duchess concludes by recounting Bullitt's smart volte-face, for she notes rather flatly that he "finally suggested that it would be just as well if I went away for a while"[12]—which of course she did. Here, as elsewhere, the Windsors' accounts invariably present their actions in a much more heroic light than was the case.

It is true, of course, that, while the battle was already going badly for the Allies, by the end of only the fifth day one would have had to have intuition to match Hitler's to be able to perceive the full extent of the threat, which evidently the duke did, or else he knew more than the Allied command itself could foretell. Clearly he would brook no delay in getting his wife away from Paris, which he suspected would soon be in the battle zone.

The duchess always found consolation in her numerous guides, whether *Fanny Farmer's Cookbook* or, as in this case, her battered copy of the *Guide Michelin*, for, clearly, even flight one had to do with aplomb. So, while the refugees already fled before the battle like birds flying before snow, the duchess was savoring fond memories of a charming little hotel at Blois where she had stayed with her companion, Perry Brownlow, on that tedious journey in 1937. It was, she recollected, the logical place to stop while assessing the situation. One presumes that, meanwhile, the duke's colleagues were assessing the growing battle.

They had a hard, slow trip, chauffeured by the faithful Ladbroke along the winding, tree-lined roads of France, crowded with cars loaded with whatever possessions families could strap on top. Moreover, when they reached Blois, disappointment faced them; there was no room at the hotel. However, the duchess appealed to the weary landlord, who eventually consented to put up for them two small cots in a tiny sitting room on the ground floor, because all the beds were otherwise taken. Ladbroke and the inevitable maids are not mentioned, but presumably they made do with the car; the duke, as we have seen, was not one to worry about that kind of thing.

By the morning the duke had decided on a change of plan and set off for Biarritz on the French Atlantic coast. It was close to the Spanish border, he told his wife, and should the Germans overrun France, they could soon nip across the border. Once again, one cannot help thinking he was taking an unduly pessimistic view of Allied prospects.

Once the duchess was safely settled into the splendid Hotel de Palais, the duke set off again for the battle zone. But, to the embarrassment of the Windsors, the Germans knew of the duchess's move to Biarritz, and their propagandists "played a most unchivalrous trick on me," she lamented indignantly. They broadcast that she was at Biarritz, giving her address and even her room number. "Instantly," she recalled, "I became the most unpopular guest in the long history of the Hotel de Palais."[13] She was of the opinion that her presence made the hotel a German target, although the Germans had no aircraft to reach it. Why she should believe that the Nazis would be chivalrous to her, however, is difficult to see, unless she expected preferential treatment; they had just raped Poland, overrun Norway and Denmark, were in the process of pulverizing Rotterdam, and were about to expunge the BEF before defeating France. But then, as Metcalfe had written earlier, the Windsors' self-centeredness was truly unbelievable. In October, when the Germans had begun to shell the Maginot Line (to which the French had replied, causing casualties to both sides) and there was an indication that perhaps the war was hotting up, the duke had been incensed over a mix-up with his chef. It seems he had been making great waves with the War Office to get his own chef for his mess. The chef, however, had been sent to a unit in the south of France, and the infuriated duke had gone off to the French High Command to sort the matter out. It was not a major general's job, he ranted to Metcalfe, but if people beneath that rank could not do it, he would have to. . . . It had been a difficult war so far.

By May 23 three separate panzer corps had reached the English Channel between Calais and the estuary of the Somme at Abbeville, encircling the BEF in a diminishing enclave around the small port of Dunkirk. This considerable British force appeared lost, for it had virtually no heavy weapons with which to hold off the massive German armored forces. There then occurred one of those quirks of history that are later called miracles but which really result from someone's miscalculations. This time it was Hitler's unaccountable order to his panzers to halt—much to the fury of its commanders—while Goering's Luftwaffe was sent to finish off the enemy, which it failed to do. The British put into effect Operation Dynamo, and the flocks of small ships went to bring home the BEF, as well as many French and Belgian troops.

Hitler's sudden change of plan at Dunkirk has baffled military historians for a long time. It was, of course, true that the panzers had reached the point where their supporting supply tail needed time to catch up and that the tanks themselves were in need of maintenance. Nevertheless, this could not have been Hitler's purpose, for he was always impatient of such administrative necessities; in any case, the tanks could have fought on the few days and fewer miles it would have taken to overrun Dunkirk. Neither does the intention of allowing the Luftwaffe the honor of the coup de grâce ring true, for once it was seen that they alone could not destroy the British forces trapped amid the dunes, the panzers would soon have moved. Hitler's reason was political, for as we shall see, he still coveted the dream of a neutral Britain guarding the rear of the crusading German Army as it drove eastward. And there is ample evidence that he firmly believed that a weakened Britain, deprived of its heavy weapons and air force—hence the use of the Luftwaffe—would be demoralized and ready to talk, as per de Ropp's message, if not under Churchill, then perhaps under a man who would see his role as a peacemaker and be ready to assume the throne once more. It was not going to be long before the Nazis made their move to negotiate with him.

Meanwhile, the remainder of the French Army, with some British formations, was still fighting before Paris. During those fatal weeks the duke continued dutifully to visit different sectors of the front, accompanied by the faithful Metcalfe, although with German columns thrusting deeper into France, this was becoming difficult, not to say hazardous. As the enemy overran the disintegrating French Army, it loosed more hordes of refugees and deserters to clog roads and hamper the efforts of the few remaining reserves to get forward.

With disaster threatened, on May 19 French Premier Rey-

naud restructured his Cabinet. He relinquished the Foreign
Ministry to Daladier and took over the Ministry of National
Defense. But the key and in retrospect fatal move was his recall
of Marshal Henri Pétain, the legendary hero of Verdun, who
had been French Ambassador to Madrid. Just prior to this
reshuffle, another intrepid figure of French history had moved
into view: newly promoted General Charles de Gaulle had been
given command of the Fourth Armored Division and had
already made resolute attacks against the Germans, unfortunately too late to have any influence on the outcome of the
battle. Another powerful figure had also returned: General
Maxime Weygand, come from Syria to take over as commander in chief in succession to Gamelin. But all these changes
were too late to alter the course of France's ebbing hopes.
Churchill had flown to Cherbourg on the 22nd, to confer with
Reynaud and Weygand, who had drawn up a new plan—but it
failed, due partly to confusion and recrimination between subordinate army commanders, including Gort.

Another factor was provoking French recriminations and
would do so long afterward, too. This was Churchill's refusal to
allow RAF fighters to be deployed in strength in France. Early
in the German offensive some squadrons had been thrown into
the fray with disastrous results, for the Battle light bombers
were obsolete and the Hurricanes too few. Churchill was really
far more pessimistic about the French Army right from the
outset than he admitted, and he evidently recognized that the
time might come when the RAF fighters would be Britain's
first line of defense. But it could be that he also knew more
about the attitudes of leading French personalities than has
been realized. It does not seem possible that Churchill had any
inkling then about the contents of de Ropp's communications
with Rosenberg, advising that the time would be right for
peace moves only when the RAF had been destroyed, but it is
very possible that that was Hitler's purpose in using the Luftwaffe at Dunkirk rather than the armor. They were in effect
dragging their coattails as bait, to which Churchill did not
respond, and because of that "Fred" never sent his message
including the fateful word "excursions." But too much is still
secret, and Churchill is long dead, so we shall probably never

know how thin was the line between Britain's survival and defeat.

In Paris, by this time, Metcalfe was as disillusioned as the duke, although for different reasons. The previous November he had discovered from talking to someone at the military mission who was concerned with pay that the War Office "have got *no authority* to pay me at all as Purvis (the Duke's A.D.C.) is the only one officially on H.R.H.'s staff," as he wrote bitterly to his wife. Metcalfe had dined with the duke that same night. "I showed him the letter & the *little tiny man* said—Nothing—He then looked at me and said 'Didn't they tell you at the W.O. that you wouldn't get any pay?'"[14] Metcalfe said the duke just looked fishy. He could not fathom that Windsor was quite prepared to do nothing for him at all, and it is clear that he would have welcomed a way out of his invidious position with the duke.

As mentioned, the duke was still visiting various units, accompanied by Metcalfe. They would then return to their quarters, and if that was Paris, the duke would go to Boulevard Suchet, while Metcalfe went to his hotel. The duchess, of course, was still at the Hotel de Palais in Biarritz. Before parting at the end of each day, the duke and his unofficial aide made tentative plans for the following morning. But on the morning of May 28, when Metcalfe telephoned the duke's house, he was flabbergasted to hear from the remaining staff that the duke had fled Paris and gone to join his wife at Biarritz. He had left at 6:30 A.M. without even bothering to inform the BMM, while Metcalfe, who had served the Duke most faithfully for several years, had been abandoned without the slightest warning of the duke's intentions. He was left to find his own way back to Britain. It was typical of the duke's self-centered attitude and his inability to see beyond his own immediate needs. In her memoirs the duchess says that the duke was given leave of absence from the BMM so that he could go to La Croë, his house in Antibes, to close it up as there was a possibility of Italian invasion. But, since the records of the BMM are not available for scrutiny, there is no way of telling, except that had his absence been official, one would have assumed he would have told Metcalfe or his official ADC, Purvis. Apart from these two men, in October Major Gray

Phillips had been sent by the War Office to join his staff, but as we shall later see, Phillips, too, was left behind and was to turn up some two weeks later at Antibes, having hitched lifts on any transport he could.

The duke moved fast, and by the following morning, May 29, his entire entourage, chauffeurs, valet, maids, and, of course, the duchess, left Biarritz in their several cars for a stately procession back to La Croë. While the German armies smashed their victorious way south and west to bring France to her knees, and while thousands of British troops fought for their lives or waded waist-deep to reach the schuyts, paddle steamers, ferries, pleasure boats, and destroyers in a fight to get out of the hell of the Dunkirk beaches, the duke had evidently decided he had had enough of war. He did not close up La Croë, as the duchess claimed, or even leave there until he had to. There cannot have been many serving officers able to do that in wartime with absolute impunity.

On May 28, Belgium had suddenly surrendered after fighting for just eighteen desperate days. This collapse was to have its own profound reflection in French thinking, for only a few days earlier, Weygand had already conceded the possibility that the French Army might soon suffer such heavy losses that it would be unable to hold the Germans. President Lebrun then made a portentous and unwelcome intervention. "What would happen if the French Armies should be scattered and destroyed?" he asked, expressing concern that the government would then be unable to respond to any German peace proposals, albeit that on March 28, a week before Reynaud had taken office, an agreement had been made with Britain forbidding France's concluding a separate peace. Reynaud promptly described Lebrun's declaration as "disastrous." But he was under increasing pressure to end the war, especially before Paris might be invaded, for as in 1914, there were powerful families who were determined at virtually any cost to save their homes and businesses. Weygand then went to Reynaud and made it clear that he wanted Britain told that "a time might come when France would find herself, against her will, unable to continue a military struggle to protect her soil."

Reynaud was then sixty-two years old and had been premier of France for less than three months. He was a staunch anti-

Nazi but his mistress, the Parisian socialite the countess Hélène de Portes, was one of those influential people who were determined that France should quickly curtail her war with the Germans and then link their industries in a vigorous trading block that would take care of the Communists once and for all. She was, many thought, a woman with a malign influence on France's destiny, and one of Reynaud's greatest failings was his deep and blinding love for this traitorous woman.

In August 1939 the Soviet-German Pact had established a strange prostitution between Hitler and Stalin, both of whom had hitherto existed only for the destruction of the other. It was typical of Hitler's cynicism that by his pact with Russia he would be able to use the extreme Left's usual blind gullibility to Moscow's instructions to his own advantage. Although today the Left indicts the Fascists, it should never be forgotten that the Communists played a decisive role in bringing Hitler to power. It was principally the Soviet Union's aid in training and experimental facilities in the 1920s and 1930s for the embryonic German army and Luftwaffe in defiance of Versailles and the blockade-busting supplies they afforded Germany in 1939 and 1940 that more than any other contribution, made Hitler's conquests possible. But Moscow's aid was more direct than that. In 1952 the historian M.A. Rossi declared that the French Communist party was acting on Moscow's orders and was the "living embodiment of the notorious 'Fifth Column.'" Paul Levenkuhn, the historian of the Abwehr, says that the Abwehr used its contacts "with members and officials of the Communist Party in Belgium to assure the distribution in France of defeatist and anti-British leaflets. Communist agents were also given directives and technical instructions with regard to sabotaging France's war industries." In Britain, too, the Communists were active on Moscow's orders, and in those vital weeks when Britain faced invasion and defeat, Communist workers in ammunition factories assured that more than half a million rounds went out with no powder in them. Hitler and Stalin had the same aim of destroying Western democracy. The duke and many other important and intelligent people in Britain, France, Belgium, and America clearly saw the Communist threat but foolishly believed that Nazi Germany's iron fist was the answer; they were like the Romans who used the barbarian German tribes to stem the eastern hordes and got eaten themselves in the process.

It was, then, the conflicting pressures from the Countess de Portes and others, all convinced that theirs was the right path to survival, that were to confuse Reynaud at that vital moment in France's history, with his nation poised for disaster. The countess even flatly contradicted him before his Cabinet colleagues and urged him to seek terms with the Germans, echoing the strident voice of old Marshal Pétain. She was an important influence on that right-wing *Fronde* that included men like Lemargue-Dubreil, pushing for a quick end to the war so that a united Europe could withstand the Soviet menace.

As early as the summer of 1934, during a brief exchange between Rosenberg and Winterbotham, Rosenberg had angrily slapped a file before Winterbotham: "If you will take a look at that," he had said, "you will see what I mean. For your information it is a list of prominent Frenchmen who are already in our pay." Winterbotham had handed it back but not before he had recognized some important names.

In these impossibly confusing conditions, Reynaud continued for a few weeks longer to try to steer France out of the catastrophe. Hélène de Portes, like so many characters in this story, also met an untimely end, for within a few weeks she was to be killed in a mysterious car crash in the mountains.

Recriminations were by then piling up on all sides. Some of these charges are still ghosts, including whether King Leopold of the Belgians betrayed his allies by surrendering. A much more fundamental controversy centers on French accusations of British betrayal. This has generally been understood to refer to Dunkirk, of the evacuation of which they were not informed for two days, which delayed the participation of numerous French warships based on Calais. Nevertheless, every effort was made to take off the French, and by the end of Dynamo well over 130,000 French troops had been rescued. One wonders, therefore, if this "betrayal" claim does not refer to some more cardinal action, perhaps the revelation of their own defense plans.

There can be no doubt that French security was poor, and as we have seen, there were numerous French people anxious that the war should be quickly concluded, but very few of them were in a position to know of the high command's strategy. The Duke of Windsor was, and there is that incredible and uncomfortable line of communication: Windsor, Bedaux, Abetz, Zech, Ribbentrop.... With the most charitable interpretation, this link was an inconceivable one for any serving British officer and a woefully foolish one for a man so garrulous, frustrated, and embittered as the duke; at the worst, it would have enabled the duke, *had he so desired,* to fulfill his belief that Germany was Britain's natural ally, a view he expressed many times. It is unlikely in any case that in the summer of 1940, the French knew about the intrigues of Charles Bedaux, although they would certainly do so when the dynamic little opportunist began to pour all his vitality and knowledge into aiding both the Germans and the Vichy authorities.

The British government was not going to be in the dark about Bedaux for much longer either. U.S. Military Intelligence records show that in September 1940 they informed British Intelligence that Bedaux was a German spy. It is interesting, however, that although the Americans were very helpful in supplying information for the preparation of this book, there is one document alone which is still so secret after forty years that it remains "unavailable." What, I wonder does it say? But in any event, the Foreign Office in London was being informed from other sources, too. In March 1941 a Mr. Norman Pleming of Associated Industrial Consultants, Bedaux's company in London, forwarded to the Trading with the Enemy Branch a letter from C. J. Carney of their New York office. This revealed that Carney had been told by a senior executive of Eastman-Kodak that "Charles Bedaux is actively engaged in the reorganization of the French coal industry for the Nazis."[15] This was only nine months after France's surrender. The Foreign Office official minutes on the letter were noncommittal, somewhat fearful of Bedaux's position, and suggested that the matter should be referred to the Ministry of Economic Warfare. However, in spite of the American official warning in September 1940 and then Pleming's letter in March 1941, an examination of that ministry's blacklists (FO 837/51-52) and the G (suspect) list (FO 837/39) for 1940 or 1941 does not reveal Bedaux's name.

Why is Bedaux's name not there as a known German spy and

active collaborator? The answer can only be because it would have immediately raised the most awful questions about his relationship with the Duke of Windsor. Remember that when Bedaux was captured in 1942, his bag of documents promptly vanished into the maw of British Intelligence, so that even the Americans claim not to know what they contained; and Bedaux did not live to stand trial.

Northern France had been overrun, and although the BEF had escaped from Dunkirk, Britain was beleaguered, with no heavy weapons to resist invasion once France fell. The Windsors, though, had settled into the luxury of La Croë once again and for a few weeks tried to take up their easy, pleasure-filled existence where it had been rudely interrupted at the outbreak of war. There is certainly no indication that the duke was closing up the house as the duchess claimed was his purpose or that she ever contemplated her nursing home either.

The Riviera was scorching hot and in full bloom with mountains of flowers basking beneath the tall palms along the Croisette at Cannes. Many of the wealthy expatriate British families were warily packing, and while still reluctant to abandon their haven from the war, they were nervously aware that just a few miles beyond Nice the Italians were strutting toward war to grab some French spoils before it was too late.

At La Croë, meanwhile, there were parties, drinks on the terrace overlooking the Côte d'Azur, splendid food and entertainments laid on by the duchess, which became a familiar routine. The duke, who seldom ate lunch, would take himself off at midday to play golf, sporting his usual outrageous trousers, or, alternatively clad in shorts, happily dug and hoed in the gardens. He always had great vitality and in the days before his marriage would coerce his gentlemen friends to abandon their wives for a vigorous afternoon hacking away at the undergrowth at Fort Belvedere. The Windsors stayed at La Croë a trifle uneasily, trying hard to assume normality but, like everyone else, could not manage entirely to forget the approaching disaster. Then, in early June, Major Gray Phillips finally caught up with them after hitchhiking from Paris on military trucks and ambulances and once again attached himself to the duke.

Since the duke had abandoned his official post, the Windsors had been receiving their news from the radio, and they were becoming acutely conscious of the dangers of their situation. Finally, on June 11, their haven fell in when Mussolini "dug his small dagger" in France's back and entered the war on Germany's side. That afternoon they had been relaxing on their sun-drenched terrace, amusing the French entertainer Maurice Chevalier, when Major Phillips arrived hurriedly from visiting friends at Nice. He urged the Windsors to get out of France before the Italian invasion troops reached them.

News of the Italian attack soon spread like a summer Riviera fire, and thousands of people were scurrying to get away to Spain or Gibraltar, the only places left. All regular shipping was fully booked, and with the powerful Italian Navy at war, the sparkling Mediterranean was clouded with menace. For many of the elegant and wealthy the only opportunity to avoid internment was in taking passage in coal boats on which they suffered terribly from discomfort, privation, and bad weather. None were spared, and among those who braved the weeks at sea to Gibraltar was the elderly novelist Somerset Maugham. For those left behind, life would soon become hazardous. Even though the south of France remained nominally in Vichy French control—apart from Nice which was grabbed by the Italians—the black Citroëns of the Gestapo were soon cruising the sunny, abandoned streets, and many Britons who did not leave were sent to concentration camps.

During the last few days, the French government had abandoned Paris for Bordeaux, where in hotels and the town hall, the final dramas of France's downfall were being enacted. Reynaud wanted to fight on but was violently opposed not only by the venerable Marshal Pétain and his supporters but also by Hélène de Portes. Despite Reynaud's courage and the support of his new undersecretary for war, General de Gaulle, the premier was not going to last much longer. The intrigues, plots, and counterplots were being hatched and dispatched in cafés and hotel rooms and even, on one occasion, in the darkest gloom of a hotel corridor.

Meanwhile the duke had other ideas for leaving France than on coal boats and still saw it as his country's duty to get himself and his wife home once more. According to the duchess's account, he immediately telephoned the British consul at Nice.

This is not true, however. In fact, Windsor first telephoned the British Legation, which was then in Bordeaux along with the other major legations, except the American, as Ambassador Bullitt decided to stay in Paris, much to Reynaud's concern, and thereby denied his considerable American moral support to the struggling French government. De Gaulle, who witnessed Bullitt's departure from Reynaud, later wrote of Bullitt's refusal to travel with the government: "The United States no longer had much use for France," which explains much of his later antipathy for America.

The duke's call eventually got through the congested telephone system to the Hotel Montre, where the British Legation was installed. It was answered by Harry Mack, the Legation's first secretary, who was in conversation with de Gaulle. The tall and imperious young general had just reached the legation where he was breathlessly recounting that the Pétain faction was about to arrest him (de Gaulle would eventually be smuggled out of the legation in disguise and thereby reached Britain to establish the Free French). Mack impatiently broke off his talk with de Gaulle to answer the tiresome duke, who forthwith wanted a British warship to be sent to Antibes to collect them. This was in the aftermath of Dunkirk, which had cost Britain six priceless destroyers, and Italian battleships and cruisers were at large in the Mediterranean to cut Britain's lifeline through the Suez Canal; so manifestly there were no warships to spare. The duke persisted until Mack, with "suave but firm politeness," suggested that the road to Spain was still open.[16] Thus it was only *after* Windsor's request for a warship was rejected that he irritably telephoned Major Dodds, the British consul at Nice.

Major Dodds could not be too helpful, either, since he and his colleagues at Menton had already received instructions to burn their papers and evacuate their posts. He told Windsor, however, that they had obtained permits from the Spanish consul allowing them to cross the border into neutral Spain. They would, he said, be traveling in a convoy of cars that would pass La Croë at noon the next day, and he advised the duke to join them.

The following morning, therefore, was busy at La Croë, for

while the duchess arranged for their villa to have the protection of the American Consul, the duke supervised the loading of their luggage onto a trailer hooked to the back of their car. At noon the Windsors, together with Major Phillips, the duchess's maid, and their friends the Woods, who also had a trailer on their car, attached themselves to the consular convoy, and they all headed off along the sparkling, sunlit road toward Marseilles and thence the Spanish frontier.

By then France was in a turmoil of fear and suspicion. The winding roads were crammed with refugees fleeing before the Germans and, by then, the Italians. Endless weary hordes of the old and the young, mostly women without their menfolk, straggled between the roadside trees, ever ready to rush into the fields at the approach of an aircraft. Their belongings were piled on carts and barrows. There was a general terror of Fifth Columnists and the dreaded German paratroopers. Through this mass, the duke's party wended its way slowly in the summer heat.

Notwithstanding these difficulties, the convoy progressed well enough until it passed the ancient town of Arles, where it crossed the mighty surge of the Rhône. But after Arles the party was delayed at every major town by barricades across the roads, at which they had to produce credentials. The Windsors had no permits, but believing that the veterans who manned the makeshift barriers would remember him, the duke called out: *"Je suis le Prince de Galles. Laissez-moi passer, s'il vous plait."* And each time the old men let him through.

They stayed overnight in a crowded hotel in Arles and pressed on the following morning, the 13th, heading southwest along the Route Nationale 9, toward Perpignan. Time was ebbing fast for France, and the valiant Reynaud was to resign the next day. It was late in the morning when they at last reached Perpignan, within sight of the towering crags of the barrier of the Pyrenees. Wearily they booked into another overstuffed hotel only to learn from the suspicious old concierge that they would need to secure visas in the town before being allowed to cross the frontier at Port Bou. Early the following morning the duke purposefully set off through the heat with George Woods to obtain the necessary papers from the Spanish consulate in the town. But it was going to prove far from being as simple as the duke assumed.

There were crowds of desperate people waiting to cross into Spain, and the duke and Woods had to wait for hours in the blazing heat of the Rousillon Plain while the consular staff laboriously dealt with the stream of refugees. They suffered the frustration of the ordinary refugee who meets with brisk, inhuman shortage of attention and consideration and desultory interest in his problems. When they returned to their hotel hours later, the duchess recalled, "David was the angriest man I have ever seen."

"To put the matter bluntly," "David" fumed, "the consul won't let us into Spain. He has the peculiar idea that we might become a charge on the Spanish government."[17] To add to the duke's angry indignation, the official had had the effrontery to pester him to sign his grandchild's autograph book, which he did in the hope the official would in gratitude relent and sign his visa, but he did not.

By this time the diplomatic wires were buzzing between London and Madrid, and Sir Samuel Hoare, the British ambassador, had received a telegram from Churchill telling him that the Windsors were held up at the frontier at Perpignan; it has never been explained how Churchill knew this. The various accounts suggest that the Windsors were not long delayed at Perpignan, but working back from their arrival in Madrid on the 23d, preceded by their two-day stay in Barcelona on the way, they must eventually have crossed the border on the 21st, which means they were at Perpignan for a week. The duchess recounts, however, that after being frustrated locally, the duke had got in touch with the Spanish ambassador to France, Señor Joseph Lequerica, who was an acquaintance, and thereby the duke took the initiative in procuring the all-important visa. But this seems to be only another attempt to magnify the duke's influence. The official story is that Hoare telephoned Lequerica, who was then at Bordeaux, where he was eagerly awaiting the moment to act as go-between for the French and Germans; only then did the Spanish authorities grant the duke a visa. One supposes, therefore, that unable to get a visa locally, the duke must have telephoned Lequerica, who then approached the British Legation about the duke, or it happened vice versa; either way the British Legation must have cabled London for instructions. That nothing seems to have been recorded by the legation is easily explained by the chaos then reigning at Bordeaux, for by then Reynaud had gone and Pétain had taken over. The end of the Third Republic was in sight, and the British Legation was getting ready to abandon France. At noon the Germans formally marched into Paris.

However, the formalities of the duke's visa were arranged; they were then quickly completed, and the Windsors and their staff and friends went across the Spanish frontier at the Port Bou crossing point. They motored on to Barcelona, where they took a much needed two-day rest. Refreshed, they traveled on by train to Madrid to be welcomed by Hoare. By then, as we saw in chapter 1, the Nazis were already plotting to reopen their direct links with the duke.

So it was that the Windsors arrived in Spain and, unwittingly or not, placed themselves at the center of the war's greatest spy story and a dangerous intrigue whose echoes have not died yet.

10

The Führer Ponders

A T NOON on June 21, while the duke was traveling from Barcelona across Spain's arid plateau to Madrid, Adolf Hitler was driving victoriously through northern France to the shady forest of Compiègne for the French surrender. William L. Shirer recalled that the day was "one of the loveliest summer days I ever remember in France. A warm June sun beat down on the stately trees—elms, oaks, cypresses and pines—casting shadows on the wooded avenues leading to the little clearing." Hitler's cavalcade arrived promptly at 3:15 P.M. and stopped some way from a clearing where the Führer climbed from his specially armored Mercedes. He wore his gray uniform jacket, his breeches and jackboots and his curiously oversized peaked cap. For a moment the Führer paused to stare malevolently at the French Alsace-Lorraine memorial statue, which had been draped under German war flags lest its sight offend him; then he turned abruptly and stumped on his way. Shirer was impressed by Hitler's expression: His face was ". . . grave, solemn, yet brimming with revenge."

France's army was beaten and her government exhausted. Four days before, the aged Marshal Pétain had requested the armistice from Hitler. During the intervening days the Führer's headquarters staff had toiled energetically to prepare the scene for the world's press to witness the historic ceremony that would humble the once-mighty France. The old

181

wooden dining car in which Marshal Foch had dictated terms to a defeated Germany on November 11, 1918, had been retrieved from its permanent display in Paris and set up on a short length of railway track in the same spot in the forest. Forty minutes after Hitler, the French officers arrived, and the surrender formalities began.

Hitler contemptuously left Field Marshal Wilhelm Keitel to complete the surrender formalities at Compiègne while he went on a pilgrimage. The powerful dictator, the master of Western Europe, wanted to fulfill a dream he had had as a frustrated down-and-out would-be architect thirty years before in Vienna: He toured the wonders of Paris with his official architect and youthful alter ego, the ambitious Albert Speer.

After seeing Paris, Hitler spent some days visiting the Flanders battlefields over which he had fought as an infantryman in the First World War, but he was both moody and exultant and could not settle down. Although his adjutant, Rudolf Schmundt, had prepared a headquarters at Tannenberg, in the Black Forest near Freudenstadt, Hitler did not want to go there. Neither was he ready to return to Berlin, although the German capital waited to give him a hero's welcome. The Führer was biding his time before staging a triumphal return to his capital, in fact awaiting some unofficial response to peace feelers he had extended to the British through Sweden. He already planned to make his formal peace offer in a speech in the Reichstag on July 6, once he knew that the British were ready to accept it. After that, he was sure, he would be free to turn the Wehrmacht east to attend to Russia in 1941. But to his fury and disappointment he got only a noncommittal answer from the British foreign secretary Lord Halifax.

This anti-Bolshevik urge was like some Wagnerian motif that inspired Hitler's private deliberations and surfaced in moments of triumph. Every time the Russians made a move, Hitler was reminded that this urge was his real raison d'etre, the dynamism behind those years of struggle. He had been deeply disturbed by the recent and inexplicable Russian armistice with Finland concluding the Winter War, in which the Russians had triumphed only after huge losses at the hands of the Finns; Hitler concluded that Stalin was bluffing about his military weakness. In Hitler's mind, however, the Russian and British problems were inseparable, for he had long recognized that he could attack Russia only after eliminating the Franco-British threat to his rear. That situation had radically changed with France's defeat, and now only the British remained, prostrate and unarmed on their island. Hitler fervently hoped that Britain would soon accept the kind of bloodless defeat that he had always envisaged for what he regarded as a brother Aryan country. An abundance of evidence in the archives of the OKW shows that in June 1940 Hitler was as well disposed toward the British Empire as he had been in the 1930s, for he feared that its dissolution would only benefit the United States, Russia, and Japan. So the problem that occupied his mind as he wandered distractedly across France was how to make Britain quickly sue for peace. Only then could he launch his mighty attack in the East to secure the Germans' Lebensraum, the granaries of the Ukraine, and the oil of the Caucasus.

Hitler was convinced that the fall of France would make the British government see reason and give in, and indeed, he had been given plenty of reasons over the years to believe this to be so. However, the German military leaders did not share his views, and already Admiral Raeder, the imperiously autocratic German Navy commander, urged him to launch immediate air raids on the main British naval bases in preparation for the seaborne invasion on which his naval staff were already at work. Hitler was not yet ready and stubbornly insisted that such an invasion would be unnecessary: "One way or another," he contended, "the British will give in." These differences of opinion between the German military chiefs who saw immediate invasion as the logical step to defeating Britain, and Hitler, who firmly believed that Britain would negotiate and so consistently put off the invasion, are evidence not so much of the Führer's lack of strategic thinking or fear of the water, as others have suggested, as of the fundamental truth that he never believed it would be necessary.

It will be recalled that on June 16 Hitler had met General Vigon, who was Spain's head of Supreme Army Defense Council. On that occasion Hitler had spoken to Vigon of the Duke of Windsor and mentioned that he wanted him detained in Spain in order to establish contact with him once more. And again, one must ask how, on June 16, Hitler knew that Windsor would be in Spain. Presumably the information was passed by Lequerica to the Spanish Foreign Office, although in those circumstances one would have expected Vigon to be telling Hitler, not the other way around.

While Hitler was pondering his future moves, in Britain Prime Minister Winston Churchill was also profoundly disturbed about the Windsors' arrival in neutral but unfriendly Spain. He reputedly growled pithy invectives at his former sovereign, of whom, in 1936, he had remained a lonely supporter during the abdication crisis. As soon as the Windsors reached Madrid, therefore, Churchill cabled Sir Samuel Hoare, instructing him to lose no time in telling the duke that he attached great importance to the Windsors' urgent return to Britain. Hoare, thereupon, hastened to explain to the duke that the prime minister wanted them to go immediately to Lisbon, where two RAF Coastal Command flying boats would be sent to carry them home. He also passed on the message that the Duke of Westminster had offered them the use of his home, Eaton Place, near Chester, thus solving their accommodation problem.

Sir Samuel Hoare was himself a very controversial political figure. He had been the center of a major political row when he was foreign secretary in 1936 because of the Hoare-Laval Pact, which decreed that Britain and France were to lift sanctions against Italy and allow it to keep its Abyssinian conquests. The ensuing outrage in Britain at the pact had forced him to resign. Diana Mosley wrote of his quick restoration to government office: ". . . it was perhaps rather typical that Ed VIII should give a dinner party for him. He was, and remained, an Empire man." The Duke had later cemented his own connection with the notorious pact when he was living in Paris by entertaining the Countess René de Chambrun, the married daughter of Pierre Laval. He had also had a long discussion with Laval, the man who would become hated and eventually be executed for his appeasement of the Nazis.

Hoare's appointment as Ambassador to Madrid was interpreted by many as a reflection of his reputation as an arch appeaser, which would make him highly acceptable to the

French, although by the time he arrived in Spain France was finished. Sir Alexander Cadogan assumed from a remark made by Lady Hoare on May 20, 1940, that she already anticipated Britain's defeat. He recorded it in his diary: "The quicker we get them out of the country the better. But I'd sooner send them to a penal settlement. He'll be the Quisling of England when Germany conquers us and I'm dead." Cadogan considered that Hoare's appointment was basically to get him out of Britain, although in fairness to Hoare, he did establish a better understanding with some members of the Spanish Junta and did much to keep that country neutral. Nevertheless, Churchill must have been dismayed in June that fate had thrown together Hoare and Windsor, two men of decided pro-German views.

Although the Duke of Windsor's selection of Spain as a refuge was very much a Hobson's choice, it was, as Churchill knew, a very unfortunate one. His royal position linked the duke to most of the reigning houses of Europe, and in Spain he had a particular connection with the Infante. Moreover, the political orientation of Spain would ensure the duke a ready ear for his own anti-Communist views. So Churchill was very anxious to get the irksome Windsors out of Spain for a number of good reasons, not least that Spain was by no means certain of staying out of the war. The country's insecurity was evident from Hoare's correspondence at the time of his appointment in May 1940.

Sir Archibald Sinclair, the air minister, had written to Hoare to explain the arrangements for his flight at the end of May, to which the new ambassador replied on May 23, "I think that I ought to bring this further question to your urgent attention. It may well be that things may go badly in Spain and that we have to leave at very short notice and in very difficult conditions. May I rely on you to send me out a machine to bring us back in these circumstances. We have to face facts in the world today and we cannot exclude the possibilities of a coup organized by German gunmen."[1]

Faced with the prospects of an indefinite sojourn in a Fascist country, Hoare was not so keen, but in the case of Spain his fears were undoubtedly justified. It was not just because the ruler, General Francisco Franco, owed his victory to German support but because Spain was by then virtually a German protectorate. On June 1, barely a week after his arrival, Hoare sent back to the Foreign Office the "Annual Report of Spain" (most of which must have been composed before his arrival as it dealt with January to June 1940): ". . . His Majesty's Government in the United Kingdom to withstand the persistent provocations of a German controlled press, a Gestapo run police, a miserably incompetent and corrupt regime in constant terror of the Germans. . . ."[2] The Spaniards had good cause to fear the Germans, too, for Madrid in 1940 was the greatest center for the German intelligence services outside Berlin.

The German intelligence services were complex organizations that need volumes themselves to be explained adequately. Basically, however, they derived from two sources. First there was the Wehrmacht's own Military Intelligence service, the Abwehr, whose origins went back to the First World War. Since January 1, 1935, the Abwehr had been controlled by Admiral Wilhelm Franz Canaris, another devious man of war. It was later found that while he was a lieutenant commander in the navy's intelligence during the Weimar Republic, he had used their secret funds to finance the rudimentary Nazi party; yet in the final years of the Second World War he actively intrigued with the Allied intelligence services to bring about the downfall of Hitler; he was eventually executed by the SS in the Flossenberg concentration camp in the closing weeks of the war.

The other principle intelligence service was the SD *(Sicherheitsdienst)*, which was a part of the all-embracing SS empire of SS *Reichsführer* Himmler. By 1943, the SS was practically a state within a state and held most of Europe in its inhuman grip, but it, too, was seeking to overthrow Hitler. In 1939 it was already the sole party intelligence and counterespionage service and was under the grip of Reinhardt Heydrich. As the SD's insidious tentacles penetrated further into Secret Service operations, however, they collided increasingly with Canaris's Abwehr, and eventually, in 1944, after years of rivalry, the Führer ordered the Abwehr to be absorbed by the SD under Walter Schellenberg. He was then head of the SS Amt VI *(Ausland* SD), that part of the vast organization specifically concerned with foreign intelligence and a direct inheritance of his activities in Spain in the summer of 1940.

Canaris had seen quite early on that the best base for Abwehr foreign intelligence operations was in the German embassies abroad, but Ribbentrop opposed this idea when it was put to him because it would have weakened his own foreign policy advice to Hitler. Canaris was not to be thwarted, though, and took the idea to Keitel, who passed it on to Hitler. This resulted in Keitel's sending a letter to Ribbentrop on the Führer's order, although actually dictated by Canaris, demanding that the Abwehr be allowed to plant its people in the German legations. This resulted in a flood of bogus diplomats, and before long the German Embassy in Madrid had a staff of 391 people, for whom separate accommodation had to be constructed, although 171 were real diplomats and the rest Abwehr. Canaris had deliberately chosen Spain because it was the only foreign country he liked; he also spoke Spanish fluently. By 1939 he had a network of spies in both Spain and Portugal and a close relationship with his old friend General Campos Martinez, chief of the Spanish Secret Service. But his success angered the SS/SD, and soon they too approached Ribbentrop for facilities. The foreign minister saw the SD as a counterbalance to the *Abwehr* and was flattered with honorary membership in the SS, even obliging his reluctant staff to wear the hated SS uniform. But it was not long before he regretted his decision as the SD began to exert its influence over foreign policy. The events at Venlo had been a confused culmination of the machinations of Ribbentrop's foreign fiddling and the SD's ruthless reaction.

Thus, by the time Windsor arrived in Madrid, there was intense rivalry between the German Foreign Office, the Abwehr, and the SD for dominance in foreign affairs. That rivalry aided by British postwar reticence has distorted and confused the realities of the so-called German kidnap plot against the duke. It was not an attempted kidnap plot but a determined and high-powered scheme to encourage the duke to go to Spain as a first step to restoring him to the British throne and so bring about the quick peace prior to the German invasion of Russia. Behind the plan was the SS/SD.

So the Spain into which both Hoare and the Windsors arrived within a few weeks of each other was indeed a nettle patch of intrigue, both between the Allies and the Axis and between the various factions of German foreign policy and intelligence. In the aftermath of German victories in the Low Countries and France, though, German fortunes and reputation were riding high in Spain, while Britain's prestige had plummeted. Hoare himself had been *en poste* only a few days when, on June 2, he was sent a memorandum by the British naval attaché, Captain A. H. Hillgarth, who was extremely worried about the state of morale in the embassy: "... in effect," he wrote, "the Embassy your Excellency has come to command is defeatist. This is not only patent in private conversation but is evident in the general interpretation of policy. As it is Spain with whom we have to deal and the Spanish viewpoint is very largely influenced by German and Italian propaganda, our belief in ourselves, which must betray itself in our words and actions, is of supreme importance...."[3] Within three weeks of Hillgarth's exhortations, the Windsors were proclaiming to the world the futility of Britain fighting on.

As we saw in chapter 1, the Windsors stayed in Madrid just over a week, during which time Hoare gave a splendid reception for them. That in itself was a strain of the embassy's resources, for in his private correspondence with the Foreign Office in London, Hoare makes it clear that food was so scarce in Madrid that he was having it brought in by truck from Portugal. But while the duke was making his portentous remarks to Weddall, the American ambassador, to which eager Falangist and Fascist ears were also tuned, the continued neutrality of Spain was by no means certain. The Duke of Windsor could hardly have chosen a worse time and place to open his mind once again, for as *The Times* reported that same morning, the Germans had officially occupied the Franco-Spanish frontier: "General Lopez Pinto and other Spanish authorities, the German Ambassador, von Stohrer, and General von Hausser, Chief of the German forces at Hendaye, on the frontier, had celebrated the occasion.... General Pinto 'pointed out the importance of Germany having made contact with Spain." *The Times* also noted that on the next day, Saturday, an entire German motorized division "is doing to cross the frontier for an official visit to San Sebastian where festivities are being arranged to welcome the visitors."[4] This visit frightened Britain, and it was with relief that Hoare later reported it had left Spain.

The days of fear, chaos, and unaccustomed helplessness in the face of foreign authority had not distracted the duke from his major preoccupation with his prestige and the recognition of his wife by the king and government at home, and in answer to Hoare's information about the flying boats from Portugal, he made it clear that his return home was still dependent upon satisfaction of his grievances. So the duke had plenty to talk about during those visits by important Spanish Falangists, such as Doña Sol, who, it will be recalled, had given the smart Fascist salute and the Infante Alfonso, that Spanish Air Force general who had bowed so low over the duchess's slim little hand while purring "Highness" to her. The special relationship the duke had with the Infante, mentioned earlier, is revealed by correspondence between the royal household and Hoare, in which the latter was requested to inquire of the duke about a royal property at Kew, to which he had granted the Infante a five-year free residence in 1936 and which was then coming up for renewal; did the duke wish the arrangement to continue . . . ?

The Windsors were kept busy with visitors and private engagements in those all-too-brief days in Spain. The duke did like Spain, though, and spoke Spanish, as is revealed by the comments of Sir Bruce Lockhart on the occasion of a visit in 1933 to Edward, then Prince of Wales, by the kaiser's grandson, Prince Louis Ferdinand: "They talked Spanish and German as well as English. Prince Louis says the Prince's Spanish is quite good and that he is the only one of his relations with whom he can talk Spanish."[5] But Prince Louis Ferdinand also told Lockhart: "The Prince was quite pro-Hitler, said it was no business of ours to interfere in Germany's internal affairs *either re Jews or re anything else*, and added that dictators were very popular these days and that we might want one in England before long. . . ." It is evident from other influential sources that Edward regarded himself as the major contender for such a role. His time in Spain and especially in Portugal only enhanced this belief of his.

The duke was undoubtedly under a great strain at that time, and Friki Mas Mendes, then a young chambermaid, remembers the duke hurrying through the lobby of the Ritz Hotel: "He looked very sunburnt, but thin. I thought him quite old. He didn't seem to notice the staff but whenever he was with his wife, he would listen very intently to her talking. She smiled a lot but I didn't like her, she was very demanding and kept re-arranging the things in their suite."⁶ His first forty years had totally unsuited the duke for the life of a private citizen, which in itself would not have been an affliction had it not been for his irrepressible drive for self-justification and his incorrigible resolve to see justice done to his wife. He was still irretrievably committed to finding a sphere of interest for himself, as he had made clear to Zech's contacts in London and as he persistently told his Spanish friends, who promptly reported to the Germans. Once settled in Madrid, moreover, the duke saw new possibilities that with Churchill as prime minister, the atmosphere in Britain would be more propitious for his return. He even thought that he might expect what the duchess termed "an appropriate job." He was distinctly hopeful, too, that he would be received back with all the respect due to him and persisted in making conditions for his return to Britain. Consequently he pretentiously announced by telegram again that unless his wife was accorded equality with the wives of his brothers and until he knew what job was proposed for him, he would not leave the Peninsula. But then all his plans were confounded once more when Buckingham Palace dashed his expectations and refused to acknowledge the duchess as Her Royal Highness. This left him even more infuriated.

The frustrated and embittered duke was so out of touch with reality that he understood nothing of the low regard that the majority of people felt for him since the abdication. The support he had in his *Fronde* was exclusively political and still covert, if potentially powerful. Actually, to the ordinary person, hardly anything that he had done in the years since abdicating was even known, because of press reticence and censorship, and most British people had simply lost interest in him; he and his wife were relegated largely to the gossip columnist. This would remain so until he died, when in a macabre sense he was resurrected in the public's notice. In June 1940, indeed, most ministers found difficulty in deciding whether to condemn the duke's egotism at that critical hour in his country's history that he had done so much to bring about or to pity his deluded hopes. In any case, though, during the following critical months when Britain awaited an imminent invasion, a good deal of Churchill's vital time had to be given to the recalcitrant duke. But it was still to no avail, as he would not budge from his position. So Churchill decided that other methods had to be employed to persuade the duke out of Iberia and, as it began to look increasingly necessary, to foil German attempts to use him. It had quickly reached the government's notice that the watching Germans in Madrid were already sending back reports of the duke's careless talk and activities to the Foreign Ministry in Berlin.

It was ironical, moreover, that while Britain awaited the imminent German invasion and the German high command planning Operation Sealion urged the Führer to act decisively, it was the Führer's very preoccupation with the duke and the belief that he would take some measure to restore his throne that was actually delaying the invasion until the opportunity was lost. Hitler still hoped that the duke and those who continued to support a British friendship with Germany against Communism would prevail and take Britain peacefully out of the war.

From early June onward, during that long, hot summer of 1940, Hitler's political posture remained a conviction that Britain could be persuded by diplomatic means to yield to his will. On June 25 one of his secretaries wrote in her diary: "The Chief plans to speak to the Reichstag shortly. It will be probably his last appeal to Britain. I believe it still hurts him even now to have to tackle the British. . . ."

Britain's refusal to accept defeat had indeed perplexed the Führer. Since the invasion of Poland he had never really expected to have to fight, let alone defeat Britain. It has hitherto been thought that this misperception stemmed from Ribbentrop's erroneous advice, but his memoranda in 1938 and 1939 make it plain that Ribbentrop had no such illusions. Until Edward VIII's abdication Ribbentrop had frequently met him, and was not just a coincidence that his change of opinion occurred in the weeks following Edward's stepping down from the throne. It is, as we have seen, much more likely that Hitler's mistake derived from conversations he had had directly with the duke and also with people such as Lord Lothian. Conwell-Evans, who accompanied Lothian on his 1937 trip to see Hitler, had assured Hitler that British public opinion was becoming more and more pro-German and that he regretted such lapses as reports in the British press alleging that German planes had taken part in the bombardment of Guernica in Spain. As Sykes put it: "So ended the interview which must have given Hitler an agreeable impression that Great Britain would not seriously resist him."[7] More recently than that discussion, though, Hitler had been getting from Rosenberg and Walter Hewel hot-off-the-press information from de Ropp that appears to have emanated from the SIS, who, if Winterbotham's opinion is typical, were bent on stopping the Soviet expansion.

Albert Speer recalled that when the Führer stalked through the shattered villages of northern France, his conversation with himself, with Schmundt, and his other companions persistently turned to his stubborn belief that Britain would come to terms. He constantly referred to the telegram he had personally sent in reply to the Duke of Windsor's only three days before the declaration of war: "I thank you for your telegram of 27th August," he had replied. "You may rest assured that my attitude toward Britain and my desire to avoid another war between our peoples remains unchanged. It depends on Britain, however, whether my wishes for the future development of German-British relations can be realized."[8] Speer says that "After the abdication of King Edward VIII, Hitler frequently referred to his apparent friendliness towards National Socialist Germany. I am certain that through him persistent friendly relations with England could have been achieved. If he had stayed, everything would have been different. . . ."[9]

There was no doubt in the minds of Hitler and the leading Nazis that the duke was firmly against a war, which he feared might bring about a revolution in Britain and Communism. The duchess herself confirmed that "He was wary of war. . . . He saw but too clearly that it could bring about only needless human suffering and a resurgent Bolshevism pouring into the vacuum of a ravaged and exhausted continent."

But it was not just the fear of an inevitable Communist

expansion—which he predicted—that gave the duke his fear of war. Between 1914 and 1918 he had seen a great deal of war, mostly through his own persistence to get actively involved, in spite of the opposition of his father and the War Office. As a staff officer with XIV Corps he had witnessed the appalling action at the Battle of Passchendaele, which began with so much enthusiasm, achieved nothing, and ended with mass death and exhaustion. He had shared the weariness and the cynicism of the soldiers and thus learned from experience to fear and hate war. Unfortunately, he could not see that for him to impart such opinions to Hitler only strengthened Nazi resolution to take advantage of a supposedly universal British reluctance to fight. But having said that, one must then question whether he would have modified his words if he had realized their effect, and to that the answer seems to be no. He respected Hitler and accepted that he was the only means to stanch the spread of Communism.

It was one thing for Hitler, as he surveyed the battlefields of two wars, to ponder the duke's attitude and potential as a Nazi sympathizer and as a leader who would take Britain out of the war, but another to make his wish a reality. The duke was not in Britain, but he *was* in Spain, at the very center of the German intelligence web in Europe. The next step was to present him with a convincing path to peace whereby Britain would emerge with honor.

While Hitler was delaying his final decision about Britain until he knew the results of his latest peace feelers, he was nevertheless under pressure from his navy and especially Goering's Luftwaffe to do something about finishing off Britain. In the second week of June, therefore, he somewhat reluctantly ordered his chiefs of staff and the arms industry to prepare for the special needs of the invasion of Britain, just in case.

On June 24, however, Ribbentrop took the first steps toward the subsequent intrigue in Spain when he sent his cable to Stohrer in Madrid inquiring as to the possibility of detaining the duke and duchess in Spain. When Stohrer assured him on June 26 that every effort would be made to do so, Ribbentrop began to plan.[10][11]

On June 25, Hitler had gone to the village of Bruly le Péche,

near Sedan, which had been cleared of its inhabitants to make
a German headquarters. He dejectedly told Speer that "The
British were cajoled into this catastrophe by emigrés and
liberal-thinking people ... now it is up to them to find some way
out of this mess." He had, meanwhile, approved a suggestion by
Walter Hewel, his liaison officer with Ribbentrop, to send a
letter to his contact in Switzerland who was close to the duke.
This was obviously de Ropp, with whom he had been in contact
at Montreux the previous October. Clearly an idea was taking
shape in Hitler's mind, and in view of Ribbentrop's communication with Stohrer, one assumes that Hewel was acting on
Hitler's prompting.

Albert Speer was with Hitler at 1:30 A.M. the night the
armistice with France became effective and recalled the scene:

> That night we sat with Hitler around a deal table in the simple
> room of a peasant's house. Shortly before the agreed time
> Hitler gave orders to turn out the lights and open the windows.
> Silently we sat in the darkness, swept by the sense of experienc-
> ing a historic moment so close to the author of it. Outside a
> bugler blew the traditional signal for the end of the fighting. A
> thunderstorm must have been brewing in the distance for as in
> a bad novel occasional flashes of summer lightning shimmered
> through the dark room. Someone, overcome by emotion, blew
> his nose. Then Hitler's voice soft and unemphatic: "This
> responsibility . . ." and a few minutes later; "Now switch the
> lights on." The trivial conversation continued, but for me it
> remained a rare event. I thought I had for once seen Hitler as a
> human being.[12]

In spite of his outward calm, Hitler was a worried man, for
during his preoccupation with a stalemate in the west he was in
acute danger of losing his opportunity to strike at Russia in the
East while his army was at peak condition. He was obliged to
keep looking over his shoulder at the activity of the equally
artful Stalin, whose Red Army had just taken Lithuania, Latvia, and Estonia and was threatening Romania and the source
of Germany's oil. On June 26, there had occurred an upheaval
in German plans that must have strongly pushed Hitler
toward the plan to initiate the moves to make further use of the

Duke of Windsor. Molotov, the Soviet foreign minister, informed Germany that despite earlier promises to avoid war with Romania over the Bessarabian region, which Russia claimed, the Soviet Union could brook no further delay and was resolved to use force if the Romanians refused a peaceful settlement. This bombshell was bad enough, but to the Führer's consternation he learned that the Russians were also claiming the Bukovina, a province that had never been a part of Russia and which contained a large population of ethnic Germans.

Seething with anger, the Führer summoned Ribbentrop and told him to refresh his memory as to the contents of the 1939 pact with Russia. Fury turned to dismay when the secret protocol negotiated by the slow-witted Ribbentrop was found to be alarmingly vague. After reference to Bessarabia, it concluded, ". . . the German party declares its total *disinteressement* in these regions." The plural "regions" was an embarrassment, but Ribbentrop had signed the document, and Hitler backed down rather than risk a conflict with the Russians for which he was not ready and which would almost certainly lose him his oil. Ribbentrop had been proved inept, and in contempt for the Foreign Ministry Hitler turned to Himmler's SS, which had already shown itself a more fruitful organ of foreign policy. Ribbentrop was, of course, furious and already bitterly resenting his earlier courtship of the SS, which had resulted in their disquieting presence in most of the German embassies. He needed a coup of his own to put himself back in Hitler's favor and promptly started searching for a way to end the war in the West and perhaps bring Britain over to be Germany's ally against Russia. It must have been then that he recalled the cable he had received from Stohrer in Spain three days before asking if he should endeavor to have the Duke of Windsor detained, to which Ribbentrop had replied that he should.

Stohrer's cable had come at the right moment for Ribbentrop. Then on July 2, there arrived on the foreign minister's heavy desk the much more significant cable from Stohrer advising of the duke's outspoken criticism of the government and the futility of continuing the war. This latter must have reminded Ribbentrop of what he had said of the duke after his visit to Hitler in 1937: ". . . something akin to a British National

Socialist." In all events it seemed to Ribbentrop an excellent chance to pursue the peace plan, now so desperately wanted by Hitler.

In Britain the duke's activities were again causing concern. Lord Halifax, the foreign secretary, telegraphed Lord Lothian, the ambassador in Washington, that the position of the Duke of Windsor was causing embarrassment, and "although his loyalties are unimpeachable there is a backwash of Nazi intrigue which seeks, now that the greater part of the continent is in enemy hands, to make trouble about him." He went on: "There are personal and family difficulties about his return to this country. In all the circumstances it is felt that an appointment abroad might appeal to him and the Prime Minister has with H.M.'s cordial approval offered him the Governorship of the Bahamas."[13] He added that the duke had accepted the appointment, although unbeknown to the duke, the incumbent, governor had very unwillingly been moved to make way for him—on an island three thousand miles from the war, where he could be expected to do little harm (although he did enough). In her memoirs the duchess explains how grateful he was and that he accepted it with good grace. As we shall see, not only did he fight tooth and nail against going to the Bahamas, but when he was there as governor and commander in chief, he still persisted in his communications with the Nazis.

The offer of the governorship was presumably made by Churchill through Hoare at the time he told the duke of the flying boats at Lisbon, although it is not clear. Halifax's letter to Lothian is interesting because of its haste to establish that the duke was "unimpeachable." Halifax evidently had his own decided views on the duke, as is apparent from a letter he sent to Hoare on July 8: "You, of course, know all about the arrangement for the Windsors. I dare say it is a good plan that they should go to the Bahamas, but I am sorry for the Bahamas. You will not, however, be sorry to be rid of them. I am glad they have had you to guide their footsteps while they were in Spain."[14]

11

The Portuguese Connection

THE WINDSORS left Madrid on July 2 and set off in their usual cavalcade for Lisbon, taking two days to travel across the baking and dusty Spanish plateau toward the Atlantic. They again traveled in two cars, accompanied by their friends the Woods and Major Gray Phillips. They were met by the British ambassador to Lisbon, Sir Walford Selby, whom, it will be remembered, the duke had known during his sojourn in Austria before his marriage. It was through Selby that, according to the duchess, it was arranged for them to stay at the home of a Portuguese banker, Dr. Ricardo do Espiritu Santo y Silva, known to embassy staff as "the Holy Ghost." Espiritu Santo had a lovely villa at Cascais, a resort some twelve miles from Lisbon on a point overlooking the Atlantic; finished in pink stucco, it had a swimming pool and was very private. Unfortunately and despite the duchess's assurances that Selby had arranged the loan of the villa, Espiritu Santo had strong German sympathies and was a constant informer. This is amply evident from German cables, especially Stohrer's of August 2, in which he says, "I immediately got in touch with our confidant the Duke's host, the banker Ricardo do Espiritu Santo y Silva. . . ."[1] If Selby did arrange the villa, it was a bad error on the diplomat's part.

Lisbon was the exact antithesis of Madrid. Where Madrid had been halfdead from depression, Lisbon was alive with a strange, restless life. From the outbreak of the war, people of all nationalities had been fleeing to Lisbon as a refuge while the war lasted. Many British, French, Germans, and especially large numbers of wealthy Jews had made it their base. With the blitzkrieg many thousands more people from Holland, Belgium, and France had fled to Lisbon in the hope of going from there to America; but accommodation was scarce and passages were enormously expensive. Consequently the great majority of refugees were marooned in Lisbon, trying to live upon the proceeds of the furs, jewels, and other valuables they had managed to carry and had wanted to sell to buy passage on ships.

The Portuguese capital was a paradox, as the huge increase in demand had already caused prices to rise to fantastic levels. The government did what it could to check inflation for the sake of its own people, but it could do little about the huge foreign influx over whom it was impossible to exercise control. Fortunes were being made and lost by reckless speculators, while dozens committed suicide each week, driven to it by despair and virtual starvation.

On the day that Windsor departed from Madrid, Stohrer promptly cabled Ribbentrop: "The Foreign Minister [Beigbeder] informed me that the Duke of Windsor is traveling to Portugal today or tomorrow to confer there with the Duke of Kent who is in Portugal in connection with the jubilee celebrations." He also affirmed the duke's resolve to return to Britain only if his wife were recognized, etc. According to Stohrer, "The fulfillment of these conditions was practically out of the question. He intended, therefore, to return to Spain where the Spanish Government had offered the Palace of the Caliph at Ronda as a residence for an indefinite period." He went on to say that Windsor had again expressed himself "in strong terms against Churchill and against this war," and concluded that Beigbeder supposed the duke was going to Portugal to "replenish his supply of money."[2] This was a curious comment, and one wonders if the Duke of Kent was perhaps carrying funds for him from Britain. Anyway, the cable could only confirm the duke's lack of inhibition in saying what he felt, which was foolishly disloyal.

Walter Monckton wrote, "With the King's straightness and

directness there went a remarkable determination and courage and confidence in his own opinion and decision. Once his mind was made up one felt that he was like the deaf adder, 'that stoppeth her ears and refuses to hear the voice of the charmer.'"[3] The determination, courage, and confidence, of course, were derived largely from the royal prerogative that no one contradicted him, and in any case he had grown up with a bevy of speech writers and advisers who spared him the challenge of original thoughts. The duke has been called impetuous and silly for his actions, but other men in wartime were called traitors for far less than that, never mind what else may have happened in France. By his continued open association with men who could not be anything but German emissaries, he was laying himself open to grievous charges, although they could never have been made.

The duke settled in at Cascais to his usual round of entertainments and discussion. Clearly he talked a lot, for on July 9 Ribbentrop received a signal from Stohrer in Madrid, whose office was continuing to handle all dispatches about the duke, informing him that the duke had sent a message to Beigbeder asking that "a confidential agent be sent to Lisbon to whom he might give a communication for the Foreign Minister"; he added that the request was being fulfilled immediately.[4]

After meeting with Beigbeder, in due course, Stohrer lost no time in going to see the Spanish minister of the interior, Ramon Serrano Suner. Hoare described Suner as the "deliberately ill-mannered, spitefully feminine, small-minded, fanatical, impetuous . . . little brother-in-law of the Generalissimo [Franco]. This hated and incredible young man, not yet forty, with his snow white hair, his hands and feet smaller than any girl's, and his quick and shifty eyes . . ."[5] Suner promised Stohrer to get Franco "in on the plot" and to carry it out. Furthermore, they would send to Lisbon the duke's old friend Miguel Primo de Rivera, who would invite Windsor to Spain for some hunting and to confer with the government. Suner would use that occasion to inform the duke about a British Secret Service plot to bump him off. Suner was also going to invite the Windsors to accept Spanish hospitality "and possibly financial assistance as well."

Stohrer sent a cable on July 12 to Ribbentrop confirming the arrangements and adding that Beigbeder had repeated that Windsor was sticking to his decision to return to Spain, as he had reported on July 2.[6]

There are a few points in this exchange between Suner and Stohrer which need a little elaborating. First, the initiative for the emissary came from Windsor, who obviously wanted to keep going some communication through Spanish officials. Secondly, Suner's talk of an invitation to Spain for hunting and "possibly financial assistance," will reappear in the package that Ribbentrop was soon to put together when he directed Schellenberg to go to Lisbon on or about July 21. Thus Suner's suggestions predate Ribbentrop's by a week at least. It appears very likely, therefore, that the original idea of the duke slipping back into Spain and a little financial inducement—fifty million Swiss francs—sprang from the duke himself! This rather dents the German "kidnap" theory.

Ribbentrop hastily replied to Stohrer from his special train at Fuschl on the 12th, telling Stohrer that he had also heard from the ambassador to Lisbon, Hoynegan Heuene, who said that Spaniards with whom the duke was associating had confidentially informed the German Legation that the appointment of the duke as governor of the Bahamas was intended only to keep him far away from Britain. The duke, apparently, believed that his return would give strong encouragement to British friends of peace, so that "his arrest at the instance of his opponents would certainly have to be expected." Nevertheless, the duke had made it clear that he was going to delay his departure for the Bahamas for as long as possible, certainly until the beginning of August, "in the hope of a turn of events favorable to him. He is convinced that if he remained on the throne war would have been avoided, and he characterizes himself as a firm supporter of peaceful arrangements with Germany." The cable then ends with a very strange footnote: "The Duke definitely believes that severe bombing would make England ready for peace. Heuene."[7]

This cable is evidently advice given in answer to inquiries made by Spanish or Portuguese friends, of whom the duke had many who were well-known Falangists and close supporters of Nazi Germany. The duke had been very put out some weeks before when his valet, Fletcher, had been drafted into the army, and he complained bitterly about his inability to manage his clothes without him. He was now agitating for the valet's return as another condition of accepting the Bahamas appointment. The fuss over his valet and his wife's maid, however, seen in the light of Heuene's cable, was a pretext to delay his departure in the belief that he would soon be needed in Britain.

Was he then delaying his departure because he was certain his hard-pressed country was being forced into a position in which surrender was the only alternative to invasion and occupation? The misguided duke, who bitterly regretted abdicating, was waiting for that opportune moment when a British people disillusioned by Dunkirk and cowed by the kind of bombing that had destroyed Rotterdam and Warsaw—perhaps after his brother and his family had fled to Canada—would look for an alternative to the indomitable Churchill, someone like Pétain, who would conclude an honorable peace with Hitler and relieve his country's suffering.

The last line of the cable, about the bombings, is almost impossible to construe except as an answer to a direct question. The significance of the answer was not lost on Hitler, who was still vacillating on how to bring about a peace with Britain. His indecision was noted by Count Ciano, the Italian Foreign Minister, who visited him on July 7 and wrote, "He is rather inclined to continue the struggle and unleash a storm of wrath and steel upon the British. But the final decision has not been reached, and it is for this reason that he is delaying his speech. . . ."[8] This speech was the long-promised address to the Reichstag, when he hoped to announce a peaceful settlement with Britain. But only two days after Heuene's cable the Führer was resolved. He wrote Mussolini a letter that he had decided on his course of action. That morning he had had a meeting at the Bergdorf, above Berchtesgaden, where he conferred with his generals. Halder, the quiet, laconic chief of staff, who was, according to Speer, put off by the Führer's vulgar dynamism and so seemed rather hapless, noted in his diary: "Hitler has at least understood the reason for Britain's refusal to make peace."[9] On July 16 Hitler issued Directive No. 16, the "Preparation of a Landing Operation against England," and, as a prelude, ordered Goering's Luftwaffe to begin the intensive bombing of Britain. These preparations, we now know, were still principally intended to frighten Britain into meeting Germany's terms and may have been connected with his aspirations for the duke, who was hanging on in Lisbon. Hitler continued to display an obvious reluctance to consider an invasion seriously, and his directives were concerned more with preparation than with an actual attempt. He did not want, in any event, to risk decimating his army against Britain. This, he was sure, was the right path: Bomb Britain into submission, frighten the country with the threat of invasion; the right man was waiting to lead them when a terrified people overthrew Churchill.

That the duke had an overriding ambition to regain a position of power under virtually any circumstances is evident from an interview he had given in 1938 to the *Daily Herald.* He said that "If the Labor Party wished and were in a position to offer it he would be prepared to be President of the English Republic." This interview was banned from publication at the time by the censor.[10]

Ribbentrop eagerly sent a copy of Heuene's cable to Stohrer, with a covering letter declaring that they were convinced the duke was surrounded by British agents who wished to get him away from Lisbon as soon as possible, "if necessary by force." Ribbentrop urged haste, although he lamely admitted he could not decide on the method to be used, especially in connection with the existing liaison between the Spanish minister and the duke. He continued:

> From here it would seem best if close Spanish friends of the Duke would privately invite him, and of course, his wife, for a short one or two week visit to Spain on pretexts that would appear plausible to him, to the Portuguese and the English agents. That would mean, therefore, that the Duke and Duchess, as well as the English and Portuguese, must believe that Windsor in any event is going to come back there. If it does not take place in that way there is the danger, according to our information about the company of the Duke, that the real reason for the return of the Duke to Spain will become known in England and that England will prevent it at all costs.

What was this "real reason" that was to be kept secret? If the duke was not going simply to live in Spain, what was he really going for?

Ribbentrop suggested that once on Spanish territory, the duke and his wife would be persuaded to remain, but failing that, Germany would reach an agreement with the Spanish government that through the obligations of neutrality, the duke would be interned as a British officer and a member of the British Expeditionary Force who had crossed the frontier as a military fugitive, thus compelling him to remain. But this was a typical bit of Ribbentrop bullying and fairly meaningless, because it was not what the Führer had in mind at all. After asking how the Spaniards would react to this, Ribbentrop concluded,

> At any rate, at a suitable occasion in Spain the Duke must be informed that Germany wants peace with the English people, that the Churchill clique stands in the way of it, and that it would be a good thing if the Duke would hold himself in readiness for further developments. Germany is determined to force England to peace by every means of power and upon this happening would be prepared to accommodate any desire expressed by the Duke, especially with a view to the assumption of the English throne by the Duke and Duchess. If the Duke should have any other plans, but be prepared to cooperate in the establishment of good relations between Germany and England, we would likewise be prepared to assure him and his wife of a subsistence which would permit him, either as a private citizen or in some other positions, to lead a life suitable for a King.[11]

Ribbentrop's remarks, one should note, constantly stress that Germany wants to make peace with Britain, and while this may be a euphemism for surrender, at this stage of the war it probably meant just that, to enable them to attack Russia. One can have little doubt they would have returned, like the Goths to Rome, with a different kind of "peace."

Within the next few days more information was sent to Stohrer, first confirming that the duke's host, Espiritu Santo, was friendly to the Germans, and second: "A report has reached me today from a Swiss informant who has for many years had close relationships with the English secret service, to the effect that it is the plan of the English secret service, by sending the Duke to the Bahamas, to get him into English power in order to do away with him at the first opportunity...."[12] This document, clearly important to an understanding of the intrigue then surrounding the duke on all sides, is another "not found," and the "plot" is known only by a reference to it on this particular German foreign policy record. The Swiss informant has to be de Ropp, who was Winterbotham's resident "sleeper" in Switzerland and who had the closest of connections with the SIS. But did the British Government really intend to "do away with" the duke? There is no answer to that except that, as we shall eventually see, no one who was intimately involved in what became one of the greatest intrigues, plots, and counterplots of the war survived; all died in strange circumstances. That Windsor did not get "done away with" might be explained by the circumstances in which he was eventually persuaded to go to the Bahamas.

The Germans, nevertheless, persistently claimed that the British were planning to "do away with" the duke, which was understandably refuted. But the German cables referring to the rumor were not for publication and so had no propaganda value. Indeed, as has been said before, the entire affair came to light only after the war, when it certainly did the Germans no good, and it has been consistently hushed up by the British government, notably Churchill.

Could such a plan to get rid of Windsor have existed? Because of his intransigent and outspoken attitudes, encouraging enemy belief that he was a serious alternative to the existing government, he could easily have become a focus for defeatism and collaboration in the mold of Pétain, had he reached Britain. If, as I believe, he had, however unwittingly, given away details of Plan D and revealed Allied strategy to the Germans via Bedaux, thereby bringing about the catastrophe of May and June 1940, then he was a real danger. He could have done so again, were he in a position that would give him access to secret plans. Had he been anyone but a key member of the royal family, it is unimaginable that his loose talk and seditious behavior would have been tolerated. But, as ex-king and brother of the reigning king, nothing could be done to restrain or censure him without playing into German hands and providing devastating anti-British propaganda of considerable harm in the dominions and in the United States. If he would not quickly go to the Bahamas, where he could do comparatively little harm, doing away with him may have indeed been a real alternative. He certainly could not be allowed to go on making traitorous remarks, for in the event of invasion his role might have become critical. British files on this aspect are not available; some will never be. Nevertheless, it is worth considering that in 1945 the Polish general Sikorsky was shot down over the Mediterranean after leaving Gibraltar in an act persistently attributed to Churchill and equally persistently denied. Before this story is ended, two other notable figures of the Second World War will have been eliminated in strange circumstances.

Within a few days of the duke's arrival in Lisbon, the Germans succeeded in making contact through Miguel Primo de Rivera, the Madrid leader of the Falange with whom the duke had become very friendly while in the Spanish capital. On July 16, Stohrer cabled Ribbentrop that the duke had sent a message through de Rivera to the Spanish foreign minister saying, "His designation as Governor of the Bahamas was made known to him in a very cool and categorical letter from Churchill with the instructions that he should leave for his post immediately without fail. Churchill has threatened him with arraignment before a court martial in case he did not accept the post."[13] This part seems to have been transmitted orally to the duke, presumably via Hoare before they left Madrid. Quite a different version is in the duchess's account of the appointment. But the Germans were clearly anxious to keep the duke within reach in Portugal or Spain, and Stohrer confirmed that accordingly Beigbeder had asked their ambassador to Lisbon, Nicolas Franco, "to warn the Duke most urgently against taking up the post."

It is apparent from the amount of cable traffic between Berlin and Madrid that the Germans and the Spanish were putting considerable pressure on the duke not to go to the Bahamas, and clearly they attached great importance to his potential as a leader. But the Germans were not the only ones straining to bend the duke to their way. British Intelligence was naturally bent on countering Nazi pressures, and they knew more about it than has been admitted.

One of the best-kept secrets of the war was the Ultra equipment. By the use of these specialized decoding machines, an example of which had been smuggled from Poland in 1939, British Intelligence intercepted the German radio signals and was able to read their coded messages. The publication of Group Captain F. W. Winterbotham's book *The Ultra Secret* revealed the extent to which this highly secret equipment was able to give vital information to field commanders and the commanders of air and naval operations and so gain great advantages for the Allies. This made me think that perhaps Ultra had listened in to the German signals about the Duke of Windsor, and so I asked Winterbotham about it. He confirmed that indeed they had intercepted these signals, but he claimed that he never knew what was in them because they were immediately seized by MI5, the internal counterespionage service. If MI5 had the signals, however, they knew in July 1940 of the duke's flirtation and collaboration with the Nazis, and that reinforces the "do away with him" idea. It also made it very easy after the war for the Intelligence Service to find all those "missing" cables; they knew exactly which ones to look for. American sources, too, confirm that in the wake of their armies as well as the British, hordes of British Intelligence men descended like locusts on all the German records they could find.

But British Intelligence was operating in Portugal, too, to counter German moves and so had up-to-the-minute information from Ultra on which to work. It is probable that Churchill knew exactly what was going on and was able to plan accordingly, for it was toward the end of July 1940 that Churchill, like Hitler, began to see a way of using the duke's involvement with the Nazis to Britain's advantage, without, it must be added, letting the duke in on the game. As the American chief of staff put it, "A secret service must be secret," and Britain's always has been. In writing their memoirs, the politicians and generals have invariably ignored the aid they received from the secret services. But the fact is that behind all the significant events in recent history have been an army of anonymous spies who have exerted far greater influence on history than those who wrote it.

On the evening of July 19 Hitler marched into the Reichstag to deliver his long-awaited speech. The assembly was packed, and the front row was a display of Nazi dignitaries: Hess, Goering, Ribbentrop, Goebbels—all waiting expectantly. It was the cleverly emotive speech of a conqueror, mixed with the sentimentality that so strongly appealed to the German people. Although inevitably sprinkled with insults to Churchill, it was, nevertheless, modest in tone and shrewdly conceived to deceive the world's neutrals and win the support of the British masses. When the thunderous applause had echoed away amid the decorative balconies of the old opera house, Hitler left jubilantly with his cronies, confident that the way to peace had been prepared.

An hour later, though, the Führer's wrath overflowed. While his cronies stood petrified and open-mouthed, he stamped and shrieked himself into a mouth-foaming frenzy: The BBC had already broadcast a determined No!

From then on Hitler was bent on bringing Britain down as quickly as possible. The Foreign Ministry had manifestly failed. What about Himmler's SS, always waiting in the wings like jackals for the carcass?

12

Enter the SD

S *BRIGADEFÜHRER* Walter Schellenberg was in his office that July morning when a friend rang from the Foreign Office to warn him to expect a call from the "old man," meaning Ribbentrop, in person. Schellenberg went on working until the call came at noon. He lifted the receiver to hear Ribbentrop's sonorous and autocratic voice, tinged with the respect due to a high-ranking officer of the *Sicherheitsdienst*—the SD. In his memoirs Schellenberg recalled the foreign minister's words:

"Tell me, my dear fellow, could you come over to my office at once? You have time, haven't you?" Schellenberg replied that he did, but added, "Could you tell me what it's about? There may be some material that I should bring along."

"No, no," said Ribbentrop, "come at once. It's not a matter I can discuss over the telephone."[1] The conversation ended.

Schellenberg was a cautious young man and knew only too well how risky it would be to embroil himself in the schemes of the foreign minister, so instead of leaving immediately he telephoned his boss, Heydrich, and told him of the call.

"I see," Heydrich said, his thin voice without a trace of humanity. "The gentleman no longer wishes to consult me—old idiot! Well, go over there and give him my best regards." Schellenberg promised Heydrich a detailed report of what Ribbentrop wanted. He had known Heydrich for many years and was as close as anyone could ever be to the merciless automaton who ran the SD. He was aware of Heydrich's pathological jealousy.

Schellenberg left his office in the SD building in the Wilhelmstrasse and walked along the sunlit street to the Foreign Ministry, which was in the same street. He was a daunting figure in his black uniform, his silver belt buckle engraved with the Führer's own device, Our Honor Is Called Fidelity.

Ribbentrop was waiting impatiently, standing behind his desk with folded arms in emulation of his Führer, a serious expression on his face. Schellenberg sat down at Ribbentrop's invitation and waited until, after a few polite comments, the foreign minister got to the point.

Ribbentrop knew about Schellenberg's connections in Spain and Portugal, which we have already learned included agents in the Spanish Foreign Office, although he also had close links through agents with many of the police and security authorities. Schellenberg nodded cautiously, unsure where it was leading, and after a while Ribbentrop impatiently shook his head in dissatisfaction at the SD general's evasive answers.

"You remember the Duke of Windsor, of course," he said suddenly, plunging to the point. "Were you introduced to him during his last visit?" Schellenberg said no. "Have you any material on him?" Ribbentrop demanded.

"I really cannot say at the moment," Schellenberg replied warily.

"Well, what do you think of him personally? How do you evaluate him as a political figure, for instance?"

Schellenberg says he had to confess that he did not have sufficient information to give a proper answer. Yes, he had seen the duke when he was in Germany and was aware of the generally accepted reasons for his abdication. He thought the British had handled the problem sensibly, that "tradition and responsibility had taken precedence over human feelings and personal emotions," but he could not say whether that was a weakness or strength of the British royal family. According to Schellenberg, Ribbentrop was very taken aback by his reply and lost no time in putting him right.

The Duke of Windsor, he declared, was one of the most socially aware and right thinking Englishmen he had ever

met. It was this, he insisted, which had displeased the governing clique. "The marriage issue had been a welcome pretext to
remove this honest and faithful friend of Germany, and the
issues of tradition were secondary in importance."

In his account, Schellenberg says he tried to interject, but
Ribbentrop impatiently gestured him to be quiet.

> My dear Schellenberg, you have a completely wrong view of
> these things—also of the real reasons behind the Duke's abdica-
> tion. The Führer and I already recognized the facts of the
> situation in 1936 [at the time of the abdication issue evidently].
> The crux of the matter is that, since his abdication, the Duke
> has been under strict surveillance by the British Secret Ser-
> vice. We know what his feelings are: it's almost as if he were
> their prisoner. Every attempt that he's made to free himself,
> however discreet he may have been, has failed. And we know
> from our reports [Stohrer's and Hewel's, via de Ropp, no doubt]
> that he still entertains the same sympathetic feelings towards
> Germany, and that given the right circumstances he wouldn't
> be averse to escaping from his present environment—the whole
> thing's getting on his nerves. We've had word that he has even
> spoken about living in Spain and that if he did go there he's
> ready to be friends with Germany again as he was before. The
> Führer thinks this attitude is extremely important, and we
> thought that you with your Western outlook might be the most
> suitable person to make some sort of exploratory contact with
> the Duke—as the representative, of course, of the Head of the
> German State. The Führer feels that if the atmosphere seemed
> propitious you might perhaps make the Duke some material
> offer. Now, we should be prepared to deposit in Switzerland for
> his own use a sum of fifty million Swiss francs—if he were
> ready to make some official gesture dissociating himself from
> the maneuvers of the British Royal Family. The Führer would,
> of course, prefer him to live in Switzerland, though any other
> neutral country would do so long as it's not outside the economic
> or the political or military influence of the German Reich.

If the British Secret Service should try to frustrate the Duke
in some such arrangement, then the Führer orders that you are
to circumvent the British plans, even at the risk of your life,
and, if need be, by the use of force. Whatever happens, the Duke

of Windsor must be brought safely to the country of his choice.
Hitler attaches the greatest importance to this operation, and
he has come to the conclusion after serious consideration that if
the Duke should prove hesitant, he himself would have no
objection to your helping the Duke to reach the right decision
by coercion—even by threats of force if the circumstances
make it advisable. But it will also be your responsibility to
make sure at the same time that the Duke and his wife are not
exposed to any personal danger.

If one examines this statement, what emerges is that perhaps reluctantly, Hitler had decided to send in the SD to *aid*
the duke to get out of Portugal and away from the security of
the British to a country of his choice. The force that Schellenberg is being told he must be prepared to use is to be directed
against anyone trying to stop them getting the Windsors out,
not against the Windsors. Later on, when the plan would be
nearing completion, in Portugal, the duke's cooperation becomes evident.

Ribbentrop continued:

Now, in the near future the Duke expects to have an invitation
to hunt with some Spanish friends. This hunt should offer an
excellent opportunity for you to establish contact with him.
From that point he can be brought into another country. All the
necessary means for you to carry out this assignment will be at
your disposal. Last night I discussed the whole matter again
thoroughly with the Führer and we have agreed to give you a
completely free hand. But he demands that you let him see
daily reports of the progress of the affair. Herewith, in the
name of the Führer, I give you the order to carry out this
assignment at once. You are ready, of course, to carry it out?

Schellenberg says that he sat stunned, unable to grasp the
whole thing. To gain time while he swallowed his assignment,
he asked: *"Herr Reichminister,* may I ask you a few questions
—to clarify my understanding of the matter?" Ribbentrop told
him to be quick about it. Schellenberg wanted to know if the
duke's sympathy for Germany, of which Ribbentrop had

spoken, meant for the German way of life, its people, or also the present German form of government. Ribbentrop replied tartly that by Germany he meant the one in which Schellenberg lived.

"May I ask," Schellenberg persisted, "just how reliable is this secret information of yours?" Ribbentrop assured him coldly that it emanated from the most reliable circles of Spanish society, adding that the details need not concern him; the ambassador to Madrid would answer any questions.

One further question, Schellenberg wanted: "Do I understand that if the Duke of Windsor should resist, I am to bring him into this 'other country' that you speak of by force?" Schellenberg thought there was a contradiction in the plan, inasmuch as to be of value, the action depended on the duke's complete cooperation.

Ribbentrop seemed to avoid a direct answer by directing that the use of force should be principally against the British Secret Service. That used against the duke should be only insofar "as his hesitation might be based on a fear psychosis which forceful action on our part would overcome. Once he's a free man again and able to move about without surveillance by British Intelligence he'll be grateful to us." Ribbentrop also assured Schellenberg that the 50 million Swiss francs was not the limit: The Führer would go higher.

As Ribbentrop exhorted him to have confidence in his own ability, Schellenberg rose, but the foreign minister said, "One moment . . ." He took up the telephone and asked the switchboard to connect him with Hitler. He gave Schellenberg the second earpiece and bade him listen. When the Führer answered in his peculiar hollow rasp, Ribbentrop reported on his conversation with Schellenberg. The SD man says he could tell that Hitler was not happy about the scheme, and his replies were curt. "Yes—certainly—agreed," and he added, "Schellenberg should particularly bear in mind the importance of the Duchess's attitude and try as hard as possible to get her support. She has great influence over the Duke."

"Very well, then," Ribbentrop answered. "Schellenberg will fly by special plane to Madrid as quickly as possible."

Hitler snapped, "Good. He has all the authorization he needs.

Tell him from me that I am relying on him." Ribbentrop stood and bowed deferentially toward the telephone. "Thank you, my Führer, that is all."

There was a brief exchange about reports, which the foreign minister instructed should be sent back through diplomatic channels, and then after a final discussion about currency and papers, Schellenberg left.

The mythology of the so-called kidnap plot against the Duke of Windsor has been derived from the account given by Schellenberg in his memoirs. But that account is itself far from complete and does not tell anything like the entire story. Even the published versions, in English, French, and German, vary in length, and all are considerably cut from his original manuscript. The idea of the kidnap in any case appears to have sprung from Ribbentrop, and this combination of offer accompanied by threat was typical of his diplomatic style. Nevertheless, he was careful to distinguish between the use of force against the Windsors and against British Intelligence. It seems fairly clear from what Ribbentrop said, according to Schellenberg, which is to some extent verified by cross-checking against the cables from Stohrer, that the Germans believed that the duke himself wanted to return to Spain but was being restrained by the presence of British agents. Schellenberg's account, then, omits much of the fine detail, thereby leaving an impression of a badly organized bit of Nazi horseplay, which has been fostered by official denials of the duke's very active participation in the Spanish-Portuguese plan.

Schellenberg also said that the Führer did not sound too happy, and that was probably true, because the Foreign Office diplomats—for whom he had little use by then—had not achieved any significant agreement with the duke up to that time. The key to his conversation seems, in fact, to depend on the date upon which it took place. Schellenberg does not tie down his autobiographical account to dates, but working from Ribbentrop's comments about what the Windsors had said in Spain and what Schellenberg said he did before leaving Germany for Madrid, we can assume this interview must have taken place on about July 21. By that time the Windsors had been in Portugal for two weeks, during which Stohrer's various emissaries had been in constant contact with the duke, who appeared to be reluctantly departing from Europe altogether for the Bahamas. Once he did that, Hitler realized, he would be lost to the Nazis' cause to all intent; hence the introduction of the SD to do what Ribbentrop's Foreign Ministry could not. Even so, Schellenberg's mission for Ribbentrop was to be something of a sideshow, a bit of window dressing for Ribbentrop's benefit, while the real business in Portugal was going on with top Nazis involved in far-reaching peace negotiations arranged by the SS/SD, of which Ribbentrop was largely unaware.

After Schellenberg left the Foreign Ministry, he went straight to SS headquarters in the Prinz Albrecht Strasse where Heydrich still retained his own office, although his SD organization was based in the Wilhelmstrasse. Heydrich was seated behind his desk and received his young subordinate rather coolly, for he was a morbidly suspicious man. There was no pretension in Heydrich's office, as Schellenberg would have noted, but a spartan simplicity in stark contrast to Ribbentrop's opulence. Heydrich fixed people with a "reptilian gaze." Schellenberg suppressed an involuntary shudder, as did most people upon whom Heydrich looked. Schellenberg's own quizzical eyes flickered over Heydrich's triangular face with its sharp, predatory nose above a large mouth with thick, cruel lips. His eyes were ice blue and dead of emotion—real "wolf's eyes" was Himmler's description, and even he, who headed the entire terrible SS-SD-Gestapo network, feared Heydrich above all. He stared at Schellenberg with his narrow head slightly lowered so that he gazed characteristically upward from under almost invisible eyebrows, the light from the window shining on his gleaming brilliantined fair hair.

Here is a strange man, was the thought that Schellenberg remembered running through his mind, and not for the first time, he recalled a comment made by Carl Burckhardt, a Swiss diplomat, after meeting Heydrich: "Two people are looking at me simultaneously." Many people had detected Heydrich's dual personality, and SS officers recounted a story of how, when drunk, he had staggered into a bathroom and caught sight of himself in the mirror. Immediately he had snatched his revolver from its holster and twice fired at the mirror, shouting, "At last I've got you, scum!" Even his own SS men called him "the blond beast."[2]

Schellenberg recalled Heydrich's opening remarks. "Well," he sneered, "and how did you get on with our old idiot gentleman?"

Schellenberg remained standing and briefly recounted what had taken place. All the while Heydrich toyed with a thin, razor-sharp paper knife, flicking it in and out with rapier-style thrusts (he was one of Germany's leading fencers and had been asked to participate in the 1936 Berlin Olympics).

> Ribbentrop always wants to use our people when he gets ideas like this [he is supposed to have said]. You are really much too valuable to me to waste on this affair. I don't like the whole plan. Still, once the Führer gets hold of such a notion it's very difficult to talk him out of it, and Ribbentrop is the worst possible adviser. You have to realize that you will be making frontline contact with our opponents, so I don't want you to travel alone. Take two reliable and experienced men with you who can speak the language. At least you will have some protection. Certainly if I were the head of the British Secret Service, I would settle your hash for you.[3]

That, according to Schellenberg, was more or less all that Heydrich said, but whether or not he did say more then, it will be obvious that a great deal was going on in that fertile, almost fevered brain. Again, this seems an attempt by Schellenberg to play down the dangerous game he was getting into and, perhaps, to escape the consequences in the postwar world.

The following day Schellenberg busied himself with preparing for his journey to Spain, gathered all the information he could, chose his assistants, and detailed the work his department was to get on with in his absence. Soon afterward, he says, Ribbentrop called him in again and abruptly asked him back to his office. On arrival he asked him whether he was ready and if he had enough money. Had he decided upon a plan, he asked. Schellenberg had not. Finally the foreign minister emphasized that everything was to be kept absolutely secret and that the "Führer would punish the slightest violation of secrecy—the

Führer had wanted him to tell me that." Schellenberg thought it typical of Ribbentrop to leave that until the last moment.

Walter Schellenberg was then a boyish-looking twenty-nine, slim though with an adolescent chubby face marred by a small scar on his right cheek which twisted when he smiled. But he was decidedly not the charming rogue—a bit of a buffoon—as several writers have described him in an attempt to discredit the whole Windsor episode as immature Nazi hooliganism. He was in fact one of half a dozen extremely tough young men employed in the Reich Central Security Office, *Reichssicherheitshauptampt* (RHSA), which André Brissaud called "as monstrous an institution as was its name" and which vied for intelligence supremacy with Canaris's Abwehr. Of the various units of the RHSA, a special branch of Amt IV called E existed for surveillance of foreign agents abroad and was headed by Schellenberg. Schellenberg was undoubtedly a gifted man. He had studied for the law and had a propensity for intrigue. He was one of those men gathered by Heydrich on whom were concentrated all the powers of spying, intelligence, arrest, torture, and execution on which the Nazi dictatorship depended. Schellenberg himself described the type of functionary envisaged by the SD: The machine must "put aside all inhibiting or traditional notions—it must at least possess that flexibility which the government of a state must have if it is to administer a country smoothly in accordance with the directives which the Führer sees fit to issue."[4]

When Schellenberg left Heydrich to his ponderings, the calculating chief of the SD set in motion his own agents to watch the Foreign Office maneuvers and, it is believed, to watch Schellenberg as well. But, as we shall see, Heydrich was initiating a plan of much wider importance and of which Schellenberg was certainly aware, despite his writings. To understand the workings of men like Heydrich, Schellenberg, and Himmler is rather like studying the actions of nuclear particles: They are invisible, but one can nevertheless study their effects and so deduce the reactions that caused the effect. In this case, what happened is evident from the signals and reports that Schellenberg sent back to Berlin, and so we have to deduce what went on in the meantime.

It is important to remember that at that time, in the summer
of 1940, the most fundamental objective of the Nazi rulers—
indeed, the very essence of their philosophy, much of it based on
Rosenberg's deliberations—was Hitler's historic determination to attack Soviet Russia. But in *Mein Kampf* he had also
declared that he would never again involve Germany in a
two-front war. France had been defeated, but Britain, which
the Nazis thought had only half heartedly entered the war
because of treaty obligations to Poland, Belgium, and France,
was still fighting on, albeit with no hope of winning or even
surviving a German invasion. But Hitler would not invade
Britain so long as there was a chance he could get her out of the
war by peaceful means. Only then could he turn East against
Soviet Communism. The defeat of Russia was also foremost in
the minds of the SS leaders. They were ready and rabid to push
on eastward in a new Teutonic crusade to purge Europe to the
Urals of the scourge of Communism. So the problem of getting
Britain out of the war was foremost in the minds of men like
Heydrich and Himmler as well.

After Schellenberg's visit, Heydrich—who, to quote Kersten, "had an infallible nose for men. . . . he saw the ways that
friends or foe would take with a clarity which was absolutely
amazing"[5]—also began studying how the presence of the Duke
of Windsor in Portugal could be used to help achieve that
eastern objective that had lain like a Holy Grail behind German dreams for hundreds of years and which underlay the SS
folklore of runes, werewolves, and dark Slavic forests.

Heydrich's response, then, was a part of the internecine
struggle between Ribbentrop and Himmler about who should
decide German foreign policy that went on until the very end of
the Reich in May 1945, but this time the SS were to win and in
so doing were to set Germany along a path of disaster that
would eventually bring down the whole Nazi edifice.

13

Schellenberg's Mission

S CHELLENBERG LEFT Berlin on Thursday, July 25, taking off from Berlin-Staaken military airfield at 10 A.M. His flight was uncomfortable, to say the least, for the Junkers 52 was very much a utility transport, drafty and very noisy; it was, he said, quite inadequate, as the passengers had only packing cases on which to sit during the long, cold, and noisy flight. The flight path was recorded in his report to Ribbentrop, and from it we know that they made an intermediate fueling stop at Bourges at 1:30 P.M. and took off again for the next leg of the flight at 2:45 P.M.[1] Eventually they approached the Spanish capital on its sunburnt plateau, which reminded Schellenberg of a lunar landscape and was stifling hot. The pilots were all special couriers for the Secret Service and therefore known to Schellenberg, who frequently visited Spain. (Spain and Argentina were the two countries in which his department, Amt IVE, had the best-developed spy networks; he also had the spy "Guillermo" in the Spanish Foreign Office.) He was invited onto the flight deck and watched as they made a sweeping approach to Madrid airport, where they landed at 6 P.M.

From the airport Schellenberg was driven into Madrid, to the large hostel that had been built specially to house the hugely inflated staff of the German Embassy, most of whom were Abwehr and SD agents. He stayed at the hostel only briefly, though, before going to a small private hotel where he "registered officially" and thence on again to a private house where he was actually to live. The reports he sent to Berlin, however, which provide details of his activities that are not mentioned in the memoirs, make it clear that he can have spent very little time at the house; it was only another front.

Having covered his tracks as well as he could, presumably to avoid surveillance by British Intelligence, who would have been watching the airport for any new arrivals, Schellenberg made his way by a circuitous route to the German Embassy for an immediate discussion and briefing by Stohrer. Stohrer explained to him the connections that he had established through Spanish and Portuguese notables to the Duke of Windsor and gave an appraisal of the duke's attitude generally. He then gave an outline of the plan to entice the duke into Spain with a hunting invitation, although, as he said, the date had not yet been fixed.

Stohrer had been continually involved in the moves that had taken place in the previous week or so to subvert the duke. On the 12th he had met again with Beigbeder, who had recounted the meeting he had had with Sir Samuel Hoare. Beigbeder had emphasized to Hoare General Franco's belief that Britain had lost the war and would soon have to sue for peace; this Hoare had denied vigorously, declaring that Britain would fight to the end. But Beigbeder doubted this and reminded Hoare that Spain had acted as the intermediary between France and Germany and could do so again in Britain's negotiations, pointing out that it was likely that he, Hoare, would be the intermediary selected for the talks. Hoare had ruefully answered, "It is possible that it will sometime come to that."[2]

Of greater importance to Schellenberg, though, was the report from Primo de Rivera on his return from seeing Windsor in Lisbon. De Rivera had had two long conversations with the duke, and during the latter the duchess had joined in the talks. The duke, Stohrer explained over dinner, had talked very openly. "In Portugal," the duke had told the emissary, "he felt almost like a prisoner. He was surrounded by agents, etc. Politically he was more and more distant from the King and the present English Government," he said, and he added that his wife and he ". . . have less fear of the King, who was quite foolish [*reichlich töricht*], than of the shrewd Queen who was intriguing skillfully against the Duke and particularly against the Duchess."

Schellenberg may well have hidden a smile, though, when Stohrer told him that the duke had said he was "considering making a public statement and thereby disavowing English policy and breaking with his brother," for this was exactly what Ribbentrop asked of the duke in exchange for that 50 million Swiss francs.

"The Duke and Duchess were very interested in the secret communication which the Minister of the Interior (Suner) promised to make to the Duke. To the question about what it concerned, the confidential emissary declared that he was not himself informed but that the report was no doubt of a serious nature." This is very confused, and obviously de Rivera was only passing messages on this topic, which was thought too confidential even for his ears, but perhaps it refers to the high-level meeting that was being set up for a few days hence. The duke had frankly admitted that they wanted to go back to Spain and thanked Suner for his hospitality, but he said he was afraid they would be treated as prisoners; this fear was dispelled by de Rivera, who assured the Windsors that the Spanish government would certainly agree to the duke and his wife living in southern Spain, perhaps in Granada or Malaga, which the duke preferred.

But the problem was, the duke explained, that sometime before he had surrendered his passports to his legation with a request for visas for Spain and France because of a "possible personal visit to his Paris residence." However, since the legation would not give him the visas, "In these circumstances he asked the Spanish Minister of the Interior to advise him how he would cross the Spanish frontier again and to assist him in the border crossing."[3]

These remarks attributed to the duke by de Rivera and recorded by Stohrer's cable to Ribbentrop suggest that far from the duke being the potential victim of a "kidnap" plot, the Germans were simply responding to appeals for aid that the duke made through the Spaniards. In view of his willing involvement with the Nazis in Portugal, the extent of which we shall shortly see, there is no reason to believe he was unaware of the German interest in his movements. The point about wanting to go back to France is so naive as to be unbelievable, for did he really imagine that he could jaunt back to the Boulevard Suchet in Paris as if the German conquest of France had never occurred? The answer is yes, he did, and moreover he took advantage of the Germans' response, too, for by then the gauleiter of Paris was Abetz. A week or so later he made his arrangements.

Stohrer had finished his cable with the news that a new emissary was going to the duke soon, "to persuade the Duke to leave Lisbon as if for a long excursion in an automobile and then to cross the border at a place which has been arranged, where the Spanish Secret Police will see that there is a safe crossing to the frontier."[4] The Abwehr were, of course, virtually in control of the Spanish Secret Police, and it is likely they were handling the matter.

The plan for a clandestine border crossing, Stohrer explained, would have been taken a step further on the 25th, when the second emissary had been due to take a letter to the duke from de Rivera explaining the arrangements. With one of Suner's secretaries, de Rivera was to meet the Windsors by chance and invite them for a short visit at an estate near the frontier on the Spanish side. That was the general outline of the plan. "In this way it is to be hoped that the Ducal couple will come unmolested over the border."[5] But who is supposed to be doing the molesting? Not the Germans obviously, so they and the duke are talking about avoiding the British agents. In the same cable Stohrer reported that although de Rivera could not be sure, he thought that Suner was anxious to warn the duke of the great danger that threatened them, presumably from the British, which accords with what Hewel's Swiss informant had also said.

There was a change of plan, though, for before this second emissary could leave, Ribbentrop sent a cable to Stohrer postponing the trip. That cable has never been found, and only Stohrer's reply confirming that he had acted quickly to cancel the emissary confirms its existence, so we do not know what else it contained. Probably it advised Stohrer to do nothing further in view of Schellenberg's imminent arrival and the likelihood of more direct action by his group.[6]

In his memoirs, Schellenberg says he learned nothing very new from Stohrer, but again this seems to be an attempt to play down his role. Over dinner that evening the portly ambassador and the slim SD *Brigadeführer* agreed they could do little more until the duke's own intentions became clearer; they would bide their time. But this was the very time-consuming attitude that Hitler wanted to avoid and was characteristic of the diplomatic deliberations and courtesies with which he had lost patience. Besides, it is soon apparent that Schellenberg was only going through the motions of cooperating with the Foreign Ministry and had his own schemes planned.

It is evident, too, from what followed, that Schellenberg had arrived in Spain with such a plan already worked out in some detail, and once he had finished his discussion with Stohrer, he got in touch with another of the key figures in the scheme. This was Paul Winzer, who was the SS police attaché in Madrid. These police attachés, *Kriminalkommisars*, were in fact the local chiefs of the SS agents based on a particular embassy. They were very much Himmler's men, and through them the SS *Reichsführer* kept control on the political activities of the Foreign Ministry's diplomats and officials, who, as may be imagined, both hated and feared them. His presence is confirmed by Stohrer's cable of July 26, speaking of Windsor's proposed trip to Spain. "... the vacation itself will be shadowed with the help of a trustworthy Portuguese police chief who is an acquaintance of Kriminalkommisar Winzer, attached to the Embassy." He went on to confirm that "There is also the closest working relationship here with the Schellenberg group."[7] Winzer is a shadowy person, like so many top SS and Gestapo men, but in 1944 he was still in Madrid and at the heart of Schellenberg's negotiations with the Americans to overthrow Hitler. Winzer subsequently died in a plane crash while on his way back to give evidence against the Abwehr chief, Canaris, then in Flossenberg concentration camp. After communicating with Winzer that evening, Schellenberg sent off the required daily report to Ribbentrop.

Early the following morning, Friday, July 26, Schellenberg sent a more detailed report of his plan to Berlin, although he does not make it clear to whom in Berlin it went. He then sent a cable to Lisbon, advising of his imminent arrival, and after spending the rest of the morning and early afternoon giving instructions to his follow-up team, he left by air at 4 P.M. By seven that evening he was in the Portuguese capital.[8] Lisbon was sultry with a moist wind off the Atlantic, which combined with the stored heat of the day to produce a humid, debilitating evening.

At this point an important development in the story takes place with the emergence of a person whose presence in the duke's Portuguese-Spanish intrigue has hitherto remained unsuspected.

Schellenberg was met in Lisbon, probably at the airport, by one of Winzer's men and through him made contact with C, who by then had arrived in Madrid.[9] C is, without a doubt, Reinhardt Heydrich himself. It is important to establish clearly that this was indeed Heydrich, for he was a powerful man indeed. André Brissaud, a noted authority on the SS, writes, "Within the secret service the letter 'C' designated Reinhard Heydrich."[10] Heydrich was a great reader of detective stories and somewhere discovered that the chief of the British Intelligence Service was mysteriously referred to as C and so began to imitate that habit. The mysterious C began to appear in the SD files—"'C' has ordered . . ." or "the decision concerned 'C' personally"; a rubber stamp was even made—"Submit to 'C.'"[11] It was all intended to enhance the mystery surrounding the nebulous chief of the SD. There can be no doubt that the C who now appears in this story was Heydrich.

The answer to why the Duke of Windsor was to become caught up in an intrigue with such a man as Heydrich lies in Heydrich's role; as absolute head of the Nazis' security and espionage service, he would soon move to Portugal to make sure that two very important people could meet in safety, secure from the attention of the British SIS. One of those men was the duke; the other, who was senior even to Heydrich, was to arrive on the following Sunday.

Schellenberg spent some time on that hot Friday evening in discussion with Heydrich who, according to Schellenberg's own report, "declares himself able to guarantee security for 'Willi.'"[12] "Willi" was by then the SD's code name for the Duke of Windsor, the nephew of the great Willi—the kaiser—and the prospective "kaiser" of Britain. Willi's identification is evident from Schellenberg's signals;[13] from his arrival in Portugal on July 26 until the duke's departure aboard *Excalibur* for the Bahamas on August 1, his use of "Willi" coincides with the known movements and actions of the duke. Thus, he frequently refers to the meetings between Willi and de Rivera, which are confirmed by Walter Monckton's account. On July 31, Schellenberg reports that the wife of one of the more important police officers is with Willi's wife, who is the duchess; and on August 1, that Willi's long-serving driver refused to cooperate, and finally that Willi left on *Excalibur*. The Germans were always fascinated by code names, and their military archives are sprinkled with codes for every conceivable occasion and person.

At some point in the discussion they consulted their ambassador, Heuene, as well, perhaps for advice about local British Secret Service operations, for Portugal was nominally Britain's ally.

In the meantime, Schellenberg's two-man strong-arm back-up squad, Heineke and Böcker, had left Madrid and was on its way westward, traveling by car along the Route National V, via Talevera, then along the valley of the River Tagus before swinging away southward across mountainous country to Trujillo. From there they descended into the valley of the River Guadiana to the important city of Badajos, just a few miles from the Portuguese frontier, which they reached at 10 P.M.; there they put up in a hotel for the night.

But Schellenberg had found time before arriving in Portugal to put into operation his own scheme to subvert the duke's household, which would provide his SD team with a continually updated flow of information. The duke was always an easy target to spy on because of his unfailing garrulousness, and in Cascais he continued to talk freely at all times. Taking advantage of this, Schellenberg had arranged while still in Berlin for a Japanese agent to be taken on as a member of the duke's household staff, which was not difficult given Espiritu Santo's German sympathies. This Japanese was almost certainly named Jikuro Suzaki, and he had been recruited some years before in Lisbon by one of Schellenberg's men, Kurt Janke, a veteran German spy from the First World War, a large man with a round, bony face and dropping eyes. The Japanese had some years earlier been employed by Schellenberg in Morocco to infiltrate French secrets there. Suzaki had since then gained access to the confidential dispatches of the Portuguese envoys in London and Washington through a venal employee of the Portuguese Ministry of Foreign Affairs and forwarded them to Schellenberg in Berlin through Erich Schroeder, the SS Police attaché and head of the SD mission in Portugal.

With Suzaki employed in the duke's house, Schellenberg had a ready source of intelligence. "He and his organization had done excellent work," he wrote. "He gave me a detailed sketch plan of the house, the number of servants, and an account of the guards furnished by the Portuguese police and of the British security forces. He had also prepared a detailed description of the daily life of the household."[14] Schellenberg also met with his "Portuguese friend" as he calls his informer, and his explanation of his friend's financial difficulties suggests it was the "venal employee" of the Foreign Office once again. Schellenberg promised him a sum of money in exchange for a complete picture of the official Portuguese situation regarding the duke. This was delivered to him an hour later, and from it it was evident that the British still exerted considerable influence in Portugal. But Schellenberg says that by spending money lavishly he was able to organize considerable undercover activity to combat the British. In view of what was going on with Heydrich, it seems likely that all this subversion on the part of Schellenberg was really a diversion to keep the Portuguese and British security services occupied while the real business was being handled covertly.

At 2:40 P.M. on Thursday afternoon, July 25, just as Schellenberg's aircraft had been taking off from Bourges, Stohrer had sent another cable to Ribbentrop, about the second emissary's talk with the Duke:

> When he gave the Duke the advice not to go to the Bahamas [Stohrer said] but to return to Spain, since the Duke was likely to be called upon to play an important role in English policy and possibly to ascend the throne, both the Duke and Duchess gave evidence of astonishment. Both appeared to be completely enmeshed in conventional ways of thinking, for they replied that according to the English constitution this would not be

possible after the abdication. When the confidential emissary expressed his expectation that the course of the war might bring about changes even in the English constitution, the Duchess especially became very pensive.[15]

Stohrer added an assurance to Ribbentrop that he had said nothing to Suner about Ribbentrop's suggestion, in his July 11 cable, about the duke ascending the throne again, and de Rivera had spoken only as an old friend of the duke. So the German ambassador was getting the Spaniards to influence the duke while they prepared their own particular coup.

The plan for the duke to escape into Spain was still being developed, and Stohrer was able to confirm on the 26th that the plan for a hunting trip was ready. Since the duke remained without a passport—despite a rumor that the legation had issued it—pressure had been put by Suner on a Portuguese frontier official "who was personally obligated to him." Stohrer confirmed that he had discussed the matter with Schellenberg. The role of the very tough SD team which he was assembling would be principally to combat the British Secret Service men, who were watching the duke closely, once they reached the frontier. *Kriminalkommisar* Paul Winzer had arranged that the journey itself, from Lisbon to the border, be shadowed by a trustworthy Portuguese police chief.

The plan was that as soon as the border crossing was reached, Schellenberg's group would come into the open and take over the Portuguese side of the crossing, presumably to fend off any attempt by British or Portuguese agents to prevent the duke's escape into Spain. Then, once the duke's party was in Spain, they would provide a tough armed escort to the estate where the Windsors were going to stay. Yet another confidential agent, this time a woman, was to make contact with the duke and, to use Stohrer's words, "also if necessary get information to the Schellenberg group." This woman has not been identified, but it is possible she was attached to Windsor's party as an extra maid for the duchess, in view of what happened on July 29. But as well as this plan, an alternative flight by plane was also prepared as an emergency escape route should British Intelligence intervene to prevent the car journey. Stohrer concluded his cable by confirming that Schellenberg was in "reliable connection with me by code" and added that he "requests that the Chief of the Security Police be informed of the planning"; that was Heydrich, who was still in Madrid at that time.[16]

The next day, Saturday, July 27, saw a further escalation of activity as Schellenberg's group started to concentrate in Portugal. His two men in Badajos continued on their way at 8:30 A.M. and reached Lisbon at 3 P.M. that hot summer's afternoon. Two hours later Winzer arrived, and he probably brought Heydrich with him, for Schellenberg reported that they then had a "detailed discussion with 'C' about security, etc., for 'Willi.'"[17] They seem to have discussed two matters. One was the detailed plan of the Spanish border, which Winzer brought to the meeting. This plan had probably been drawn only that morning by the Heineke-Böcker team, for they had taken well over six hours to drive the straight 150-mile route from the border town of Badajos to Lisbon, the same time they had taken the day before to drive the much more difficult 250 miles from Madrid to Badajos. This plan was then discussed between Schellenberg, Winzer, and Heydrich. But Heydrich was not in Lisbon only to attend to the border planning, which could be well enough handled by the highly experienced Schellenberg; no, Heydrich had arrived principally to be on hand for the arrival on the following day, Sunday, of "Viktor," a man even more important than Heydrich, who was acting in his role of chief of the Security Police to protect his superior in the Nazi party.

While Schellenberg was controlling the team of SS-SD men then in Portugal, the duke in the meantime was under careful surveillance. The ease with which Schellenberg was able to insinuate the Japanese agent and others into the villa raises again the question of Espiritu Santo's connections with the Germans. He had, remember, moved out of the villa to his Lisbon home expressly for the Windsors. This strongly suggests that the banker was a willing partner in this reorganization of his staff. With the duke's well-known habit of talking in front of anyone, it explains the working of the system: The agent in the house reported either to Espiritu Santo or direct to Schellenberg. On July 30, Stohrer cabled that "Minister von Heuene has, according to the information of Herr Winzer, reported to Berlin that the Duke had on occasion expressed to his host (Espiritu Santo) a desire to come in contact with the Führer."[18]

Schellenberg was also busy and had by then contacted Hoynegan Heuene. Ambassador Heuene, it is generally agreed, was anti-Nazi and a man very different from the Nazi Stohrer in Madrid. Schellenberg perceived that the ambassador "was somewhat surprised at the authority I had been given, but said repeatedly that he was completely at my disposal."[19] It could not have been pleasant for the anti-Nazi ambassador to find himself unexpectedly involved with the intimidating SD, but Heuene was nevertheless at great pains to avoid any suggestion of a lack of enthusiasm on his part. On the same day, Saturday, Schellenberg contacted his Japanese friend. Within two days, Schellenberg had entwined the Windsors in a net of informers. "I had even managed to replace the Portuguese police with my own people. I was able to place informants among the servants, so that within five days I knew of every incident that took place in the house and every word spoken at the dinner table."[20]

With his preliminary arrangements completed, Schellenberg began a series of incidents intended to scare the Windsors into accepting the offer of German protection and reinforce their own wish to go. Once in Spain, it would ensure that the duke was on hand and available for the discussions they were sure would follow the intrigue that was about to take place in Lisbon. The intimidation went on. One warm night Schellenberg and two of his men got into the garden of the villa—which shows a surprisingly lax security—where, among the trees and bushes, heavy with scent and alive with the chirping of cicadas, they threw stones to break a number of windows. The duchess, in particular, became alarmed at this incident, but both Windsors attributed it to British agents, who they imagined were trying to scare them into getting away to the Bahamas. After that, anyway, they no longer ventured into the garden at night. Although the incidents perpetrated by the SD seem harmless enough, they were intended to discredit the British and provoke the Windsors into rash action.

During this time there had been a flurry of telegrams flying back and forth between the duke and Churchill. These had, of course, to be in code and so were routed through the harassed ambassador, Sir Walford Selby. For two long, sultry nights the Windsors had little sleep as they dealt with these exchanges, which arrived at all hours at Cascais, having been sent by courier from the embassy in hot and humid Lisbon. According to the duchess, she was pacing the floor while the duke, in his dressing gown, chewed on a pencil as he contrived his replies. It is not difficult to imagine the duke's deliberations; most of his life such trivialities as answering correspondence had devolved to a few scribbled lines that would be enlarged to an appropriate communication by a secretary or aide. Curiously enough, none of the duke's telegrams mentioned his dealings with the Germans and Spaniards.

The duke also sent cables to Lord Lloyd, the colonial minister, who was responsible for the Bahamas. At some time since arriving in Portugal on July 4, the duke had detached his aide Major Gray Phillips and sent him to London especially to see Churchill for an explanation of the Bahamas appointment, which the prime minister had hoped would be accepted. He had ended his message, "At any rate, I have done my best."[21] Having by then reluctantly accepted the appointment, the duke was, nevertheless, still throwing a smokescreen of conditions and demands. In his telegram of July 18, he insisted on being allowed to go to Washington on the way, adding, "Have been messed about quite long enough and detect in Colonial Office attitude very same hands at work as in my last job, strongly urge you to support my arrangements I have made otherwise will have to reconsider my position."[22] Churchill was vehemently opposed to the duke visiting America because he feared the duke's outspoken criticism of Britain's efforts at a time when he was pressing Roosevelt for more support. Many believed that the duke was the most accomplished conversationalist in the world, but it was there that the danger lay. A phrase askew in the duke's conversation would be disastrous, a friend lost and perhaps even an enemy created. Roosevelt, too, disliked the idea of the duke's visit because he would be obliged to treat him as a royal visitor who also happened to be from one of the belligerent countries. He was about to fight a difficult election and could not afford any more controversy.

The tiresome duke was still not finished, though, and next

began agitating for the return of his valet, Fletcher, and his wife's maid, Webster, insisting they could not manage without them. When Gray Phillips was unable to obtain Fletcher's release from the army, the duke angrily responded with another cable: "Absolutely essential that Fletcher rejoins me here as if you can as a military officer, surely he can as a soldier in plain clothes." Only hours later he followed this up with another cable: "Have asked Prime Minister to see you, I feel sure he does not know the red tape we are up against."[23] So while the prime minister was forstalling American demands for cash payments for arms and dealing with Italian operations in East Africa and the increasing German air raids preceding the invasion, the duke, like some demented Bertie Wooster, saw nothing more important than the prime minister's intervention in the matter of his valet. For several days more there was a shuffle of cables back and forth, until by July 24, Churchill was so exasperated that the duke's private servants mattered little compared to getting him to the Bahamas. He compromised and cabled the duke details of the ship on which he was to travel, but ended testily, "Sir, I have now succeeded in overcoming War Office objections to the departure of Fletcher, who will be sent forthwith to join you." Yet still the duke played for time, obviously awaiting some appointment before he was due to leave, and he cabled again for confirmation that "I should not set foot on American soil during my term of office in the Bahamas?"[24] Churchill caustically replied, "He would have to consult the Secretary of State" (for colonial affairs).[25]

All this while the duke was repeating his troubles to de Rivera, who was meeting him almost daily for lengthy discussions in the cool privacy of their Cascais villa. Having heard the duke's complaints, though, and listened sympathetically to the duchess's fearful relation of their persistent harassment, de Rivera, who was by then regarded as a close friend of the Windsors, suggested that he and his wife should get away from the villa at Cascais to a resort in the mountains near the Spanish border—obviously the harassment was having the desired effect and de Rivera, the trusted friend, carefully prodding them in the right direction. Windsor replied that he very much desired to go back to Spain.

But the duke's time in Portugal was drawing to a conclusion, and the coming weekend was to see the climax of the intrigues into which he had been led by his fraternization with de Rivera and through him with the Nazis. In his morning cable to Berlin, Stohrer confirmed that "'Viktor' is expected."[26]

14

The Deal Is Done

ON SUNDAY, July 28, 1940, came the climax of the duke's clandestine intrigues with the Nazis. His own country was by then facing its gravest crisis in 150 years—not since Napoleon had there been the remotest possibility of an enemy invading Britain—but on that hot summer's day in Lisbon, the duke was preparing to embark on momentous discussions with his country's enemy in a way that could have led to its defeat. In his telegram to Berlin at 11 A.M., Schellenberg referred to "two possibilities" on which guidance had been requested—we may assume this referred to the alternative means of getting the Windsors into Spain, for he says he had had discussions with Heydrich and Winzer. He then confirms that "'Viktor' was with 'Willi.' The latter asked for forty-eight hours' time to think it over."[1]

We have previously identified Willi as the duke, and we will shortly return to the subject of the forty-eight hours' delay that he requested. The important question is the identity of Viktor.

Viktor was Rudolf Hess, the man Heydrich had gone to Portugal to protect, the man with whom the duke was already familiar from prewar meetings in Germany from 1937 onward and who was the Deputy Führer of Germany.

It was vital to the subsequent prosecution of the war that Hess's brief visit to Portugal and the result of his negotiations there should remain secret, equally in Britain and Germany.

After all, whatever arrangements the Deputy Führer made had behind them the authority of the Führer himself. Afterward there could be no drawing back or hiding behind excuses, which was why Hitler had to deny all prior knowledge of Hess's subsequent flight to Britain. In both Britain and Germany his mission to Britain was made to appear an irrelevance perpetrated by a madman, which is also why a man still lingers in solitary imprisonment in Spandau. It was the result of those negotiations in Portugal that had to remain secret and why so many papers are "lost" or otherwise cannot be revealed. Thus, nowhere does the name of Hess appear in the records, although we can identify him by the evidence available in other signals and records, in the same way that Heydrich is not mentioned by name although there is no doubt about his identity as C.

The key figure in this intriguing web of secrecy is again Schellenberg—the link man in the whole episode—for although his published memoirs make no mention of Heydrich by name or by his code C, or of Hess or his code Viktor, I have obtained German cables[2] that are palpably attributed to Schellenberg and contain indisputable references to both Hess and Heydrich as well as to de Rivera, Winzer, Blumenstrauss, and others not mentioned by Schellenberg in his memoirs either.

Rudolf Hess was an experienced pilot who had kept himself up-to-date by flying aircraft he was loaned by Messerschmitt. He had one particular aircraft in which he made a number of flights before his final flight to Britain. Winterbotham wrote of Hess, "He was a good pilot and used to fly his own aeroplane about Germany; his flight to Scotland in the early part of the war was quite in character." The particular aircraft he normally flew was a Messerschmitt 110 twin-engined fighter bomber, its number *VJ-OQ*, giving it the call sign V, Viktor, an obvious choice for a code name. Stronger evidence, however, is available to identify Hess from another telegram sent by Schellenberg on July 28, the day Viktor arrived. It was addressed to "A. H." and read, "Just a note to keep you informed. Our friend 'Tomo' met with 'C' and 'Willi' this morning. Seven points plan was discussed in detail. Meeting again on 29.7. Urgent you contact the old lady as soon as possible. S."[3] How does this help identify Viktor as Hess, and who was A. H.?

Hess's foreign policy influence was considerable within the

Nazi party and stemmed from his association with the Haushofer family. After a distinguished military service in the First World War, Hess had resumed his studies in Munich where he had been greatly influenced by Professor General Karl Haushofer, who in 1921 had become the professor of Geopolitics. By the late 1920s, however, Karl Haushofer was no longer the main influence in Hess's life, although they remained close friends and Hess got to know his son, Albrecht Haushofer, a brilliant student of foreign affairs. This association with Albrecht was to have momentous consequences because through his friendship with Hess, he became an influential behind-the-scenes figure in German foreign policy and a major influence on Hess. Following secret missions to Prague in 1936 and again in 1937, Albrecht Haushofer wrote an important letter to his father, Karl, in which he gave an account of his discussions, showing intellectual disdain for the dictator whom he thought he could manipulate. For obvious reasons, though, Albrecht began referring to top Nazis by using Japanese code names: *Tomodaichi*, meaning "friend" was used for Hess; *Fukon*, meaning "I will not deviate" was Ribbentrop; *O'Daijin*, meaning "Master Great Spirit" was Hitler.[4] Haushofer continued to use this very personal code to his father although frequently Hess's code name was shortened to "Tomo." From this practice we may, therefore, deduce that Schellenberg's cable of July 28 was to Albrecht Haushofer (A. H.) and his reference to "Tomo" can only mean Hess. Also on the same day Schellenberg sent a summary to Berlin confirming "'Viktor' was with 'Willi.'"[5] Therefore we now have an equation: "Viktor" is "Tomo," who is Hess.

Another piece of evidence toward the identification of Hess in this situation has been provided by the historian Hugh Thomas. Thomas has an intimate knowledge of the man in Spandau who has been assumed to be Hess, and he declared in conversation with the present writer that when researching his book *The Murder of Rudolf Hess* in Dusseldorf, he had met a former SS officer who mentioned that "Hess met the Duke of Windsor in Lisbon." This information, it should be emphasized, was imparted by Thomas without his being aware of the findings that form the substance of the present book and is added confirmation of Hess's clandestine visit to Lisbon.

The duke met, then, for discussions with Rudolf Hess, the Deputy Führer of Germany. Why, though, should Schellenberg, the ruthless SD *Brigadeführer*, be communicating surreptitiously with the intellectual Albrecht Haushofer in the code he had hitherto reserved for correspondence to his father? The answer to that lay in the future of both men.

Albrecht Haushofer, as we shall see, tried in the early war period to bring about peace and failed. Later he associated himself with the anti-Hitler clique that attempted to overthrow Hitler in July 1944, for which he was sent to a concentration camp. Acting on Himmler's instructions, Schellenberg was by the summer of 1944 also working for the overthrow of Hitler, and there is strong evidence that the SS was deeply involved with the July plot, but they had the foreknowledge and ability to turn tail and with bloodthirsty and callous efficiency eliminated all who could point the finger at them. Albrecht Haushofer was executed just a few days before the end of the war on the specific orders of Himmler, no doubt to prevent himself from being incriminated by the Allies with whom he hoped to come to terms. Finally, both Haushofer and Schellenberg were seriously involved in clandestine intrigues in Spain throughout the war years. There is yet another connection between Haushofer, Schellenberg, and Hess in Schellenberg's mention of "the old lady." Later communications from Albrecht Haushofer to Hess prior to his flight to Britain several times refer to a Mrs. Roberts, a contact of Haushofer's in Portugal. So the number of Hess's aircraft, Schellenberg's cable to Albrecht Haushofer using the latter's hitherto exclusive code name Tomo, and finally the reference to "old lady," all point firmly to Viktor being Hess.

One might ask why Hess would have made this secretive visit to meet the duke, for he is generally characterized as dealing with the more mundane matters in the background of Nazi affairs. But this is erroneous and attributable to Hess's reserved nature. In fact Hess initiated many of the most important developments in the Nazi organization.

Hess had been one of the first members of the new Nazi Party in the immediate postwar years, remained a staunch supporter of Hitler, and had coined the term "Führer." He was inevitably alongside Hitler at all the big Nazi events, standing erect and darkly saturnine, glowering at the world from beneath his bushy eyebrows, arms folded arrogantly. Until 1934 it had looked as though Hess would become Hitler's designated successor, but this accolade went eventually to the infinitely more charismatic Reichsmarschal Hermann Goering, although Hess remained the Deputy Führer. By 1937 he was, nevertheless, being increasingly overshadowed by Martin Bormann, who succeeded him as *Parteiführer* after Hess flew to Britain in 1941. But Hess continued to have great authority within the party and had a large influence on foreign policy; he was also a link between the party organization and Himmler's SS.

As early as 1934 it was Hess who declared that the SD was to be the sole party counterespionage service, and through his interest in the SS/SD he became increasingly involved with Himmler, who was always nibbling at the edges of foreign policy. Then, in 1936, Hitler charged Hess with responsibility for all Germans abroad, and Hess formulated the *Volksdeutsche Mittelstelle*, (Reference Office for Racial Germans), (VOMI) which was responsible for coordinating the work of all government and party offices concerned with questions affecting Germans abroad. For a while VOMI floundered along under various chiefs, until Hess looked for some more disciplined and efficient organization to run it properly and selected Himmler's SS; Hess thereupon asked him to appoint a suitable person. This gave the greedy Himmler a chance at last to get his hands on an area of German foreign policy, and not long afterward VOMI was absorbed into the SS. The SD subsequently made good use of VOMI's countless connections abroad to set up its network of observers and listening posts, using VOMI personnel as cover, thus giving Schellenberg a ready organization in Spain and Portugal where VOMI was especially strong. This also consolidated the link with Hess who technically was still the overseer of VOMI. It can be seen that Portugal brought together all the essential elements of Hess's special "empire"—VOMI, the SD, and Schellenberg's connections.

The other thread of Hess's increasing overlordship of foreign policy was through Albrecht Haushofer. In late 1933 Hess had put Haushofer in touch with Ribbentrop, to whom he was made an unofficial adviser with the *Dienstelle Ribbentrop*, which was also under Hess's supervision. Haushofer was quite happy in this capacity, which he saw as a more influential role in foreign affairs than if he had joined the Foreign Ministry. In his advisory role Haushofer became increasingly involved in covert foreign relations deals, such as that developed in Portugal in July 1940 with Windsor. That personal involvement began over Czechoslovakia after Haushofer had written to Hess praising the Nazi authorities for their influence, which was offsetting the paucity of ideas emanating from the traditional Foreign Ministry.[6] This advice at once fell on fertile ground, for at that time Hitler was trying to circumvent the Foreign Ministry's important but long-winded negotiations with other countries, mainly because he didn't trust the diplomats. Hitler, therefore, encouraged Hess and Ribbentrop to develop these alternative diplomatic maneuvers and to recruit specialists who could determine Nazi foreign policy. In 1936 Haushofer and Graf Zu Trauttmannsdorf were sent by Ribbentrop, on Hitler's orders, to contact the Czechs for secret talks but "they were strictly forbidden to have any contact with the German diplomatic mission in Czechoslovakia and with the German Foreign Minister, von Neurath."[7] Thus, even in 1936, Hitler was using his own specialists to bypass the Foreign Ministry, just as he would in July 1940 in Portugal.

In the months following his visits to Prague—which led to the coded letters to his father—Haushofer was used by Hitler and Hess for several other missions abroad, and although he was obviously hoping to influence the Nazis for peace, in this he was singularly unsuccessful. Hitler, nevertheless, continued to regard Haushofer as a useful and well-informed expert ably supported by Hess.

It was with regard to Britain that Haushofer's most important contribution was made. He often visited London and as early as 1932 had written reports for the German Foreign Ministry. After 1934 he constantly forwarded data on Britain to Hess and was inevitably in the background of any diplomatic exchanges or visits by eminent politicians. Haushofer was a strong advocate of peaceful coexistence with Britain, which he believed was possible, and influenced Hess accordingly. In April 1935, Haushofer wrote for the *Zeitschrift für Geopolitik* a

"Report from the Atlantic World," stressing his belief that it was absolutely essential for Germany to live in a state of peaceful coexistence with Britain: "The final decision on the fate of Europe—as was the case at turn of the century—is in the hands of Britain. . . ."

Hess, then, was by no means the ineffectual party functionary he has been characterized; he was an important man, shunning the limelight in the same manner as his successor Bormann, and indeed that kind of personality was undoubtedly an asset when working close to the morbidly suspicious Führer. Hess had fingers in many pies—foreign policy, the SD, VOMI, and an all-embracing watchdog role ensuring that the Führer knew everything that happened.

During the French campaign Hitler and Hess had a lengthy conversation about strategy, and Hess later admitted that his plans for a secret mission stemmed from that date. That was the conversation referred to by Dr. Kersten in his diary for June 24, 1940, when he had treated Hess. In the course of his treatment Hess spoke to Kersten about an era of Franco-German cooperation, and when Kersten raised the British question, pointing out that they were a stubborn people, Hess replied, "We'll make a peace with England in the same way as with France. Only a few weeks back the Führer again spoke of the great value of the British Empire in the world order. Germany and France must stand together with England against the enemy of Bolshevism. That was why the Führer had allowed the English Army to escape at Dunkirk. The English must see that and seize their chance. I can't imagine that cool, calculating England will run her neck into the Soviet noose instead of saving it by coming to an understanding with us."[8]

It is significant that Hess's plans should have stemmed from June 24, for that was the day on which Hitler received Stohrer's cable asking for confirmation that he might be interested in establishing contact with Windsor, according to the conversation the Führer had with General Vigon. The secret mission Hess referred to, hitherto assumed to be his flight to Britain in May 1941, is more likely a reference to his imminent trip to Portugal to confer with the duke. Hitler's conversation with Vigon and the subsequent Nazi actions all indicate that

Hitler knew that Windsor was going to Spain, if not Portugal, and it is probable that after Dunkirk he was already intending to open negotiations to get Britain out of the war. Hess, as we have seen, had already been very much influenced by Albrecht Haushofer's dedication to a peace with Britain. There was never any question of Hess's patriotism or his devotion to Hitler, and his active involvement in a peace attempt with Britain was, as Winterbotham concurred, certainly done with Hitler's full knowledge. Hess's peace motives were not derived from any friendly feelings toward Britain but simply because, as Hugh Thomas put it, "If a settlement could be made with England, it would leave Germany free to tackle the *real* enemy, Soviet Russia."[9] In that mission Hess's main adviser was still Albrecht Haushofer, who had friends in Britain and also numerous contacts in Spain and Portugal, as did Hess. According to Hess's wife, Ilse, early in 1941 she knew he was flying abroad but thought he was planning a visit to Pétain to cement a longterm peace plan with France, although, Hugh Thomas says, "a stronger possibility is that he meant to fly to Stockholm, Madrid or even Lisbon, neutral capitals in which he might meet an emissary from England," as he had done in July 1940.

It was Hess's secret visit to Portugal and his far-reaching negotiations with the duke, which also involved an important British government minister, that gave the impetus for Hess's flight to Britain in May 1941. From Kersten's recollections it is evident that in June 1940 Hess had the same trend of thought that Rosenberg and others had gleaned from important British contacts in the 1930s, including the duke and his younger brother, Kent. Rosenberg was also close to Hess, as Winterbotham reported after he had talked with both man on several occasions and they maintained this close association up to the very end. The intention to "make peace with England in the same way as with France" suggests they expected a leader to emerge who would collaborate in Pétain's fashion—the Duke of Windsor. So Hess was not the awkward imitator of the Führer, the mindless errand boy portrayed by history after his flight to Britain; that, as will become evident, was the cost of his tarantella with the duke.

After Windsor's departure for the Bahamas, we find a great

deal of activity by Hess and Haushofer, and it is evident that they were indeed awaiting some response to a proposition made to England. And, oddly enough, on the very evening of Hess's flight to Britain, a reply arrived for Haushofer, from Stohrer in Madrid, indicating that Sir Samuel Hoare had agreed to an exploratory meeting. By then it was too late, though, and Haushofer was said to be furious that Hess had wrecked his carefully prepared peace plan; but then he had never been let into the whole of the affair. It is relevant to quote Winterbotham once again, because he was one of the few British people who knew Hess: "Despite his lack of self-confidence he had ample courage. He must have realized that for all the endeavours of the Nazis to keep Britain out of World War Two, she looked like fighting on, and that this would be a disaster for Germany. His flight was a last attempt to persuade the British to make peace." That it may have been, but the first act had taken place in Lisbon the previous July.

When Hess landed in Scotland in May 1941, he brought with him details of a peace plan that contained seven essential points, and in two cables Schellenberg had referred to the seven-point plan.[10] Hess obviously expected the British government to treat him with respect as the representative of the Führer and knew that the peace plan had already been discussed with British representatives. Thus he could not understand why he was treated like a criminal. On that Sunday, July 28, 1940, in Lisbon, it will be recalled, Schellenberg's report substantiates that discussions took place between Hess and the duke, for he reported that Hess spent some time with the duke while Heydrich was in conference with Winzer. Thus the two chief negotiators were together while the two policemen watched over the security arrangements. It will also be recalled from page 233 that the duke had asked for forty-eight hours to think it over. Evidently, whatever proposition was put to the duke was beyond his power to give an immediate decision. If the peace plan that Hess produced in Scotland nine months later is examined, it is clear they were thinking in terms similar to those the duke had been expounding for years. Hess does not appear in the cables again, and evidently he left after the meeting with the duke, leaving Heydrich and Schellenberg to await the answer.

That same day, however, Schellenberg sent another telegram in which he said that the Windsors intended to move out
of the villa at Cascais and into the Hotel Aviz in Lisbon. He had
his Portuguese agent immediately contact the duke and warn
him that the hotel was the center of the British Secret Service
and of the "hostile intentions of the Churchill Government,"
following which he remained at Cascais. Schellenberg also
says that the duke told him that he was expecting the "prearranged arrival of a friendly English minister" that day, and it
seems likely he was coming with the government's answer to
Hess's peace plan. Clearly the Germans knew the minister was
arriving, for Schellenberg informed Berlin in his telegram
Number E 035156. He also confirmed in his regular telegram,
"the departure to America is postponed until September 1,"
and asked the German security forces to report to him.[11]

The duke, in fact, would be leaving as scheduled within a few
days, at the beginning of August, and it seems likely that the
British government's answer contained the proviso that the
duke should leave immediately as a prerequisite to agreement.
It seems conceivable that at this stage it was used as extra
leverage to get him away. Only later was the full implication of
Hess's proposals realized. By his actions when he got to the
Bahamas it is evident he expected something more. In any
event the duke proceeded to buy himself some extra time in a
most peculiar way, which again reveals the lengths to which he
was prepared to collaborate with the Nazis and which relates
to the conversation about visas he had had with de Rivera a few
days before. To enhance their growing cooperation with the
duke and delay his departure as long as they could, the Germans seized upon the Windsors' well-known preoccupation
with recovering objets d'art from their house in Boulevard
Suchet. Paris was, of course, by then under a rigorously ap-
plied German occupation. But the German gauleiter in Paris
was Herr Otto Abetz, the friend of Charles Bedaux, who was
also in France. A series of exchanges between Stohrer and the
German foreign minister produced an arrangement whereby
the SD, acting for Abetz, would protect the Windsors' house.
Stohrer had the duke informed confidentially through de Rivera that the "Foreign Minister is looking out for its protection."

The telegram, signed by "Schmidt," added, "No written statement whatever is to be made."[12]

The duke was quite contented with this arrangement, despite the well-known evidence that the Nazis were looting the art treasures of Europe. In September 1940 Rosenberg, who by then headed a special bureau for systematic looting, the *Einsatzstab Reichleiter Rosenberg*, was gleefully reporting the vast hoards he was taking in France. Nevertheless, the duke sent a message of thanks to Stohrer, who sent off the inevitable cable to Berlin: "The Duke of Windsor expressed his thanks for the co-operation on the matter of his house in Paris and has made a request for a maid of the duchess's to be permitted to travel to Paris to pack up various objects there and transport them by van to Lisbon, as they were required by him and the duchess for the Bahamas."[13]

The French lady's maid left with German approval on July 29 and went to Paris, which was then experiencing the first terrors of Nazi occupation and the food shortages that would get worse as winter approached. She evidently saw Gauleiter Abetz, for on August 3, he reported that she told him, "The duke has no intention of embarking to take up his new post and would await further events in Europe and Lisbon." An already complicated story becomes even more intriguing at this point, for while the Germans had suggested protecting the Windsors' house and readily agreed to the maid's journey, which had been the duke's idea, Stohrer was not taking any chances of his departing once the maid rejoined him with the valuables, so he deviously arranged for the maid to be stopped on the Spanish border on her return trip, as a means of holding the duke up.[14]

But why did the maid go to see Abetz anyway? They could get all the information they wanted through de Rivera or the new direct contacts just established. But then ladies' maids do not usually travel fifteen hundred miles through enemy-occupied territory. So was she a German plant who had been with the Windsors since Paris—hence the Germans' constant knowledge of the duke's movements? In the latter case she was probably being given the chance to clear out without arousing the duke's suspicions. Whoever she was, Abetz sent a signal to Stohrer on August 2, confirming that he had spoken with "Miss Fox" about security for "Willi" and adding, "Miss Fox travels back to San Sebastian at 18:30 hours. Abetz."[15] In his own report on August 1 Schellenberg too mentions a "Miss Fox (San Sebastian)" without revealing who she was, but it is likely she was an SD or *Abwehr* agent. Whoever she was, it would be generous to think that in his usual way, the duke had played into German hands in the naive belief that they would do special favors for him; unfortunately, the evidence is that there was no such naiveté in his actions.

Events were by then moving toward a confused conclusion. The day after the maid left, which was Sunday, July 29, and the same day that the duke met with Hess, the duke's lawyer, Walter Monckton, flew into Lisbon.

Walter Monckton was then minister for information, a small, bespectacled man who wielded considerable authority at home and was a close confidant of Churchill. But why did he fly so precipitately to Lisbon, avowedly only to persuade the duke to embark on the ship to the Bahamas. Even the duke's biographer Donaldson, who is usually generous to the duke, queries this. "All the same," she wrote, "one cannot help wondering if it is true that Monckton was ignorant of everything that was going on except the attempt to persuade the Windsors that they were threatened by the British, because, if so, the Duke withheld a good deal of information from him." In a footnote she adds: "Monckton also withheld a good deal. His notes on the Abdication and its aftermath purport to be an account kept at the time for the benefit, it seems reasonable to assume, of future historians. But they regularly stop short of the more interesting facts and it is quite impossible to believe that in June 1940 a member of the government was sent to Lisbon either as a courtesy to the Duke of Windsor or with no particular reason beyond a general desire to speed him on his way."[16]

In that sentence Donaldson has hit the nail on the head. Monckton must have been sent there for some much more important purpose. Churchill knew what was going on there, for as Winterbotham made clear, MI5 was being fed the output of the Ultra listening posts. He had made it abundantly clear to Windsor that he was going to the Bahamas, and the presence of quite a number of SIS operatives should have been enough to ensure that the duke did not bolt for Spain, as he surely intended. Churchill had already arranged a ship: the American Export Lines had been persuaded to divert the SS *Excalibur* to Bermuda from Lisbon, where it would connect with a Canadian ship sailing to the Bahamas.

Monckton's arrival was noticed by the Germans, and Schellenberg reported, "Today there arrived at the Duke's as announced the English Minister who calls himself Sir Walter Turner Monckton, a lawyer from Kent." Espiritu Santo, the duke's host, had promptly called Schellenberg to let him know what was going on but insisted the man was a "confidential agent." Schellenberg is supposed to have agreed with Santo that ". . . a cover name is involved and the man is an agent named Camerone."[17] It was unlike Schellenberg to make a mistake, especially since he had himself talked with "C" and "Willi" that day "concerning report to Berlin." He also reported that "'Willi' does not want to go (to Bahamas)."[18] Since Schellenberg met with Willi (the duke) that day, and Windsor had helpfully told him that an "English Minister" was coming, it does not seem likely that he would have confused Monckton with "Camerone," and therefore it is probable that there was another person with Monckton, who may well have been an agent or perhaps someone from the Foreign Office.

Monckton's declared task was to counter the Spanish-German influence by persuading the Windsors that they were in no danger from the British and that the duke should hasten to his appointment as governor of the Bahamas. But Monckton did quickly recognize the German interest and influence and wrote rather incredulously that "It sounds fantastic but he (de Rivera) managed to impress the Duke and Duchess." But, as Donaldson says, Monckton was not one to record everything for posterity, and his published reports were half-truths. The strange fact is that this man who sought to weaken Spanish influence over the duke had at least one lengthy discussion with de Rivera. It is likely he was in the background to other talks as well, for the duke again met his "enemy" associates, and by Tuesday morning, July 30, Schellenberg could report to Berlin, ". . . since it has been established without doubt that 'Willi' will cooperate."[19] However, by then Monckton had also ensured that the duke and duchess would sail on the *Excalibur* to Bermuda on Thursday. Nevertheless, both sides seemed satisfied and began to disperse. Winzer left for Madrid on Tuesday, and as he had accompanied Viktor to Lisbon, it is reasonable to assume they left together once their task was done. Certainly the intrigue is nearly over. Two strange episodes alone remain to be acted out.

During the last days at Cascais the duke incessantly pondered his next moves, chain smoking as he walked in the garden. Every day the duke saw de Rivera, who was not going to be pushed out of the duke's confidences. He went again to the villa the day after Monckton arrived and had another lengthy private conversation with the distressed duke, who told de Rivera that he had not yet made up his mind. But he was strongly impressed by the reports of British intrigue and no longer felt secure, declaring miserably that they could not move a step without surveillance. Nevertheless, de Rivera was pleased to hear that the duke had not given up the idea of being an intermediary between Hitler and the British government, although asserting that ". . . the situation in England at the moment is still by no means hopeless, therefore he could not act now, by negotiations carried on contrary to the orders of the English Government, let loose against himself the propaganda of his English opponents which might deprive him of all the prestige when he might possibly take action."[20] Is this an admission that he has *already* negotiated some deal with Hess, which Monckton has warned him against trying to fulfill for the moment? It sounds like it, and it fits the situation.

There is a touch of pathos in this time: The lonely ex-King wandering in the gardens with a foreign emissary who held out the promise of so much new prestige, but bemoaning his impotence to take action. No doubt a part of Monckton's task had been to convince the duke that Britain was far from finished and that if he entertained ideas of suddenly taking over when his country collapsed, it was not going to be for a while yet. One wonders what other messages Monckton brought from London. Nevertheless, the ever-optimistic duke seems to have cheered up after talking with de Rivera, for he added that "He could, if the occasion arose, take action from the Bahamas,"[21] which he tried to do several times.

When this report reached Ribbentrop a few hours later, he quickly sent a long message back to Heuene in Lisbon, with

instructions to contact Espiritu Santo immediately and get
him to talk confidentially with the duke before he departed for
the Bahamas. He was to tell him that "Basically Germany
wants peace with the English people. The Churchill clique
stands in the way of this peace. Following the rejection of the
Führer's last appeal to reason Germany is now determined to
force England to make peace by every means of power. It
would be a good thing if the Duke were to keep himself prepared to co-operate with them for further developments. . . .
Germany is likewise prepared to co-operate with the Duke
to arrange for the Ducal couple in accordance with their
wishes."[22]

The duke sanguinely explained to Espiritu Santo that he
could intervene only if he were convinced he had the support of
the majority in Britain, otherwise his return might provoke
civil war. But he earnestly assured his Portuguese host that he
could return by air in twenty-four hours from Bermuda, where
he would change ships—he clearly expected a swift change in
Britain, perhaps as a result of his deal with Hess, which
Monckton was taking back. Santo telephoned Heuene soon
after that conversation, and the German ambassador quickly
got a cable off to Berlin that "Undiminished though his support
for the Führer's policies are, he thinks it would be premature
for him to come right into the open at present."[23] The duke had
been checkmated.

The duke was also under pressure from the duchess and had
to turn his attention to his wife's maid, then on her way to Paris.
The duke was pressed to get in touch with the U.S. Embassy in
Lisbon and ask for their assistance in finding her, although she
had left only the day before. In view of the fact that she had
hardly had sufficient time to arrive, the duchess seems suddenly to have had reservations. Could it be that she had at last
realized what they had been doing and with their departure
imminent began to panic for fear they were going to be found
out?

The U.S. authorities, however, promptly passed the message
on to the British Foreign Office, which decided, with some
acerbity, "The next step, if any, appeared to be with H. R. H.,
who had carefully refrained, apparently, from approaching
either Sir W. Selby or Sir S. Hoare. I was reluctant to place on

the shoulders of overworked Madrid and Lisbon the search for a nameless French woman, particularly when the person principally interested had not asked for this to be done."[24] Of course the duke could not ask British diplomats to aid him, for he knew only too well that he had been in communication with his country's most inveterate enemies.

One aspect of the German attempt to frighten the Windsors into staying in particular is clouded by official denials. It has long been rumored that a bomb was placed on the ship but always denied by the British government. Yet in his report on Tuesday, July 30, Schellenberg uses the phrase: "Construction of an infernal machine [*Höllenmaschine*] with 'C.'"[25] An infernal machine was the German name for a time bomb! The time bomb was indeed constructed as suggested by Heydrich and was placed aboard the *Excalibur* by one of Schellenberg's men, named Blumenstrauss. But, as Blumenstrauss reported on Wednesday, July 31, the crew arrested a suspect on the ship, and he informed about the bomb plot. This led to a general examination of all the passengers to search for any more plotters. The ease with which the bomb was found suggests it was intended only to warn the duke that he should flee to Spain.

Meanwhile de Rivera kept almost constant company with the duke, urging him to accede to the seven-point plan. The duchess was in the care of the wife of a senior Spanish Secret Police official, whether to "protect" her from the British or in preparation for a last-minute dash for Spain is not clear, although it is evident from Schellenberg's report on Thursday that a dash for Spain might still have to be considered. The police official's wife, though, was apparently also entreating her to use her considerable influence with the duke. Something was certainly going on, and there were hurried exchanges between Lisbon and Madrid and Berlin. Schellenberg had a further brief meeting with Heuene, who was the Germans' direct link to the duke through Espiritu Santo, while a signal from Madrid informed him that "nothing of importance had happened." Perhaps this implied that either Hess or Hitler had not ratified the proposals. Meanwhile a mysterious message from Stohrer reports in similar vein about that "which was requested by 'Willi.'" Then, in the night of Wednesday, July 31, the tension breaks: "Ribbentrop's answer comes in, von Heuene takes immediate action," which usually means that he got in touch with Espiritu Santo once more. Following this comes the cryptic, "In the night of August 1st, the execution of the 7 points"[26]—so agreement had been reached.

By Thursday the intrigue was nearly over, although the signal traffic reveals that plenty was crammed into the remaining hours. At 7 A.M. Schellenberg was with Heuene yet again, and it looks as though a very last attempt was to be made for that dash for Spain. A report that "Phillips was worked over by a man . . ."[27] is hard to understand, since he is not otherwise identified. Although the duke's aide, Gray Phillips, is not recorded as having returned to Lisbon from London, the duchess nevertheless remarks that Gray Phillips telephoned the duke from the embassy, although the timing of the call is omitted. But it is possible that "Phillips" got in the way of a German attempt to move the duke. Certainly Schellenberg's men approached "'Willi's' long-serving driver (who refuses to accompany us on our attempt)," confirming that an attempt was made, and the fact that the bomb had been discovered rather easily suggests that it was all a part of the last-minute tactics to excuse the duke bolting for Spain.

Reading between the lines, however, it appears that the final details of the seven-point plan had been agreed upon, although Schellenberg notes that some bargaining, or at least negotiations, continued. His report shows that Schellenberg met with Heuene and Heydrich, after which the ambassador had a talk with "F," who is not otherwise identified; F, whoever he was, then went and talked with "S," "L," and Monckton.[28] So the British government minister was still there talking through arbitrators with Heydrich and the German ambassador. F is not known, but S was Schroeder, the SS Police attaché in Lisbon, Winzer's Portugal-based counterpart, while L is probably Lorenze, the VOMI agent in Lisbon. The business must have been satisfactorily concluded, however, for that afternoon the Windsors departed.

There was one last attempt to divert them when one of their cars was waylaid and was an hour late reaching the dock, but it carried only the luggage. The Windsors had a last meeting with de Rivera and Portuguese President Salazar, and then at 6:30 P.M. the *Excalibur* sailed. The ship was crammed with stranded Americans also making their way home, and on the ship, with the huge United States flag painted on her sides to declare its neutrality to lurking U-boats, the Windsors were quickly absorbed among the other passengers as honored traveling companions. The duchess, though, admitted they saw Europe fade over the horizon with a sense of being removed "from the centres of action, from the main theatre of war...." Her memoirs make her sound sorry to be going.

The duke had finally departed from Europe, after negotiating some deal that Monckton had concluded with the Nazi representatives. The deal has never been admitted, but what else could Monckton have been doing there with the Nazis? The duke certainly left in the belief that his departure was only a convenient interlude, for on August 15, just two weeks later, Hoynegan Heuene again wired Berlin, "The confidant (Espiritu Santo) has just received a telegram from the Duke of Windsor from Bermuda asking him to send a communication as soon as action is advisable. Should any answer be made."[29]
Monckton had evidently succeeded in getting the intransigent duke to leave for the Bahamas only after assuring him that serious consideration, if not an actual agreement, would be given to the German peace proposals contained in the seven-point plan presented by Hess as Hitler's official representative on July 28. The duke, therefore, had gone believing that soon there would be negotiations with the Germans and a peace formula agreement that would satisfy German demands for hegemony in Europe while protecting the British Empire.
The duke's telegram of August 15 further confirms his cooperation with the Nazis and also makes it abundantly clear that his arrangements were working too slowly for him and that he expected to be recalled from the Bahamas either by the British, ready to replace the Churchill government, or by the Germans, who would put him back on his throne.
A lot was to happen in the next months, including the climax to the duke's intrigues in Portugal, which in its way was to provide a turning point in the war. But the frustrated, embittered duke still did not give up, and on August 5, 1941, he sent off another telegram, which the German ambassador, Heuene, dutifully passed on: "The intermediary familiar to us from re-

ports at the time, has received a letter from the Duke of Windsor confirming his opinions as recently expressed in a published interview that Britain has virtually lost the war already and that the U.S.A. would be better advised to promote peace not war." This was from the commander in chief and governor of a British colony.[30]

But he was too late. The last trick had been played, and far from being finished, his struggling country had been given a new lease on life as a result of the intrigues in Portugal. It has been one of the best-kept secrets of the war and the biggest double cross ever, as we shall see in the concluding chapter.

15

The Turning Point of the War

WHEN THE Windsors left Lisbon, away from the Nazis and the war in Europe, the British government must have been thankful that an embarrassing episode had at last been closed. But had it?

Two weeks later Windsor sent his telegram requesting the reopening of contact with the Nazis, but by then events had already moved on. Hitler had been persuaded by Goering to let his Luftwaffe bring tottering Britain to her knees, thereby hastening the British desire for peace. Hitler had, however, also taken an even more fateful decision. Greatly alarmed at Russian expansion in both the Baltic and the Balkan regions, he was under pressure from his intelligence services and his generals to strike at Russia before the Red Army grew too strong. In the belief that he had an agreement with Britain within his grasp, therefore, he ordered preparations to begin for "Barbarossa," the invasion of the Soviet Union.

In his book *The Nazi Connection*, F. W. Winterbotham relates how he visited East Prussia in 1938 in the company of Erich Koch, the gauleiter of East Prussia. After seeing the immense amounts of work being carried out there by the military, Winterbotham had asked when the work would be finished and was told three years at least. "So it was to be 1941 at the earliest in the East," he concluded. Winterbotham had then worked out the timetable after talking with Koch.

... If the Russian invasion was to start in 1941 it must begin in the spring as soon as the snows melted in early May. That in turn meant that if the Germans were determined to have a *Blitzkrieg* attack on France and the West they would have to complete it by October 1940 in order to give themselves time to refit their divisions and re-deploy them from the West to the eastern Russian front. ... It was partly the knowledge that the Germans had to invade Britain before the end of September 1940 or not at all, because of their Russian commitment, which helped us to recognize the Battle of Britain, when it came, for what it was; a critical turning point with a definite time limit for the Nazis.[1]

These dramatic developments must have alarmed Rudolf Hess, who had expected his peace initiative to move more quickly. Although Hitler's plan for invading Britain was nearing completion, nevertheless, the Führer remained reluctant to embroil his land forces in a battle for Britain that he was by no means confident of winning. Such a battle—against superior British naval forces, a very active RAF, and an obvious obstinacy to fight from the beaches to the hills and never surrender—offered little glory and could only grind up increasing numbers of German divisions already earmarked for Russia. Nobody was more aware of this than Hess.

On August 31, at his Alpine cabin, Hess met his old friend Karl Haushofer, who still acted as his occasional political adviser. The burly professor general afterward wrote to his son Albrecht on September 3, telling him about his meeting: "with 'Tomo' from 5 o'clock in the afternoon until 2 o'clock in the morning. ..."[2] He recounted that although Hitler was making preparations for invading Britain, he was still hoping for a peaceful way out, and Hess had asked whether a peace feeler could be made through a British intermediary in a neutral country. Now, while Schellenberg's cable of July 28 to "A. H." is almost certainly to Albrecht Haushofer, there is no evidence that he in turn had discussed it with his father, Karl, and indeed there would have been sound reasons why he should not disclose his close and dangerous contacts with an SS/SD operation. Albrecht's mother was Jewish, and it was only Hess's patronage that protected her. That fact alone would have been a powerful reason for this devoted son to keep his father as far removed from his SS contacts as possible. We also know that Hess kept his forthcoming flight to Britain a secret from even his closest aides, so he may have cautioned Albrecht to confide in no one. We do not know why Hess met with Karl alone at that time, but neither do we know the whereabouts of Albrecht, who may have been otherwise engaged. In any event Hess seems to have been probing Karl for alternative contacts with Britain in the frustrated belief that the Lisbon trail had gone cold.

Hess, the Führer's determined disciple, had realized that the Lisbon arrangements were not leading anywhere and possibly suspected that the agreement was being held up until it was seen how the Battle of Britain turned out. Hess disliked Ribbentrop vehemently and wanted to develop his own connections without involving the scheming foreign minister. In his own singularly determined way he was seeking a solution that would restore him to Hitler's favor at the expense of Ribbentrop and the SD.

Karl Haushofer eagerly prattled to Albrecht his news about Hitler's intentions, writing, "But before this decision, which is perhaps inevitable, the thought once more occurs as to whether there is really no way of stopping something which would have infinitely momentous consequences." He plunged on enthusiastically, "There is a line of reasoning which I absolutely must pass on to you because it was so obviously communicated to me with this intention. Do you, too, see no way in which such possibilities could be discussed at a third place with a middle man, possibly the old Ian Hamilton, or the other Hamilton?"[3]

Neither of these men was a very likely lead. General Ian Hamilton had once lunched with Hitler and Hess, while Karl Haushofer had met the Duke of Hamilton in Munich just once. His reason for choosing either is not clear, and the Duke of Hamilton claimed he had never met Hess and had only a single, quite casual meeting with Karl. A possible explanation for the choice of the latter, however, lies in the fact that through the years de Ropp, the contact between SIS's Air Intelligence branch and the Germans, had maintained that he was acting for the Air Ministry and given the impression that the Air Ministry was keen to see the war over quickly. In a cable of

October 5, 1939, de Ropp's contact in Switzerland had reported the British Air Ministry's view that it would be able to act only after a substantial part of the British Air Force had been destroyed. "It believed that then the views represented by the Air Ministry would have to be taken into account, since the Empire could not permit its air strength to be reduced beyond a certain point. For these reasons the gentlemen in the Air Ministry believe that it would be only then that they could make use of our authoritative statement on Germany's intentions."[4] So it was not unreasonable for Hess and the Haushofers to believe they had been dealing with the Air Ministry, and what better reason for contacting the Duke of Hamilton, who was a slight acquaintance of Karl Haushofer and a ranking RAF officer. The Haushofers were obviously searching for contacts, and the Duke of Hamilton, with his title, fitted the bill, since the Nazis had a misperception that all titled people in Britain had access to the prime minister and the king, probably as a result of their prewar contacts with the Cliveden Set.

According to Otto Dietrich, Hess sought assurance at this time from Hitler that the Führer's policy toward Britain remained unchanged and was assured that he still desired an Anglo-German understanding.[5] This has been interpreted to mean that Hitler was approving Hess's inquiries through Haushofer, but since Hitler had ordered the original contacts made by Schellenberg and Ribbentrop the previous July with Windsor, it is more likely that Hitler was confirming that contact should be maintained. Winterbotham, too, when I asked about Hitler's foreknowledge, was quite emphatic that he knew all about Hess's flight in advance, and I assume this had been communicated to him by de Ropp. Winterbotham believed that had Hess's mission succeeded, Hitler would have taken credit for the "peace coup" but was prepared to deny him in the event of failure, as is the lot of most secret agents.

On September 23, 1940, Albrecht Haushofer wrote his letter to the Duke of Hamilton. It was signed "A" and consigned via Mrs. Roberts, the "old lady" in Lisbon. In late September it was intercepted by the British Censor. It has never been explained how or when Haushofer's letter was intercepted, and its very existence remained a secret for five months.

It was the end of February 1941 when Hamilton received a

letter, dated February 26, 1941, from Group Captain F. G. Stammers OBE, asking whether Hamilton might be in London soon as he wanted to have a chat with him. It was halfway through March when Hamilton, who was stationed in Scotland, visited Stammers at the Air Ministry. To his surprise Stammers asked him what he had done with the letter Albrecht Haushofer had written him. Hamilton thought he was referring to a letter Albrecht had sent him in July 1939 and replied that it was in his bank. Before long, though, they realized that they were talking about two different letters, and Stammers produced a photographic copy of the intercepted handwritten letter, which Hamilton had never seen before.

During the five months between the interception of the letter and the time when the copy reached Stammers, it had been with MI5. The Air Ministry claimed that the delay in contacting Hamilton resulted from the need to inquire who "A" was, but also said that the letter had been misplaced for a long period. Bearing in mind that we now know that "Ultra" had intercepted all signals about the Duke of Windsor and passed them to MI5, it is probable that they knew well enough the identity of A. By then the Intelligence authorities had discovered that A was Haushofer and an important person with connections to the German Foreign Ministry. However, if MI5 believed that Haushofer was so important, it is surely inconceivable that they would have "lost" the letter. It began,

> My Dear Douglo,
>
> Even if there is only a slight chance that this letter should reach you in good time, there is a chance, and I am determined to make use of it.... [It went on with friendly personal greetings and then:] If you remember some of my last communications to you in July 1939, you—and your friends in high places—may find some significance in the fact that I am able to ask whether you could find time to have a talk with me somewhere on the outskirts of Europe, perhaps in Portugal. I could reach Lisbon any time... within a few days after receiving news from you. I do not know whether you can make your authorities understand so much, that they give you leave.[6]

He concluded by suggesting writing to a contact in Lisbon.

Haushofer's letter must have contained more than good wishes and condolences and no doubt mentioned the arrangements that had been made with Windsor and Monckton. If this was so, then the letter was not misplaced but deliberately delayed while MI5 and Churchill, too, wondered what to do next. The obvious course was to use the letter to induce some further German action, but it was impossible to do so without passing it on to Hamilton; therefore the letter had had to be altered. All the Intelligence services employed skilled forgers, and it would have been a simple matter to rewrite this letter. The ensuing photographing process would have masked any inaccuracies, type of paper, and so on. The original has never been available for inspection.

But if they altered Haushofer's letter, they also replied, sending to Haushofer, whom Intelligence would have known to be acting for Hess, some further inducement. That it was delayed may be accounted for by the need for some careful timing if their plot was to work.

After Hamilton's meeting with Stammers, little happened for more than a month, until he was ordered to report to Group Captain D. L. Blackford at the Air Ministry, where they met on April 25. Also present was Colonel T. A. Robertson, who was one of the most brilliant directors of MI5's Department B1(a), which had developed the "Double Cross" system, whereby enemy spies were manipulated and often encouraged to land in Britain with false messages. Those spies that would not cooperate were, it is said, executed at a secret establishment at Ham Common in Surrey. They wanted Hamilton to go to Portugal and learn all he could from Haushofer. Hamilton was reluctant to do so unless ordered, and he eventually agreed, provided he was allowed to consult with the British ambassador to Lisbon and also to explain to the Foreign Office what he was doing. These were sensible precautions lest he later be accused of collaborating with the enemy, but Intelligence was far from happy at his request. If he met Selby, the Lisbon ambassador, he could have found out what had been going on there, and it is almost certain that the Foreign Office were never let into the plot, anyway.

Events caught up with the Air Ministry and MI5 planners, however, for on the night of May 10 a lone Messerschmidt 110, numbered *VJ-OQ*, approached the Northumbrian coast and flew over southern Scotland; later that night a man parachuted to the ground near Hamilton's ancestral home. Rudolf Hess had arrived.

The details of Hess's flight and his startling arrival are well known. Suffice it to record that Hess, who gave his name as Oberleutnant Horn, asked to see Hamilton, who went to Glasgow the next day, puzzled as to who Horn could be. When they met, Hess asked to see Hamilton alone, whereupon he identified himself and declared he was on a mission of humanity. After explaining how Germany would inevitably win the war and outlining Hitler's peace terms, he requested Hamilton to see the king and ask him to give him his parole as he had come unarmed and of his own free will.

Hamilton promptly traveled to Ditchley Park, near Oxford, where Churchill was staying. The prime minister feigned skepticism, but late in the evening he went into the matter thoroughly and for three hours submitted Hamilton to every conceivable type of question. Hamilton confirmed that the man was Hess. Outstanding among Hess's arguments was his opinion that the British had been cowed by the bombing, an opinion suspiciously like that expressed by Windsor in July 1940. The outcome was that Hamilton was sworn to secrecy and left with the feeling that Churchill was not entirely clear as to how the matter should be explained.

In the next few days a succession of top Foreign Office experts went to interview Hess, including Sir Ivone Kirkpatrick, who was Eden's German expert. He too opined that the man was Hess, although he had never actually met him before. Paradoxically, Winterbotham, who was one of the few Britains who did know Hess, was not allowed to see him.

When Hitler heard that Hess had arrived in Britain, he flew into a rage and arrested Hess's adjutants, although they were later released. He knew that Hess had gone to Britain and why, but he had to maintain secrecy in view of the high stakes for which both sides were playing.

In Britain, too, Hess's arrival caused great consternation. Contradictory statements were issued. Churchill described him to Roosevelt as a war criminal who would have to go on trial eventually, while Harold Nicolson, private secretary to the minister of information (Monckton), wrote in his diary that he was sure Britain was hiding something because no propaganda was being made of Hess's defection. Later he was obliged to make the fatuous statement to the House of Commons that Hess could not be used for propaganda because "Such ignominy should not be put on this fundamentally decent man," which completely contradicted Churchill's war criminal pronouncement.

It is, however, apparent that when Hess arranged his flight to Britain, he fully intended to return soon after to Germany. He wrote to Reichleiter Richard Darré, on May 9, the day before his flight, "I am contemplating an extensive journey and I do not know when I shall be back. I therefore cannot as yet tie myself down to a fixed date. I shall get in touch with you again after my return."[7]

On the day of his departure Hess had invited his old friend Rosenberg to an unusually early lunch at his house. Rosenberg, like Hess and Haushofer, had long believed that Germany's destiny lay in joining Britain in an attack upon Russia, and he had, of course, been instrumental in opening the original German contacts in Britain and to Edward. Ilse Hess was unwell that day and did not join her husband and Rosenberg over lunch, at which Hess had instructed his servants not to disturb them. Rosenberg left soon after 1 P.M., after which Hess rested a while and then changed into Luftwaffe uniform before bidding his wife a normal goodbye—nothing emotional or out of the ordinary, and flew to Scotland.[8]

Hess was supposed to have been interrogated by MI5 after being taken to London by train on May 16. He is supposed to have spent four days in the Tower of London at the suggestion of the War Office. According to author Hugh Thomas in his book The Murder of Rudolf Hess, he was interrogated by MI5, although the existence is denied of any records to confirm this or of any expert interrogation of the Number Three Nazi. In view of the thoroughness with which MI5 handled other German agents, it is inconceivable that no attempt was made to obtain the myriad secrets Hess carried in his head, for he was a priceless source of intelligence. It has to be assumed that he was questioned and revealed information considered potentially so dangerous that it could never be exposed. It must have been confirmation of his negotiations with Windsor but also the aftermath of that and the reason for his arrival in Britain.

One is forced to conclude that the British had Hess interrogated by MI5 but decided either simply to cover up that fact or to hide something even more sinister. Hugh Thomas claimed that Hess is long dead and based his hypothesis that the man still in Spandau is not Hess on convincing medical evidence. Therefore he assumed that Hess never arrived in Britain, an imposter having taken his place in Germany. In spite of Thomas's reasons for the Germans doing so, there was really nothing to be gained by such an action. So if one accepts that the real Hess did land in Scotland (and in view of his dealings in Portugal and the other evidence of his desire to make peace, it seems conclusive that he did) and Thomas's seemingly irrefutable medical evidence that the man in Spandau is not Hess, then one is left with the truth that a false Hess was substituted in Britain.

Thomas states, "To this day members of the Foreign Office are so shifty and evasive when asked questions about the Hess affair that the second alternative [i.e. that the man in Spandau is not Hess] seems the more probable. Several times in the course of my enquiries I put questions either directly or through intermediaries about whether there is any suspicion in the Foreign Office that the last prisoner in Spandau may not be Hess at all. On every occasion the enquiry produced a sudden silence, a marked fall in temperature, or an off-hand remark, such as, 'I shouldn't be surprised' or some equally inadequate response."[9]

It is also significant that two Foreign Office files on Hess were removed, according to Thomas, from the Public Records Office in July 1978 by the Foreign Office and not returned for six months, after which they showed signs of having had all contentious material removed.

In his book *The Secret War of Charles Frazer-Smith*, the latter relates how one night in May 1941 he was called in by MI5 to make an exact copy of the captured Rudolf Hess's German uniform in just four hours, while Hess lay deliberately drugged in the Tower of London. The copy was duly made and delivered, he said. Why would that suit have been needed? Frazer-Smith evidently was not told the reason. It must have been that MI5 knew that Hess was coming, because of the doctored letter they had sent to Haushofer and realized how vital it would be to the extremely devious plan that British Intelligence was hatching, based on the Windsors' deal in Lisbon, that Hess should never be able to reveal the truth. Therefore Hess had to be eradicated. That was why he was never exploited for propaganda, photographed, or released. But there were important political reasons why he could not be seen to have died in Britain, and so he had to be replaced by a surrogate. Given that Intelligence knew he would arrive in Britain at some date in the near future—and timing was crucial to the scheme—they would have had time to search among the thousands of German prisoners of war, or maybe internees, to find one who resembled Hess; statistically there had to be one. In all probability, then, Hess never arrived at the Tower of London and the man for whom Frazer-Smith made the suit was Hess's double. That man was then subjected by the "Double Cross" group to a prolonged period of brainwashing and reeducating with the details of Hess's life. Only then, after more than a year, was he transferred to Abergavenny in South Wales, itself a publicized trip witnessed by the press, from a suitable distance. In South Wales he was permitted to walk in the hills and was frequently seen, which proved he was still alive. But he was never allowed contacts; reporters were kept at a distance, and the only man known to have photographed him was arrested and dismissed from the service of the hospital where Hess lived, and his film was destroyed. All the available literature about this man, this "surrogate Hess," makes it plain that he was disoriented, behaved in ways that were uncharacteristic of Hess, and frequently had lapses of memory.

What then happened to the real Rudolf Hess? Another source of information says that Hess went to the highly secret Intelligence establishment at Ham Common, the place where the uncooperative spies were eradicated. The dreadful truth may be that Hess was enticed to Britain with the inducement of fulfilling his Lisbon peace initiative but in reality so that British Intelligence could enact another devastating strategy. In Britain Hess was deliberately killed once it was soundly established that he was indeed Rudolf Hess, the Deputy Führer.

This effectively covered up Hess's involvement with Windsor as well as the British Intelligence plan that was being foisted on the Nazis, the ramifications of which could themselves never be revealed.

That intrigue cost Hess his life and imprisoned for life his substitute. Heydrich, too, was assassinated in 1942 on the orders of British Intelligence, while Bedaux died of an overdose of sleeping tablets. Even the Duke of Kent, who had certainly been in contact with his brother in Lisbon, died in a mysterious plane crash that the Germans insisted had been arranged by British Intelligence. Everyone was silenced. Why?

What was the deal negotiated in Lisbon by which the Duke of Windsor was persuaded to leave for the Bahamas, at least momentarily believing he had got the peace he wanted and on which the Nazis set such store?

Remember that the whole basis of Hitler's expansion and aggression since 1933 was his declared intention to attack Russia. To do that, as we have seen, he had to eradicate Russia's western ally, France, and to neutralize Britain. France had gone under in June 1940, and only Britain remained, obdurate and stubborn. But Britain was reeling. The Battle of Britain had staved off a German invasion, which may or may not otherwise have been launched—we cannot be sure—except that, in that deal in Lisbon, Hitler may have thought he had negotiated a peace with Britain and thereupon delayed too long. Winterbotham's intelligence reports in the 1930s had established that 1941 was to be the date for the invasion of Russia, and that meant that the war in the West had to be concluded by October 1940 at the latest. That it was not was a bitter blow to Hitler's hitherto well-regulated timetable.

By the spring of 1941 Britain was in desperate straits. The mounting U-boat offensive was crippling her shipping. A winter of appalling air raids had devastated Britain. In Africa British forces were being pushed back by the combined German-Italian army and were about to be besieged in Tobruk. In the Near East, German forces were reinforcing Syria, stoking up Rashid Ali's revolt in Iraq, and seemed bent on sweeping into Iran and Britain's oil. In the spring, too, Yugoslavia and Greece, Britain's last remaining allies, were defeated, and the imperial troops were again pushed out of Europe. Britain could not go on unless the relentless German pressure was taken off her.

Hess came to Britain on May 10, anxious to conclude the peace plan that would leave Germany free to attack Russia. The German war machine was ready; it had been diverted by the brief Balkan campaign, but even that had in turn freed her southern flank from a possible counterattack. Only Britain remained, battered almost to collapse.

On August 7, 1940, the end had seemed imminent when repeated German air raids against the vital fighter stations had just about wrecked Fighter Command in the decisive "invasion" sector. Then Churchill had played a deliberately ruthless hand and ordered RAF Bomber Command to attack Berlin. That raid so enraged the Führer that he immediately ordered the Luftwaffe to devastate London in retaliation. London was bombed and set on fire for months, but the fighters had been saved, and in time the Luftwaffe was defeated. In spring 1941 another masterstroke was needed to avoid defeat, and so the mine that had been laid under the Germans in Lisbon was sprung.

In July 1940, while the Duke of Windsor was in Portugal, Churchill had sent Sir Stafford Cripps to Moscow to warn Stalin that Germany would attack Russia if Britain was defeated. The Russian dictator immediately informed the Germans that Britain was trying to get Russian aid, for Stalin had no desire to see Britain survive.

But in the Lisbon negotiations the Germans had revealed their hand too well. They wanted Britain out of the war to leave them free to attack Russia, and they negotiated some kind of deal, probably guaranteeing the British Empire in return for British neutrality. That it was not acted upon was because Churchill's aim then had been to satisfy Windsor's ego and prize him from the German rock to which he was so attached. By spring 1941, however, matters were much more serious. Through continuing contacts in Portugal and probably by the Intelligence Service's use of the Haushofer letter to Hamilton, they had reopened the negotiations. Hess had come to Britain believing that the British were then willing to sign the peace

treaty to save themselves from further punishment and thereby free Germany in the West.

Evidence that such a scheme existed is contained in a letter
which Sir Samuel Hoare wrote from the British Embassy in
Madrid to Anthony Eden on May 20, 1941, ten days after Hess
arrived in Britain. It was headed "Personal & Secret" and,
after opening remarks, continues,

> ... I fully agree with Winston and you that I could not leave here
> unless we were all three satisfied that it was reasonably safe. I
> will therefore watch the course of events and send you my views
> about them as you suggest in a few weeks time.
>
> I have just written Winston a short personal note in view of
> the fact that he took so much interest last year in agreeing to
> our plans. I thought that he would like to know that during the
> last two or three weeks they have worked out very much as we
> hoped.
>
> I am enclosing a curious and very secret note that has just
> been sent me from Beigbeder (Spanish Foreign Minister). The
> suggestions in it bear a remarkable resemblance to what I
> imagine Hess has been saying in England. You will therefore
> no doubt wish to take it into account in connexion with anything
> that you get out of Hess. . . .[10]

The "curious and secret note" from Beigbeder has not been
found in the records, but on May 31, 1941, eleven days after his
letter, Hoare sent another "Most Secret" memorandum, headed "Subsequent Note on the Candid Proposals of DJB Dated
11:30 P.M. 31st May 1941."

This memorandum referred to a visit to Hoare by his friend
DJB (Don Joachim Bar), who had himself been visited by
Ribbentrop's Paris agent, Señor Gardeman. It detailed proposals that DJB should act as mediator between Hoare and the
Germans in peace proposals, which, it will be recalled, Haushofer had referred to but condemned as spoiled by Hess's
precipitate flight to Britain. The memorandum also contained
the usual German "big stick" threat that "Ribbentrop ... could
not understand the blindness of England which will be
attacked between 15th June and the 15th July with new de-

structive methods so terrible . . . that anything done hitherto
will seem mere childs play. . . ."[11]

But the German bluff was being called, for toward the end of
April, only three to four weeks before, Cripps in Moscow had
been informed of the date on which the Germans intended
attacking Russia, and he told Stalin. On April 24, the German
naval attaché in Moscow sent a message to the naval high
command in Berlin: "The British Ambassador in Moscow pre-
dicts June 22 as the day of the outbreak of war."[12]

The information was said to have been learned of through a
British agent. The German admirals were surprised at its
accuracy, while the naval attaché, who knew nothing of his
country's intentions, described it as "manifestly absurd." It is
obvious that the British deliberately leaked that information to
ensure that it got back to the Germans, who were put in a
dilemma, for they were then aware that the Russians knew
Germany was about to attack. Now, while Stalin continued to
ignore British warnings, the Germans did not know whether
he was bluffing while secretly mobilizing the huge Red Army.

At Nuremberg the British prosecutor suggested that Hess
flew to Britain to arrange a peace settlement enabling Germany to attack Russia. The Russian prosecutor said he was
sure of this. Stalin also insisted that, to quote Shirer, "some
deep plot was being hatched between Churchill and Hitler that
would give Germany the same freedom to attack the Soviet
Union that the Russian dictator had given her to assault
Poland and the West." In October 1943 Churchill visited Moscow and tried to assure Stalin that no such plot existed, but
Stalin would have none of it and insisted that Britain knew that
Hess was going to arrive. Now Stalin was almost certainly
correct, for it had been negotiated in Spain and Portugal, and
the reason Stalin knew was that the leading SIS agent at the
time was Kim Philby, who is now known to have been a Russian
spy since the 1930s and who eventually defected to Russia. To
quote Ladislas Farrago, "In 1934, on orders from Moscow, he
became one of the first propaganda agents the Nazis dug up in
England." He goes on: ". . . he found a niche in Section V of MI6,
as Major Cawgill's chief assistant in charge of counterespionage on the Iberian desk. Although Section V was not the only
British security organ battling German agents in Spain,

Philby was given virtually unrestricted authority and he made the most of it."[13] What Philby revealed to Stalin was to bedevil Western relations with Russia ever since.

The trap was sprung. The Germans were committed to launching their attack on Russia because they knew that the Russians were expecting it, and Germany could not, therefore, back away for fear of a Russian counterattack.

On Sunday morning, June 22, 1941, as predicted, Hitler's armored, mechanized, and hitherto invincible armies drove into Russia. Because of Britain's deception, Germany had taken on 200 million Russians, and Britain was no longer fighting alone. Germany was inevitably on the path to defeat as she took on the Russian colossus in the two-front war that Hitler had sworn to avoid. Britain was able at last, after two terrible years, to draw breath and begin again. With the Luftwaffe pressure lifted and the threat of invasion deferred, her factories gathered momentum enough to supply new weapons not only to her own growing armies but to the Russians as well.

The Russians were to suffer terribly in the years to come, but they had, after all, allowed Hitler to attack the West, and they were in turn reaping the whirlwind. In the end, though, they advanced Communism westward, just as Winterbotham, the Intelligence services, and, it must be admitted, the Duke of Windsor had said they would.

The Duke of Windsor and his wife remained in the Bahamas until May 1945, by which time he was eager to quit a post not marked by success. He did not wait for his tenure to end but, just as he had done in Paris five years before, simply left, this time for New York. Eventually he went back to France, where he spent the next thirty years in frivolous luxury, fêted wherever he went, except in Britain, where he was never welcome.

Meanwhile an aged, unknown man shuffles around the bleak solitude of Spandau. . . .

16

Postscript:
The Cover-up

WHEN I began writing this book it quickly became apparent that whatever evidence existed of the momentous intrigues that took place in the hectic, traumatic summer of 1940 was likely to be well hidden in secret files. It was only by following every possible lead and by connecting small pieces of a diverse, barely discernible puzzle, pieces scattered in many documents and histories and in the memories of a few remaining people, that I eventually became aware of those hitherto unrevealed negotiations. Consider the impact of such a revelation: that the Duke of Windsor, the former King Edward VIII, conducted highly secret and controversial negotiations with the Nazis at a time when Britain was being written off by most of the world, who expected her imminent surrender to German might. The negotiations, moreover, were intended to expedite Britain laying down her arms, for despite Hitler's promises of friendship, Germany could never have tolerated a Britain, however inadequately armed in the summer of 1940, to remain a latent threat to German hegemony in Europe. If such an agreement had become known at the time, it would have weakened British and Empire resolve and surely dissuaded the Americans from aiding Britain; afterward Britain's veracity would ever have been in doubt and relations with Eastern Europe and Russia especially would have been soured. But there can be no doubt that the intelligence services used the contacts with Hess to lead the Germans into attacking Russia in the belief that Britain was about to seek peace. It took the pressure off Britain and saved the country. For obvious reasons successive governments have preferred that these events should remain secret and therefore contrived to ensure that most of the evidence has been hidden or destroyed.

We have seen that when he was a major general on the staff of the British Military Mission, the duke maintained a close relationship with Charles Bedaux. All the evidence reveals without doubt that Bedaux was a German spy. The British government, moreover, knew by September 1940 that Bedaux was a German agent, for the Americans then passed on the evidence; although the Ministry of Economic Warfare was also warned of Bedaux's work for the Nazis, Bedaux was not even blacklisted before his arrest in 1942. What were those documents of Bedaux's which U.S. Intelligence says were taken by British Intelligence and never seen again? That nothing was ever revealed could be only because of his embarrassing connection with the duke. Why are the documents relating to the duke's service with the BMM also secreted in the Public Records Office and unavailable? He complained bitterly of his mundane duties, so what could have been so secret about his service during these months between September 1939 and when he discharged himself in June 1940 that can never be revealed? Was it because, inadvertently or not, he betrayed the Allies to Germany through Bedaux? In fact hardly any evidence of Bedaux's complicity with the Germans exists in British records; the evidence has emerged from American and French sources.

The evidence that the duke intrigued with the Nazis in Portugal is very strong, despite sustained official attempts to distort it. Most of that evidence is entwined with SS *Brigadeführer* Walter Schellenberg, who was officially dismissed as a Nazi thug, although whatever else he was, he was an intelligent, cunning man. His own published memoirs about the so-called kidnap attempt in Portugal, however, are sketchy to say the least, and he obviously had plenty to hide. He made no mention of either Heydrich or Hess or any other lesser Nazi officials and their roles, although his own signals to Berlin are irrefutable evidence that they were there.[1] It is, though, generally known that Schellenberg's published version is much shorter than his original manuscript from which much was omitted. Schellenberg himself was an enigma. He was a man who rose to control one of the most sinister secret police forces of all time; the SD was feared throughout occupied Europe and beyond; he was deeply implicated in the organization of the *Einzatsgruppen* that exterminated millions of Jews in Eastern Europe; he was the foremost minion of the notorious "Hangman" Heydrich; he was a top man in the SS. Yet Schellenberg served only nine years in prison before being released on health grounds. His comrades were executed. At the time of writing, former SS officer Klaus Barbie, the "Butcher of Lyons," has been arrested and Professor Erhardt Dabringhaus, a former U.S. Intelligence officer, has explained that Barbie was protected by the Americans from the French in the late 1940s in return for his assistance. Was Schellenberg perhaps also protected, his sentence reduced in return for his silent cooperation about the duke's role? Would the Soviet prosecutors at the war crimes trials have tolerated such a light sentence for such a man? The evidence is that Stalin had been warned of the German invasion and chose to do nothing—a monumental mistake. Maybe he was thankful not to have voiced abroad the fact that he had been tipped off about the German invasion in advance.

The evidence that I have unearthed for the duke's meeting with Hess, the culmination of his intrigues in Portugal, is based ultimately on Schellenberg's cables to Germany. Those cables have not appeared elsewhere so far as I can find. Indeed, my entire research began, as I mentioned in the Foreword, with the Schellenberg signals,[2] which I obtained accidentally, inasmuch as they were mixed up with other documents acquired for a previous book. How did those papers escape being destroyed? As one American source put it: At the end of the war the British sent teams of intelligence men into Germany to grab all they could find. What were they looking for? The following article appeared in the *South Wales Echo:* It concerns Kim Philby's associate Anthony Blunt—the so-called fourth man:

> TRAITOR ANTHONY BLUNT had a secret mission to retrieve any captured German records of conversations between the Duke of Windsor and Hitler, and other prominent Nazis, it is claimed today.
>
> Chapman Pincher, writing in the *Daily Express*, says that the former surveyor of the Queen's pictures, who served in MI5 and the KGB during World War II, carried out the secret mission for the Royal Family in 1946. Blunt was selected when MI5 were asked to provide a "totally trustworthy and discreet" officer to visit Germany.
>
> Nobody else was told the nature of the task, but Pincher quotes MI5 officers who believe his mission was to retrieve the records of conversations between the Duke of Windsor and Hitler.

The article concludes:

> It was not until 1963 that Blunt was exposed to MI5 after American Michael Straight told the FBI about him. Straight was recruited to the Soviet cause by Blunt while both were at Cambridge in 1937. After Straight's confession there followed "an appalling story of contrived bungling and legal manipulation by MI5, which had one major purpose; the fixing of the circumstances so that it would be impossible for Blunt to be prosecuted or otherwise exposed to public censure." A major cause for the coverup, he says, was Blunt's royal connection.[3]

Who were the "other prominent Nazis" mentioned? The reference is more firm evidence that the British government has been desperate to conceal the duke's misdoings. This point raises another; there have always been rumors of a "fifth man"—Burgess, Maclean, Philby, Blunt, who? Conceivably that other man, like Philby and Blunt, also has a royal connection which protects him. Was Blunt protected because he found that vital evidence of the duke's complicity with the Nazis? Did he, perhaps, know exactly what he was seeking, because he had been told by Philby? There are many unanswered questions.

Remember, too, that in the Foreword I referred to the British government's extreme reluctance to have published the German Foreign Policy Documents, and when they had no option but to publish, they attached an innocuous disclaimer of the duke's role—surely an unfortunate example of the adage *qui s'excuse s'accuse.*

Schellenberg's cables from July 24 to August 1, 1940, are clear evidence of the extent of the intrigues. Schellenberg's papers must have been a prime target for British Intelligence's search, but because Schellenberg's cable to "A. H."[4] used Haushofer's own Japanese code (*Tomodaichi* or *Tomo* for Hess, *O'Daijin* for Hitler, etc.) it slipped past searchers. Since Haushofer's use of *Tomo* for Hess is irrefutable, then surely Schellenberg's use of it to communicate with Haushofer is equally conclusive evidence that *Tomo* and *Viktor* and Hess are the same person? This is established, therefore, in the cables of July 28, 1940, one to Haushofer and one to Berlin, a "Euclidean proof" if ever there was one.

Another source of evidence has so far remained unavailable and untapped: the private papers of Walter Monckton. As we have said previously, the duke's biographer, Frances Donaldson, believed Monckton hid the real reason for his visit to Lisbon. But the evidence is again in Schellenberg's cable of July 28 in which he confirms the arrival of Monckton and again of August 1 when he reports Monckton had a meeting with the so far unidentified "F."[5] Why didn't Monckton ever mention these meetings? What was he really doing in Lisbon?

Finally, the documents relating to the duke's wartime activities as a whole are officially closed and, it is declared, will never be opened. Well, never is a long time, and presumably someone will, one day, open them, and then like some regal Pandora's box, out will tumble the complete truth of the duke's intrigues with the Nazis and in particular with Hess.

Chapter Notes

Chapter 1
1. *German Foreign Policy Documents* (GFPD), vol. 10, Docs. 378, 456
2. *GFPD*, B15/B002531
3. *GFPD*, 136/74207
4. *GFPD*, B15/B002533
5. *GFPD*, B15/B002538
6. *Chips, The Diaries of Sir Henry Channon*, Robert Rhodes James, ed. (London, 1967)
7. *Baffy, The Diaries of Blanche Dugdale, 1936-47* (London, 1973)
8. *Foreign Relations of the United States 1940*, volume III, 1939/ 4357
9. *The Diaries of Sir Alexander Cadogan, 1938-45*, David Dilks, ed. (London, 1971)
10. *GFPD* B15/B002538
11. *The Game of the Foxes*, Ladislas Farrago (London, 1972)

Chapter 2
1. *Von Kaiserhof zur Reichskanzler*, Joseph Goebbels (Munich, 1936)
2. Quoted by William L. Shirer, *The Rise and Fall of the Third Reich* (London, 1964)
3. *Mein Kampf*, Adolf Hitler
4. *GFPD* 5740/HO 30995-031018
5. *Secret & Personal*, F. W. Winterbotham (London, 1969)
6. The *Times*, February 3, 1933
7. *Who Financed Hitler: The Secret Funding of Hitler's Rise to Power, 1919-33*, James and Suzanne Pool (London, 1979)

8. Ibid.
9. *The Nazi Connection*, F. W. Winterbotham (London, 1978)

Chapter 3
1. Shirer, op. cit.
2. Ibid.
3. British Foreign Office Documents, C115/4/18
4. Shirer, op. cit.
5. British Foreign Office Documents, C1438/4/18
6. *Secret and Personal*, Winterbotham, op. cit.
7. *GFPD*, 5740/HO 31457-61
8. *Chips*, op. cit.
9. *Edward VIII*, Frances Donaldson (London, 1974)
10. *GFPD*, 5482/E382057-78
11. *GFPD*, 7620/E544964-69
12. *Donaldson*, op. cit.
13. *The Woman He Loved: The Story of the Duke and Duchess of Windsor*, Ralph G. Martin (London, 1974)
14. *Baldwin*, K. Middlemas and J. Barnes (London, 1969)
15. *Chips*, op. cit.
16. *Nancy, The Life of Lady Astor*, Christopher Sykes, (London, 1972)
17. British Foreign Office Documents, C1501/4/18
18. British Foreign Office Documents, C151/4/18
19. *GFPD*, 6710/E506679
20. *Inside the Third Reich*, Albert Speer (London, 1970)
21. Shirer, op. cit.
22. Ibid.
23. *The Fateful Years*, André François-Poncet (London, 1949)
24. *Hitler's Interpreter*, Paul Schmidt (London, 1951)

Chapter 4
1. Donaldson, op. cit.
2. *Monckton Papers*, as quoted by Donaldson, op. cit.
3. *GFPD*, 8015/E576522-4
4. Martin, op. cit.
5. Donaldson, op. cit.

Chapter 5
1. Records of the War Department, Military Intelligence, Washington, RG 165, DW nos. 10505-27
2. *Grand Rapids Herald*, July 3, 1917
3. *The Heart Has its Reasons*, The Duchess of Windsor (London, 1956)
4. Donaldson, op. cit.
5. Ibid.
6. Ibid.
7. Ibid.

Chapter 6
1. *Monckton Papers*, op. cit.
2. Donaldson, op. cit.
3. *New Yorker*, Profile, September 22, 1945.
4. *The Woman He Loved*, Ralph G. Martin (London, 1974)
5. Pool, op. cit.
6. *My Three Years with Eisenhower*, Captain Harry C. Butcher (New York, 1946)
7. Quoted by Donaldson, op. cit.
8. *My Life With Goering*, Emmy Goering (London, 1972)
9. Schmidt, op. cit.
10. Martin, op. cit.
11. The Duchess of Windsor, op. cit.
12. Martin, op. cit.

Chapter 7
1. *Der Spiegel*, November 13, 1963
2. Donaldson, op. cit.
3. Ibid.
4. Ibid.
5. Harold Nicolson—unpublished essay written for Michael Astor
6. *GFPD*, F1/0039–48
7. Ibid.
8. *The Mountbattens*, Alden Hatch (London, 1966)

Chapter 8
1. Duchess of Windsor, op. cit.
2. War Office 106/1678
3. Martin, op. cit.
4. *GFPD*, 124/122667–68
5. Donaldson, op. cit.
6. Quoting Simone de Beauvoir, Martin, op. cit.
7. Donaldson, op. cit.
8. *GFPD*, 21/119527
9. *GFPD*, 7433/E539977
10. *GFPD*, 7433/E539980
11. *GFPD*, 7433/E539982
12. Bundesarchiv Documents MS-P-215
13. *The Other Side of the Hill*, Sir Basil Liddell Hart (London, 1948)
14. Donaldson, op. cit.
15. *Nazi Secret Service*, André Brissaud (London, 1972)
16. *World War II*, chapter 3 (London: Orbis Publishing Ltd., 1972/8)

Chapter 9
1. *GFPD*, 124/12269
2. Donaldson, op. cit.
3. Martin, op. cit.

4. Donaldson, op. cit.
5. *GFPD*, 124/122671
6. *World War II*, op. cit., chapter 3
7. *Diana Cooper*, Philip Ziegler (London, 1981)
8. *World War II*, op. cit., chapter 12
9. Ibid.
10. Ibid.
11. The Duchess of Windsor, op. cit.
12. Ibid.
13. Ibid.
14. Donaldson, op. cit.
15. British Foreign Office Documents, W2880/7/49 in FO 371/ 28741
16. *The Week France Fell*, Noel Barber (London, 1976)
17. The Duchess of Windsor, op. cit.

Chapter 10
1. Lord Templewood, Private Papers (Cambridge University Library)
2. Ibid.
3. Ibid.
4. The *Times*, July 1940
5. *The Diaries of Sir Robert Bruce Lockhart, 1915–38*, ed. Kenneth Young (London, 1973)
6. Private correspondence
7. Sykes, op. cit.
8. Donaldson, op. cit.
9. *Inside the Third Reich*, Albert Speer (London, 1970)
10. *GFPD*, 136/74207
11. *GFPD*, B15/B002533
12. Speer, op. cit.
13. Donaldson, op. cit.
14. Templewood Papers

Chapter 11
1. *GFPD*, B15/B002632–33
2. *GFPD*, B15/B002538
3. *Walter Monckton*, Lord Birkenhead (London, 1969)
4. *GFPD*, B15/B002545
5. Templewood Papers, op. cit.
6. *GFPD*, B15/B002552–53
7. *GFPD*, B15/B002549–51
8. *The Ciano Diaries*, Count Galeazzo Ciano (New York, 1946)
9. *Hitler als Feldherr*, Franz Halder (Munich, 1949)
10. Quoted by Jill Edwards, *The British Government and the Spanish Civil War, 1936–9* (London, 1979)

11. *GFPD*, B15/B002549
12. *GFPD*, B15/B002549-51
13. *GFPD*, B15/B002652

Chapter 12
1. *Memoirs*, Walter Schellenberg (London, 1956)
2. *The Order of the Death's Head*, Heinz Hohne (London, 1969)
3. Schellenberg, op. cit.
4. Hohne, op. cit.
5. *Totenkopf und Trueu*, Felix Kersten (Hamburg, 1952)

Chapter 13
1. Bundesarchiv Document no. R SS/1236
2. *GFPD*, B15/B002556
3. *GFPD*, B15/B002582-83
4. *GFPD*, B15/B002581-83
5. *GFPD*, B15/B002583
6. *GFPD*, B15/B002590 & FO Telegram 421
7. *GFPD*, B15/B002591-93
8. Bundesarchiv Document no. R SS/1236
9. *Die SS*, Josef Wulf (Bonn)
10. *Nazi Secret Service*, André Brissaud (London, 1972)
11. Wulf, op. cit.
12. Bundesarchiv Document no. R SS/1236
13. Bundesarchiv Documents nos. E 035156 and R SS/1236
14. Schellenberg, op. cit.
15. *GFPD*, B15/B002588
16. *GFPD*, B15/B002591-93
17. Bundesarchiv Document no. R SS/1236
18. *GFPD*, B15/B002611-12
19. Schellenberg, op. cit.
20. Ibid.
21. Foreign Office Series no. 136
22. Ibid., no. 149
23. Ibid., no. 152
24. Ibid., no. 173
25. Ibid., no. 176
26. Bundesarchiv Document no. R SS/1236
27. Ibid., no. 176
28. Bundesarchiv Document no. R SS/1236

Chapter 14
1. Bundesarchiv Document no. R SS/1236
2. Ibid.
3. Bundesarchiv Document no. E 147120
4. *Motive for a Mission*, James Douglas-Hamilton (London, 1971)
5. Bundesarchiv Document no. R SS/1236

6. Ibid., HC 833, etc.
7. *Motive for a Mission*, James Douglas-Hamilton (London, 1971)
8. *The Kersten Memoirs*, Felix Kersten (London, 1956)
9. *The Murder of Rudolf Hess*, Hugh Thomas (London, 1978)
10. Bundesarchiv Document nos. R SS/1236 and E 147120
11. Telegrams 28.7.40, Bundesarchiv Document no. E 035156-7
12. *GFPD*, B15/B002536
13. *GFPD*, B15/B002563
14. *GFPD*, B15/B002603
15. IWM Document no. T9-46
16. Donaldson, op. cit.
17. *GFPD*, B15/B002610
18. Bundesarchiv Document no. R SS/1236
19. Ibid.
20. *GFPD*, B15/B002619
21. Ibid.
22. *GFPD*, B15/B002617-18
23. *GFPD*, B15/B003632-33
24. FO Document FO 371.24263 4612, 23.10.40
25. Bundesarchiv Document no. R SS/1236
26. Ibid.
27. Ibid.
28. Ibid.
29. *GFPD*, B15/B002655, footnote to B15/B002632-3
30. *GFPD*, no. 1862, volume V, 8. 108869

Chapter 15
1. *The Nazi Connection*, F. W. Winterbotham (London, 1978)
2. Douglas-Hamilton, op. cit.
3. Ibid.
4. *GFPD*, 7433/E5339980
5. *The Hitler I Knew*, Otto Dietrich (London, 1952)
6. Douglas-Hamilton, op. cit.
7. Ibid.
8. *The Myth of the Master Race: Alfred Rosenberg and Nazi Ideology*, Robert Cecil (London, 1958)
9. *The Murder of Rudolf Hess*, Hugh Thomas (London, 1978)
10. Templewood Papers, op. cit.
11. Ibid.
12. Shirer, op. cit.
13. *The Game of the Foxes*, Ladislas Farrago (London, 1972)

Chapter 16
1. Bundesarchiv Document nos. R SS/1236 and E147120
2. Ibid. R SS/1236
3. *South Wales Echo* 21.1.83
4. Bundesarchiv Document no. E147120
5. Ibid. R SS/1236

Bibliography

Abetz, Otto. *Das offene Problem.* Cologne, 1951.

Airlie, Countess. *Thatched with Gold.* London, 1962.

Ambruster, Howard Watson. *Treason's Peace.* New York, 1947.

Andrus, Burton C. *The Infamous of Nuremberg.* London: Leslie Frewin, 1969.

Articles de la Dépêche du Centre Ouest. May and June 1937.

Atholl, Duchess of. *Working Partnerships.* London, 1958.

Atlee, C. R. *As it Happened.* London, 1954.

Auswartiges Amt. *Berlin Weissbuch,* no. 5.

Avon, Earl of. *An Unpublished Page of History.* London, 1937.

Avon, Earl of, *The Reckoning.* London, 1965.

Baldwin, Monica. *An Unpublished Page of History.* London, 1957.

Barber, Noel. *The Week France Fell.* New York, 1976.

Baudoin, Paul. *Private Diaries (March 1940 to January 1941) of Sir Charles Petrie.* London, 1948.

Beaverbrook, Lord. *The Abdication of King Edward VIII.* London, 1966.

Belgian Ministry of Foreign Affairs. *Belgium: The Official Account of what Happened, 1939-40.* New York, 1941.

Bernadotte, Folke. *The Fall of the Curtain.* London, 1945.

Best, S. Payne. *The Venlo Incident.* London, 1950.

Bird, Eugenie. *The Loneliest Man in the World.* London, 1974.

Birkenhead, Lord. *Walter Monckton.* London, 1969.

Bloch, Marc. *Strange Defeat.* New York, 1949.

Blumentritt, Guenther. *Von Rundstedt.* London, 1952.

Bocca, Godrey. *She Might Have Been Queen.* London, 1945.

Bois, Elie. *Truth on the Tragedy of France.* London, 1941.

Bolitho, Hector. *Edward VIII.* London, 1937.

Bonnet, Georges. *Fin d'une Europe*. Geneva, 1948.
Boothby, Robert. *I Fight to Live*. London, 1947.
Boothe, Clare. *European Spring*. London, 1941.
Bor, Peter. *Gesprache mit Hitler*. Wiesbaden, 1950.
Bove, Dr. Charles F. *A Paris Surgeon's Story*. London, 1956.
Brissaud, André. *Nazi Secret Service*. London, 1972.
Bullock, Alan. *Hitler—A Study in Tyranny*. London, 1952.
Burdick, Charles. *Germany's Military Strategy and Spain in World War II*. Syracuse, N.Y., 1968.
Butcher, Harry C. *My Three Years with Eisenhower*. New York, 1946.
Calic, Edward. *Unmasked*. London, 1971.
Cecil, Robert. *The Myth of the Master Race: Alfred Rosenberg and the Nazi Ideology*. London, 1958.
Churchill, Sir Winston. *The Second World War*. London, 1948–54.
Ciano, Count Galeazzo. *Ciano's Diplomatic Papers*. London, 1948.
Ciano, Count Galeazzo. *Ciano's Hidden Diaries, 1939–43*. New York, 1946.
Ciano, Count Galeazzo. *The Ciano Diaries, 1939–43*. New York, 1946.
Cole, Hubert. *Laval*. London, 1963.
Colvin, Ian. *Chief of Intelligence*. London, 1951.
Conseil général d'Indre et Loire—procès-verbaux. Paris, 1973.
Cooper, Diana. *The Light of the Common Day*. London, 1959.
Cooper, Duff. *Old Men Forget*. London, 1953.
Crankshaw, Edward. *Gestapo: The Instrument of Tyranny*. London, 1956.
Dahlerus, Birger. *The Last Attempt*. London, 1947.
Das Bundesarchiv und Seing Bestande. Boppard am Rhein: Harald Boldt Verlag.
Deacon, Richard. *Spy*. London, 1980.
Detwiler, D. S. *Hitler, Franco und Gibralter*. Wiesbaden, 1962.
Dietrich, Otto. *The Hitler I Knew*. London, 1952.
Dilks, David, ed. *The Diaries of Sir Alexander Cadogan, 1938–45*. London, 1971.
Documents and Materials Relating to the Eve of the Second World War, 1937–39. Moscow: Foreign Language Publishing House, 1948.
Documents of British Foreign Policy, 1919–39. London: HMSO.
Documents on German Foreign Policy. London: HMSO, Series C, volume IV; Series D, volume I; Series D, volume VIII; Series D, volume X.
Dokumente der deutschen Politik, 1939–40. Berlin.
Donaldson, Frances. *Edward VIII*. London, 1974.
Douglas-Hamilton, James. *Motive for a Mission*. London, 1971.
Doussinagge, Jose M. *España tenia Razón, 1939–45*. Madrid, 1950.

Downes, Donald. *The Scarlet Thread—Adventures in Wartime Espionage.* London, 1954.

Dugdale, Blanche. *Baffy: The Diaries of Blanche Dugdale, 1936-7.* London, 1973.

Edwards, Jill. *The British Government and the Spanish Civil War, 1936-9.* London, 1979.

Farrago, Ladislas. *The Game of the Foxes.* London, 1972.

Feisling, Keith. *The Life of Neville Chamberlain.* London, 1946.

Files of the Document Center

Files of the Central Archives of the NSDAP, on microfilms. Hoover Institute, USA.

Foreign Office Series

Foreign Relations of the United States, 1940, vol. 3.

Forward, 13.11.37

Francois-Poncet, André. *The Fateful Years.* London, 1949.

Frank, Hans. *Im Angesicht des Galgens.* Munich: Beck Verlag, 1953.

Frazer-Smith, C. *The Secret War of C. Frazer-Smith.* London, 1981.

Frischaller, Willi. *Goering.* London, 1953.

Garret, Richard. *Mrs. Simpson.* London, 1975.

Gamelin, General Maurice Gustave. *Servir.* Paris, 1949.

Gilbert, Felix. *Hitler Directs his War.* New York, 1950.

Goebbels, Joseph. *The Goebbels Diaries.* New York, 1953.

Goebbels, Joseph. *Von Kaizerhof Zur Reichskanzler.* Munich, 1936.

Goering, Emmy. *My Life with Goering.* London, 1972.

Guides to German Records microfilmed at Alexandria, Va. No. 9, Records of Private German individuals. Washington, D.C.: The National Archives, Washington.

Hagen, Walter. *Die Geheime Front.* Vienna, 1950.

Halder, Franz. *Hitler als Feldherr.* Munich, 1949.

Halifax, Lord. *Fullness of Days.* London, 1957.

Hanfstaengl, Ernst. *Hitler: the Missing Years.* London, 1975.

Hardinge, Helen. *Loyal to Three Kings.* London, 1967.

Harris Smith, R. *OSS: The Secret History of America's First Central Intelligence Agency.* University of California Press, Berkely, 1972.

Harvey, John. *The Diplomatic Diaries of Oliver Harvey, 1937-40.* London, 1960.

Hassell, Ulrich von. *The von Hassell Diaries, 1938-44.* London, 1948.

Hatch, Alden. *The Mountbattens.* London, 1966.

Henderson, Sir Neville. *Failure of a Mission.* London, 1940.

Hess, Ilse. *Prisoner of Peace.* Edited by George Pile. Britain's Publishing Co., 1954.

Hess, Ilse. *England—Nürnberg—Spandau.* Durbfell Verlag, 1968.

Hess, Rudolf. *Reden.* Munich: Eher Verlag, 1938.

Hesse, Fritz. *Hitler and the English.* London, 1954.
Hibbert, Christopher. *Edward: The Uncrowned King.* London, 1972.
Hitler, Adolf. *Mein Kampf.* Boston, 1953.
Hitler's Secret Conversations, 1941–44. New York, 1953.
Hoettl, Wilhelm. *The Secret Front: The Story of Nazi Political Espionage.* London, 1955.
Hohne, Heinz. *Canaris.* London, 1979.
Hohne, Heinz. *The Order of the Death's Head.* London, 1960.
Hood, Diana. *Working for the Windsors.* London, 1957.
Hull, Cordell. *The Memoirs of Cordell Hull.* London, 1948.
Hutton, J. Bernard. *Hess, the Man and his Mission.* London, 1976.
Inglis, Brian. *Abdication.* London, 1966.
Irving, David. *Hitler's War.* London, 1977.
Irving, David. *The War Path.* London, 1978.
Jacobsen, Hans-Adolf. *Fall Gelb.* Weisbaden, 1957.
James, Robert Rhodes, ed. *Chips: The Diaries of Sir Henry Channon.* London, 1967.
Kelley, Douglas M. *Twenty-two Cells in Nuremberg.* London, 1947.
Kersten, Felix. *The Kersten Memoirs.* London, 1956.
Kersten, Felix. *Totenkopf und Trueu.* Hamburg, 1952.
Kimche, John and David. *The Secret Roads.* London, 1955.
Kirkwood, David. *My Life of Revolt.* London, 1935.
Langer, William L. *Our Vichy Gamble.* New York, 1947.
Laski, Harald. *The King's Secretary.* London: *Fortnightly Review,* 1942.
Laval, Pierre. *The Unpublished Diary of Pierre Laval.* London, 1948.
Leasor, James. *The Uninvited Envoy.* London, 1962.
Le Livre Jaune Francais. Documents diplomatiques, 1938–39. Ministères des Affaires Étrangeres.
Liddell-Hart, Sir Basil. *The Other Side of the Hill.* London, 1948.
Lindbergh, Charles A. *The Wartime Journals of Charles A. Lindbergh.* New York, 1970.
MacKenzie, Compton. *The Windsor Tapestry.* London, 1938.
Magnus, Philip. *King Edward the Seventh.* London, 1964.
Manstein, Field Marshal Eric von. *Verlorene Siege.* Bonn, 1955.
Martin, Kingsley. *The Crown and the Establishment.* London, 1962.
Martin, Ralph G. *The Woman He Loved.* London, 1974.
Maurice, J. *Monts et son passe, synthèse historique.* Tours, 1968.
Middlemas K. and Barnes, J. *Baldwin.* London, 1968.
Minney, R. J. *The Private Papers of Hore-Belisha.* London, 1960.
Mosley, Diana. *The Duchess of Windsor.* New York, 1981.
Murphy, Charles, J. V. and Bryan, James. *The Windsor Story.* New York, 1979.
Neave, Airey. *Nuremberg, a Personal Record.* London, 1978.

New Yorker, Profile, 22.9.45
Nicolson, Harold. *Diaries and Letters*. London, 1956.
Nicolson, Harold. *King George V, His Life and Reign*. London, 1958.
Nouvelle republique: l'ordinateur après la romance, Friday, June 2, 1978.
Parliamentary Debates, House of Commons.
Pool, James and Pool, Suzanne. *Who Financed Hitler: The Secret Funding of Hitler's Rise to Power, 1919–33*. London, 1979.
Reynaud, Paul. *In the Thick of the Fight*. London, 1955.
Ribbentrop, Joachim von. *Zwischen London und Moskau*. Leoni, 1961.
Seabury, Pau. *The Wilhelmstrasse: A Study of German Diplomats Under the Nazi Regime*. London, 1955.
Servie, R. Archives départmentales, Paris.
Schellenberg, Walter. *Memoirs*. London, 1956.
Schmidt, Paul. *Hitler's Interpreter*. London, 1951.
Shirer, William L. *The Rise and Fall of the Third Reich*. London, 1964.
Spanish Government and the Axis. Washington, D.C.: U.S. State Department, 1946.
Speer, Albert. *Inside the Third Reich*. London, 1970.
Stipp, John. *Devil's Diary*. London, 1941.
Sykes, Christopher. *Nancy: The Life of Lady Astor*. London, 1972.
Tansill, Charles. *Backdoor to War*. Chicago, 1941.
Templewood, Lord. *Nine Troubled Years*. London, 1952.
Templewood, Lord. Private Papers. Cambridge University Library.
Terraine, John. *The Life and Times of Lord Louis Mountbatten*. London, 1968.
Thomas, Hugh. *The Murder of Rudolf Hess*. London, 1978.
Thyssen, Fritz. *I Paid Hitler*. London, 1941.
Trevor-Roper, Hugh. *Hitler's Table Talk*. London, 1953.
Trial of the Major War Criminals before the International Military Tribunal, Nuremberg.
Tschmi, Gabriel. *Royal Chef*. London, 1954.
Vanderbilt, Gloria and Thelma, Lady Furness. *Double Exposure*. London, 1959.
Volkischer Beobachter, 1939–40.
Weiszacher, Ernst von. *The Memoirs of Ernst von Weizsacker*. London, 1951.
Wheeler-Bennet, John. *King George VI*. London, 1958.
Windsor, The Duchess. *The Heart has its Reasons*. London, 1956.
Windsor, The Duke. *A Family Album*. London, 1960.
Windsor, The Duke. *A King's Story*. London, 1960.
Winterbotham, F. W. *Secret and Personal*. London, 1969.
Winterbotham, F. W. *The Nazi Connection*. London, 1978.

Woodward, Sir Llewellyn. *British Foreign Policy in the Second World War.* London: HMSO, 1962.
Wulf, Josef. *Die SS.* Bonn, 1954.
Young, Kenneth, ed. *The Diaries of Sir Robert Bruce Lockhart, 1915–38.* London, 1973.
Ziegler, Philip. *Diana Cooper.* London, 1981.

Index